American Heart
Association®

Learn and Live ℠

S0-BHZ-574

Quick & Easy
cookbook

ALSO BY THE AMERICAN HEART ASSOCIATION

American Heart
Association®
Learn and Live℠

Quick & Easy
cookbook

more than 200
healthful recipes you
can make in minutes

Clarkson Potter/Publishers
New York

Your contribution to the American Heart Association supports research that helps make publications like this possible. For more information, call 1-800-AHA-USA1 (1-800-242-8721) or contact us online at *www.americanheart.org*

Published by Clarkson Potter/Publishers, New York, New York. Member of the Crown Publishing Group.

Random House, Inc. New York, Toronto, London, Sydney, Auckland www.randomhouse.com

CLARKSON N. POTTER, POTTER, and colophon are trademarks of Random House, Inc.

Originally published in hardcover by Times Books in 1995. Published in paperback by Times Books in 1998.

Printed in the United States of America

Art Direction by Naomi Osnos
Book Design by Charlotte Staub
Line illustrations by Sally Mara Sturman

Library of Congress Cataloging-in-Publication Data
American Heart Association quick and easy cookbook / by the American Heart Association.—2nd ed.
Includes index.
1. Heart—Diseases—Diet therapy—Recipes. 2. Heart—Diseases—Prevention. 3. Low-fat diet—Recipes. 4. Low-cholesterol diet—Recipes. I. American Heart Association.
RC684.D5A45 1995
641.5'6311—dc2094—19973

ISBN 0-307-23753-2

10 9 8 7 6 5 4 3 2 1

Second Paperback Edition

Acknowledgments

⬤⬤⬤⬤⬤⬤⬤⬤⬤⬤

This book would not have been possible without the combined efforts of a talented and dedicated group of people. Special thanks go to Jane Ruehl, director of Consumer Publications, who handled the editorial process of making a collection of recipes into a book.

The delicious recipes were created and tested by Linda Foley Woodrum. They were analyzed by the Nutrition Coordinating Center at the University of Minnesota at Minneapolis.

The food photography was done by Cece Cox. The food styling for the photos was done by Patricia Fly.

I think you'll agree that the end result is a wonderful book of delicious recipes and beautiful photographs. I am grateful to this team of professionals for their efforts and for the opportunity to work with them on this project.

Mary Winston, Ed.D., R.D.
Science Consultant
American Heart Association

Preface

Struggling to eat tasty, nutritious meals while racing against the clock is a big challenge that many busy people face today. With less time to cook, we sometimes bypass good nutrition in favor of convenience. The great majority of us (83 percent of adults in a recent survey) are concerned that what we eat will affect our health. With this book, we hope to convince you that great-tasting, nutritious food and convenience can go hand in hand. Just look at the more than two hundred palate-pleasing, kitchen-tested recipes that were developed with an eye toward quick and easy preparation.

With this book in hand, delicious, heart-healthful meals are just moments away. Here's to good food and good health!

American Heart
Association®
Learn and Live SM

Quick & Easy
cookbook

Introduction

Years ago the image of a typical family included a stay-at-home mom, a working dad, and a couple of children. The typical woman in this traditional family cooked what she considered a healthful, tasty dinner every day. That was the beginning of a family evening at home together.

That image has changed dramatically over the past several years, and more change is expected. Research reveals that the typical household today is different from what it was twenty-five years ago. Many households are run by single parents. Others are headed by two parents, each working full time. A very large number of people live alone. There are some stay-at-home moms and dads, but more and more adults are working outside the home.

Whatever the household structure, there's no arguing that careers and hectic lives give us less time in the kitchen. Many people find themselves caught in a mealtime rush hour. Our recipes are designed just for these people. We simplified food preparation to make it easy for people to eat healthful, delicious meals without working overtime in the kitchen.

We started by keeping the preparation time short. Every recipe in this book has a preparation time of 20 minutes or less. We also paid close attention to the cooking time for the recipes. Many of these recipes can be cooked in only a few minutes. In fact, most of the recipes in this book take 30 minutes or less to prepare and cook. That's total time—start to finish!

Some things, like baked chicken and homemade bread, can't be rushed. Using the recipes in this book, you will find that there are ways to make even these dishes relatively quick and easy. The secret is to spend a little time preparing the food and a lot of time relaxing, talking with friends, or just doing whatever you want while the meal cooks in the oven or crockery cooker.

In this book we offer you main dishes, side dishes, appetizers, and desserts that are good for you. They are low in total fat, saturated fat, and cholesterol, and they are moderate in sodium. All this is done without sacrificing an ounce of flavor.

Basics of a
Healthful Diet

Many scientific studies confirm that high blood cholesterol is a major risk factor for heart and blood vessel disease. The nutritional solution to minimize this risk is relatively simple: lower your blood cholesterol. The best way to do this is to significantly reduce the foods you eat that are high in cholesterol and saturated fat. Rest assured that the recipes in this book keep a close eye on cholesterol content as well as fat and sodium content. These are the basic principles of the American Heart Association Dietary Guidelines. Most important, these recipes will help you prepare delicious and appealing dishes for all occasions.

The American Heart Association
Dietary Guidelines

The American Heart Association recommends the following dietary guidelines to reduce blood cholesterol and prevent or control high blood pressure.

- Eat at least 5 servings of fruits and vegetables daily.
- Eat at least 6 servings of grain products daily.
- Eat no more than 6 ounces (cooked weight) of lean meat, fish, or skinless poultry per day. Have at least 2 servings of fish per week.

- Balance food intake with physical activity to achieve and maintain a healthy weight.
- Choose a diet low in saturated fat, trans fat, and cholesterol and moderate in salt (sodium) and sugar. Eat less than 10 percent of your calories as saturated fat. Limit yourself to less than 300 milligrams of cholesterol and less than 2,400 milligrams of sodium daily.
- Include fat-free and low-fat dairy products, legumes, poultry, and lean meats in your eating plan.
- If you drink alcohol, limit yourself to one drink per day if you are a woman and two drinks per day if you are a man.

Knowing what foods to eat for a healthy heart is an important step in any eating plan. Here's a breakdown of the nutrients we consume on a daily basis and a guide for making smart choices in each category. We've also included some tips on eating a varied diet and the importance of exercise.

Fat

When it comes to eating with your heart in mind, the most important thing you can do is limit the amount and kinds of fat in your diet. That's because certain fats (saturated fat, trans fat, and cholesterol) raise bad cholesterol.

Saturated Fat, Trans Fat, and Cholesterol

Saturated fat comes from both animal- and plant-based foods. Animal-based foods high in saturated fat include butter and whole-milk dairy products, organ meats, lard, and beef, pork, and chicken fat. Plant-based foods containing saturated fat include coconut oil, palm kernel oil, palm oil, and cocoa butter. You should get less than 10 percent of your calories from saturated fat.

Trans fats are created when vegetable oil is hydrogenated (hydrogen is added) to make it solid. Some of the main sources of trans fats are margarine and commercially baked products such as cookies, crackers, and breads. Check ingredient labels so you can limit hydrogenated or partially hydrogenated oils. Select liquid or tub margarine when possible.

Cholesterol in foods comes only from animal products. It's in all meats, poultry, seafood, and animal fats, such as butter and lard. The richest sources are egg yolks and organ meats. Keep your dietary cholesterol to less than 300 milligrams per day.

Polyunsaturated and Monounsaturated Fats

With this information in mind, you can see that if you're going to cook with fat, it's wise to choose the polyunsaturated and mono-unsaturated varieties. They don't raise bad cholesterol.

You'll find polyunsaturated fats in vegetable oils such as safflower, sunflower, soybean, and corn. You'll also find it in some fish and fish oils. Olive and canola oils are the best sources of monounsaturated fat.

Carbohydrates

Think complex. By increasing your consumption of complex-carbo-hydrate foods (such as grains, potatoes, whole-grain breads, rice, and pastas), you'll be decreasing your consumption of fats. Be sure to leave off the butter and fatty sauces that sometimes accompany these healthful foods.

Protein

Considered the body's construction material, protein is the body's main source for growth and tissue repair. The fact is, most of us eat twice as much protein as we need for good nutrition. Some good low-fat protein choices are vegetables, legumes, grains, and seeds. Unfortunately, most of us eat high-fat protein foods, such as meats, poultry, fish, seafood, and dairy products.

Sodium

This vital element helps our bodies maintain the balance of fluids. The recommended guideline of no more than 3000 milligrams of sodium per day applies to most adolescents and adults. However, if you have high blood pressure or a history of it in your family, your doctor may advise you to reduce your sodium intake further. Examples of high-sodium foods are salt, soy sauce, Worcestershire sauce, pickles, and chicken broth.

Alcohol

Alcohol contains only empty calories—calories with no additional nutritional value—and an excess can lead to many medical and social problems. Nonalcoholic versions of wine and beer are a nice substitute for alcoholic beverages and work well in cooking.

Calories

Calories measure energy—the energy our bodies use and the energy in the foods we eat. Calories are needed for a number of body functions—such as digestion, physical activity, and breathing. When you consume more calories than your body needs, you gain weight. When you eat fewer calories than your body needs, you lose weight. So naturally, when you eat the same number of calories that you burn, then you maintain your weight. Your doctor or a dietitian can help you determine your ideal weight and can help you decide whether you need to reduce or increase your caloric intake.

Variety

Variety, balance, and moderation are the keys to a well-planned, healthful diet. Choose heart-smart foods that you enjoy and that fit into your lifestyle. If an eating plan doesn't fit your likes and needs, you probably won't stick to it. You'll find a wide variety of recipes in this book that will fit perfectly into your healthful-eating agenda.

Exercise

There's no doubt that good nutrition plays a key role in our well-being. Now merge it with being physically active and you have a healthy marriage that any heart would love. Aim for at least moderate-level activity, such as brisk walking, for a total of 30 minutes or longer on most days. If you are over 40 or if you have any medical problems, check with your doctor before beginning any exercise program.

Eating Plans and Shopping

Planning Your Meals

Invest a few minutes in meal planning and you might be surprised at the potential benefits: improved nutrition and savings in time and money. Planning your meals is as easy as writing down your entrées or entire menus for a few days or a week at a time. This gives you the opportunity to plan well-balanced meals for yourself and family without repeating the same main dish or meal very often. Even though it takes a little time up front, the more you do it, the faster you will become at meal planning.

Glance through the main-dish recipes in this book and pick out a few that appeal to you. Now fill in the rest of the meal with easy side-dish recipes or healthful store-bought items, such as whole-grain bread or ready-to-cook frozen vegetables.

When planning your menu, include the following for each adult:

- No more than 6 ounces (cooked weight) of meat, fish, or poultry a day, including at least two servings of fish a week;
- Dried beans, peas, lentils, or tofu in place of meat a few times a week;
- Whole-grain or enriched bread or cereal products each day;
- At least five servings of fruits and vegetables each day (include one serving of citrus fruit or vegetable high in vitamin C and one serving of dark-green leafy or deep-yellow vegetables);
- Two or more daily servings of nonfat (skim) or low-fat milk or other dairy products (three to four servings for children and adolescents);

- Five to eight teaspoons of polyunsaturated and monounsaturated fats and oils in the form of margarine, cooking oil, and salad dressing each day (the amount may vary according to your caloric needs).

The Shopping List

When you go to the store, don't forget to take along your best friend—your shopping list. This handy list will save you time as you search out your healthful food choices. It will also help you avoid some not-so-healthful impulse purchases. Start your list when you plan your meals and add to it as you think of other items you need. Keep your list where other family members can add to it, too.

If you know the layout of your store, try to list items in the order that you encounter them as you walk through the store. For instance, group fruits and vegetables at the top of your list under the heading "produce" if that's where you begin your shopping. Place the frozen-food items last on your list under "frozen foods" if that's your last stop in the store.

To save time in preparing foods to put in a recipe, you may choose to buy the items in the form you need them. It is more costly than buying the items in bulk, but you will save time in the kitchen. For example, you will shorten the preparation time if you choose shredded or sliced cheese, boned and skinned chicken breasts, and cut-up fresh vegetables. You can also save time by buying bread crumbs, bottled minced garlic, and packaged cleaned spinach.

Go ahead and plan on leftovers. It's a great time-saving technique for any busy cook. Just be sure to double the amount of ingredients on your shopping list, too. You can use leftovers creatively in salads, stir-fries, soups, casseroles, or sandwiches. Or freeze leftovers for longer storage and simply thaw and reheat them at a later date. Good freezing choices are soups and one-dish meals.

If you want to avoid leftovers, go ahead and halve a recipe, if necessary. For recipes that contain a sauce, the ingredients for the sauce may not need to be halved.

Shopping for a Healthy Heart

At the grocery store, beware of foods in every aisle that are waiting to sabotage your healthful shopping outing. Here are a few guidelines to help you fill your cart with heart-healthful foods.

Meat

Be picky as you ponder your choices at the meat counter. The three grades of beef you'll find in the grocery store most often are prime, choice, and select. Prime meat contains the most fat, referred to as marbling. Select contains the least amount of fat. We give a thumbs-up to select grades of round steak, flank steak, sirloin tip, tenderloin, and extra-lean ground beef. All these cuts are quick to fix, too. For all whole cuts of meat, look for separable fat that you can slash off.

Choosing the leanest ground beef available is as easy as reading the package at the meat counter. Look for extra-lean or 90 percent lean (or 10 percent fat) right on the label. In some stores, you can buy a ground-beef product that is 95 percent lean. This product replaces some of the fat with water and plant-derived ingredients to maintain moisture during cooking. Better yet, select a well-trimmed piece of steak, lean stewing beef, or lean chuck roast and ask the butcher to grind it for you.

Thanks to modern-day pig farmers, pork is much leaner than it was just thirty years ago. That means you get more meat and less fat if you choose the right cuts of pork. Select lean pork, such as tenderloin, loin chops, rib or loin roasts, low-fat and low-sodium ham, and Canadian bacon.

Fat watchers will find lamb a cut above the rest if the meat is chosen correctly. Most lamb from the United States is marketed fresh, although a small amount may be frozen. When buying lamb, look for meat that is finely grained and reddish pink or dark red. The leanest portion is the leg. Other lean cuts include leg sirloin chop, center roast, center slice, and shank. If leg chops aren't available, use rib chops instead. With all cuts of lamb, be sure to trim away the heavy covering of fat on the outside before cooking.

Veal is the young, tender meat of a calf that has not yet put on adult fat. That makes it a good choice for healthful eating. The most expensive and tender cuts come from milk-fed veal, which has a creamy pink, almost white, velvety appearance. Grain-fed veal comes from calves that have had grass or grain added to their diets, making the meat rosier in color, with a slightly stronger flavor and a coarser texture. The leanest cuts of veal are leg cutlet, arm steak, sirloin steak, rib chop, loin chop, and top round.

Some wild game is very lean. Venison, rabbit, squirrel, and pheasant are examples of low-fat game. Duck and goose are not.

Processed meats should be eaten only if they contain no more than 10 percent fat, or 3 grams of fat per ounce. Be aware that many processed meats are high in sodium.

Eat high-cholesterol organ meats—such as brains, liver, kidney, and sweetbreads—only occasionally.

Fish and Shellfish

Most fish are delightfully low in fat and make excellent low-fat choices. Lean varieties include cod, haddock, halibut, flounder, sole, red snapper, and orange roughy. All fresh and frozen fish are healthful options.

Canned fish, such as tuna, should be packed in water. For a nice alternative to tuna, choose canned salmon. The boneless and skinless variety will save you time in the kitchen.

Shrimp, lobster, crab, crayfish, and most other shellfish are very low in fat. But ounce for ounce, some varieties contain more sodium and cholesterol than poultry, meat, or fish. Choose these occasionally, and they can fit into the guidelines of 300 milligrams of cholesterol per day.

Some fish are high in omega-3 fatty acids, which may help lower the level of triglycerides, one type of lipid (blood fat). Choose from Atlantic and coho salmon, albacore tuna, mackerel, carp, lake whitefish, sweet smelt, and lake and brook trout.

Poultry

If you're looking for a tasty, versatile, and nutritious food, then poultry is your wish come true. Remember that poultry skin harbors a great deal of fat and cholesterol. When roasting a whole chicken or turkey, remove the skin before eating. When cooking chicken or turkey pieces, be sure to buy skinless poultry or remove the skin before cooking. When buying ground poultry, be sure to select the kind ground without skin.

Look at the type of poultry you are choosing. Light meat is leaner than dark meat, and it should be your first choice.

Biggest is not necessarily best with poultry. Larger, older birds, such as roasters and capons, are fattier than smaller and younger birds.

Avoid goose and duck, which are high in saturated fats.

Dairy Products

When it comes to milk, you have some excellent choices. Put non-fat (skim) or low-fat milk at the top of your list for the best low-fat, high-calcium drink. Cross light cream off your list and add evaporated skim milk. It's a flawless low-fat substitute for cream in cooked sauces. Don't forget buttermilk. Although its name sounds like high fat, it's low in fat, since it's made with cultured skim milk or low-fat milk.

Choose cheeses that are naturally lower in fat, such as part-skim mozzarella cheese, farmer cheese, part-skim ricotta cheese, sapsago cheese, or Parmesan cheese. Check the dairy case for specially made low-fat versions of cheddar and other hard cheeses that are usually high in fat. Light cream cheese, Neufchâtel cheese, and nonfat cream cheese are heart-smart stand-ins for cream cheese.

For dessert, reach for ice milk, nonfat or low-fat frozen yogurt, sherbet, and fruit ices.

Avoid dairy substitutes that are high in fat and saturated fats. Nondairy coffee creamers, canned sour-cream substitutes, and whipped-cream substitutes often contain coconut or palm-kernel oil, which are high in saturated fats. Read labels carefully and choose dairy products and substitutes that are low in fat and saturated fat.

High-fat cheeses—such as Brie, Camembert, and cheese spreads—can wreak havoc on a low-fat diet. Leave them in the cheese case.

Eggs

Watch out for those yolks! One large egg yolk contains 213 to 220 milligrams of cholesterol, which is almost your entire daily allowance.

Go ahead and eat as many egg whites as you like. They don't contain a bit of cholesterol, and they are an excellent source of protein.

When cooking, you can often use egg whites in place of whole eggs. For instance, substitute two egg whites for one egg. Or use egg substitutes, which contain little or no cholesterol. To avoid the possibility of salmonella poisoning, never eat raw eggs.

Fats and Oils

Although it's a good idea to limit the amount of fat in your diet, your body needs small amounts of certain fats. Polyunsaturated and monounsaturated oils are the kind to look for.

Buy margarine in place of butter. Look for a margarine that lists liquid vegetable oil as the first ingredient. These usually contain no more than 2 grams of saturated fat per tablespoon. Diet margarine contains water, so use it as a spread but not as a cooking substitute for regular margarine. Use nonstick vegetable-oil sprays in place of butter or margarine for cooking or coating baking pans.

Select vegetable oil made from safflower, corn, sesame, sunflower, soybean, olive, or canola oil. Avoid coconut oil, palm kernel oil, and palm oil because they contain high amounts of saturated fats.

Supermarket shelves are well stocked with a vast array of salad dressings, ranging from high-fat to no-fat-at-all. Look for reduced-calorie, low-calorie, nonfat, or no-cholesterol dressings. Some are very high in sodium, so be sure to read the nutrition label if you're monitoring your sodium intake. Or make your own heart-healthful dressing (see index for recipes).

Vegetables and Fruits

Most fresh vegetables and fruits contain little or no fat, are low in sodium, and are high in fiber and vitamins. The exceptions are coconut meat and avocados. Coconut meat (shredded or flaked) is high in saturated fat, and avocados are high in unsaturated fat. Eat these only occasionally.

Canned and frozen fruits are healthful alternatives to fresh. For less sugar and calories, choose frozen fruits without added sugar and fruits canned in water or their own juice.

Scan the frozen-food aisle and read the label of any frozen vegetables you are considering. Try to buy no-salt-added frozen vegetables whenever possible, and avoid any made with butter or sauces.

Breads, Cereals, Pasta, and Starchy Vegetables

Choose from a delicious variety of enriched breads, such as whole-grain, whole-wheat, rye, pumpernickel, cracked wheat, French, and Italian. Most contain lots of nutrients with relatively few calories.

Check the labels on baked goods and try to avoid those made with whole milk and egg yolks. Bypass most commercially baked products—such as muffins, croissants, and doughnuts—since they contain high amounts of fat. One exception is store-bought angel food cake, which is made with egg whites, rendering it fat-free.

Select a variety of tasty whole grains, such as brown rice, bulgur, millet, and wheat berries. They are low in fat and high in fiber.

Dried beans and lentils make an excellent substitute for meat in casseroles, stews, and soups. To save preparation time, choose canned beans. Just be sure to rinse them well with water and drain them before using. If you are watching your sodium, look for varieties without added salt.

Don't forget about hot cereals, pastas, and rices. They are low in fat and contain almost no sodium (except the instant ones)—just omit the salt (and butter) when cooking them.

Cold cereals are relatively low in fat but may be high in sugar or sodium. Read the labels to help you make a healthful choice.

Snacks

Healthful snacking is easy, thanks to the growing variety of low-fat crackers and cookies to choose from. Be sure to read the labels and keep a close eye on sodium.

Nuts and seeds make tasty natural snacks. Choose unsalted dry-roasted versions to cut down a little bit on fat and sodium.

Most chips are high in fat and sodium. Look for chips that are low in salt and baked, not fried. Jazz them up with some fresh-tasting fat-free Fresh and Chunky Salsa (see page 48).

Hands down, the best snacks are fresh fruits and vegetables, which are available all year round.

Miscellaneous Foods

Choose canned soups that are low in fat and sodium. Look for them in the grocery aisle with other soups.

Wet your whistle with a variety of healthful beverages, such as 100 percent fruit juices and bottled water. Be sure to read labels to avoid drinks high in sodium. If you drink alcohol, it's best to limit your intake to one to two ounces per day.

Are you on the lookout for sodium? Then watch out for these salty foods and use them in moderation: soy sauce, steak sauce, ketchup, chili sauce, monosodium glutamate (MSG), meat tenderizer, pickles, relishes, seasoning salts, bouillon granules or cubes, and salad dressings. Choose low-sodium versions of these foods whenever possible.

Nutrition Labeling

Once you are at the store trying to make your healthful food choices, take some time to read labels. You'll discover that healthful eating has never been easier, thanks to the nutrition label found on most foods in the grocery store. Most supermarket foods must have a nutrition label and an ingredient list. You can buy with confidence, since claims like "low cholesterol" and "fat free" can be used only if a food meets legal standards set by the government.

Reading food labels is like looking inside the package without opening it. Ingredients are listed in order by weight, the largest amount first and the smallest last.

You'll find other important information on a nutrition-facts label:

- *Serving size:* The serving size for all foods must be consistent, allowing you to easily compare the nutritional values of similar foods.
- *Calories and calories from fat:* The label will list the number of calories per serving and include the number of calories coming from fat.
- *Daily values for nutrients:* This section will show you how a food fits into your overall daily diet. These values tell the food's nutritional content based on a 2000-calorie-per-day diet. The nutrients listed are total fat, saturated fat, cholesterol, sodium, total carbohydrate, dietary fiber, vitamins A and C, calcium, and iron.
- *Maximum and minimum amounts of daily values:* Near the bottom of the label are six nutrients and the maximum and minimum amounts that you should try to eat every day, depending on your caloric intake. Remember that these numbers are based on a daily intake of 2000 calories, so if your caloric intake is less or more, these values will change.

A sample label

More nutrients may be listed on some labels.

Nutrition Facts

Serving Size ½ cup (114g)
Servings Per Container 4

Amount Per Serving

Calories 90   Calories from Fat 30

	% Daily Value*
Total Fat 3g	**5%**
Saturated fat 0g	**0%**
Cholesterol 0mg	**0%**
Sodium 300mg	**13%**
Total Carbohydrate 13g	**4%**
Dietary fiber 3g	**12%**
Sugars 3g	
Protein 3g	

Vitamin A	80%	•	Vitamin C	60%
Calcium	4%	•	Iron	4%

* Percent Daily Values are based on a 2000-calorie diet. Your daily values may be higher or lower, depending on your calorie needs:

	Calories	2000	2500
Total Fat	Less than	65g	80g
Sat Fat	Less than	20g	25g
Cholesterol	Less than	300mg	300mg
Sodium	Less than	2400mg	2400mg
Total Carbohydrate		300g	375g
Fiber		25g	30g

Calories per gram:
Fat 9   •   Carbohydrate 4   •   Protein 4

Key Words on Food Labels and What They Mean

When you see certain words on a food label, you can rest assured they mean what they say as defined by the government. For example:

Key Words	What They Mean
Fat-free	Less than 0.5 gram of fat per serving
Low-fat	3 grams of fat or less per serving
Lean	Less than 10 grams of fat, 4 grams of saturated fat, and 95 milligrams of cholesterol per serving

| Light (Lite) | One-third fewer calories or no more than half the fat of the higher-calorie, higher-fat version; or no more than half the sodium of the higher-sodium version |
| Cholesterol-free | Less than 2 milligrams of cholesterol and 2 grams or less of saturated fat per serving |

Labeling Regulations About Health Claims

To Make Health Claims About . . .	The Food Must Be . . .
Heart disease	Low in fat, saturated fat, and cholesterol
Blood pressure and sodium	Low in sodium
Heart Disease (in relation to fruits, vegetables, and grain products)	A fruit, vegetable, or grain product low in fat, saturated fat, and cholesterol that contains at least 0.6 gram soluble fiber, without fortification, per serving

Other claims may appear on some labels.

Stocking Your Kitchen

There's no such thing as the perfect pantry, but here's a good start. It's a list of shelf-stable and frozen foods that are used in the recipes in this book. Use this list as a guide to stock your kitchen. With a pantry full of the basics, you can simplify your shopping list and purchase only the fresh items needed for the recipes on the following pages. Most of the items are available from your local grocery store. A few items, such as quinoa or steel-cut oats, can be found at health-food stores.

Herbs, Spices, and Seasonings

Allspice	Caraway seed	Cumin
Asian-style cooking sauce	Cardamom	Curry powder
	Chili powder	Dillweed
Basil	Cinnamon	Dry mustard
Bay leaves	Cloves	Fennel seed
Bouillon granules	Coriander	Garlic

Garlic powder
Ginger, powdered
Gingerroot
Ground red pepper
Horseradish,
  prepared
Imitation bacon bits
Italian seasoning
Lemon pepper
Marjoram
Nutmeg
Onion powder
Oregano

Paprika
Pepper, black,
  crushed red, ground
  red, white
Peppercorns
Poppy seed
Red hot pepper
  sauce
Rosemary
Saffron
Sage
Salt
Savory

Sesame oil
Sesame seed
Soy sauce (reduced-
  sodium)
Taco seasoning mix
Tarragon
Teriyaki sauce
Thyme
Turmeric
Vanilla
Worcestershire sauce

Grains, Pastas, and Mixes

All-purpose flour
Bulgur
Corn tortillas
Cornbread stuffing
  mix
Cornmeal, finely
  ground yellow
Corn-muffin mix
Gingerbread cake
  and cookie mix
Granola, low-fat
Hot-roll mix
Light fudge brownie
  mix
Light white cake mix
Light wild blueberry
  muffin mix

Light yellow cake
  mix
Macaroni-and-
  cheese mix
Millet
Noodles, medium
Oat bran
Oats, steel-cut, rolled
Pasta, bow-tie, fet-
  tuccine, linguine,
  elbow macaroni,
  alphabet pasta,
  angel-hair pasta
  (capellini)
Pearl barley
Pumpkin quick
  bread mix

Quinoa
Reduced-fat baking
  and pancake mix
Rice, quick-cooking
  brown, aromatic
Rye bread
Sourdough French
  bread
Unprocessed wheat
  bran
Wheat germ
Whole-grain bread
Whole-wheat berries
Whole-wheat flour
Whole-wheat flour
  tortillas

Frozen Foods

Artichoke hearts
Asian-style frozen
  vegetables
Asparagus, cut, no-
  salt-added

Broccoli, florets, and
  chopped, no-salt-
  added
Brussels sprouts, no-
  salt-added

Carrots, whole baby,
  no-salt-added
Cauliflower, florets,
  no-salt-added
Corn, no-salt-added

Green beans, Italian-style, cut, no-salt-added
Lima beans
Loose-pack vegetables, no-salt-added
Mixed vegetables, no-salt-added

Orange juice concentrate, unsweetened
Pearl onions, no-salt-added
Peas, no-salt-added
Peas and carrots, no-salt-added

Pineapple–orange juice concentrate, unsweetened
Rhubarb, cut
Spinach, chopped, no-salt-added

Miscellaneous

Almonds, sliced and slivered
Anchovy paste
Apple juice, unsweetened
Apples, sliced, canned in water
Applesauce, unsweetened
Apricots, dried
Baking powder
Baking soda
Barbecue sauce
Beans, canned, black, garbanzo, Great Northern, kidney, navy, pinto
Beer, light or nonalcoholic
Blueberries, dried
Bourbon
Bread crumbs, plain, dry
Brown sugar
Candy sprinkles, multicolored
Capers
Cereal, toasted rice, toasted oat

squares, whole-grain flakes
Champagne
Champagne vinegar
Cherries, dried
Chicken broth, canned, low-sodium
Chicken or turkey gravy, low-fat bottled
Chocolate chips, milk or semisweet
Chocolate-flavored drink mix
Chocolate-flavored syrup
Chocolate sandwich cookies
Corn, canned, no-salt-added
Cornflake crumbs
Cornstarch
Couscous
Crackers, fish-shaped or other bite-size, low-salt
Cranberries, dried
Cranberry sauce
Cream of chicken soup, condensed, reduced-fat

Cream of mushroom soup, condensed, reduced-fat
Croutons
Currants
Dates, dried
Dried fruit bits
Dry sherry
Evaporated skim milk, canned
Fruit cocktail, canned, juice-pack
Green chili peppers, canned
Hoisin sauce
Honey
Jalapeño peppers, chopped
Jelly, jalapeño
Ketchup
Lasagna noodles, no-cook variety
Lemonade drink mix
Mandarin orange sections, canned in light syrup
Maple syrup, light
Marmalade
Marshmallows, miniature
Mashed potatoes, instant

Mayonnaise or salad dressing, nonfat or no-cholesterol
Melba toast rounds
Milk, nonfat dry powder
Molasses
Mustard, Dijon and other prepared
Oil, olive, sesame, vegetable
Olives, pitted, ripe
Peaches, strained (baby food)
Peanut butter
Peanuts, unsalted, dry-roasted
Pear halves, canned in light syrup or water
Pecans
Pesto, bottled
Pineapple, canned tidbits, chunks, crushed, unsweetened
Plum sauce or plum jam

Popcorn
Potatoes, canned, whole
Pretzels, miniature, no-salt-added
Prunes, dried, pitted
Pumpkin, canned
Ramen noodles
Raisins
Red wine, dry
Refried beans, canned, fat-free
Rice or popcorn cakes, fat-free
Salad dressing, bottled nonfat Italian
Salmon, canned, boneless and skinless
Salsa
Spaghetti sauce, bottled, meatless, low-fat
Spreadable fruit, jelly, jam, or preserves
Sugar, brown, granulated, confectioners'

Sun-dried tomatoes, packed in oil
Thousand Island salad dressing
Tomato preserves
Tomatoes, canned, chopped or diced
Tomatoes, canned, stewed
Tomato paste, no-salt-added
Tomato sauce, no-salt-added
Tomato soup, condensed, reduced-fat and -sodium
Tuna, canned, white chunk, water-packed, low-salt
Unsweetened cocoa powder
Vegetable oil spray
Vinegar, white wine, rice wine, and balsamic
Walnut pieces, unsalted
White wine, dry

Getting Organized

Is your kitchen organized with efficiency in mind? If not, here are a few suggestions.

- Try to keep clutter off the kitchen counters. Newspapers, mail, homework, and the like have a way of taking up valuable counter space that should be kept clear for cooking.
- Keep cooking equipment near the location it is used in most. For example, store pots, pans, and pot holders near your stove, and store cutting boards near your knives.
- Keep your knives sharp. Chopping and slicing are much easier with sharp blades than with dull ones.
- You may want to fill a sink with hot soapy water before you start to cook. This allows easy clean-up for measuring utensils and pots and pans. It also keeps preparation utensils clean and free of bacteria, especially when preparing raw poultry.
- Assemble all the recipe ingredients on the counter before beginning to cook. This way you'll know immediately if you have all the ingredients on hand before you begin.

Kitchen Equipment

You don't need fancy kitchen equipment to put together a healthful meal using these recipes. Saucepans, skillets, baking dishes, knives, cutting boards, measuring cups (dry and liquid), and measuring spoons are a good start. But if you're in the market for some time-saving equipment, check out these options:

- For large amounts of chopping or combining foods in a jiffy, food processors or blenders are ideal. If possible, leave these appliances on the counter so you will use them more often. But for smaller jobs, it is sometimes quicker to chop foods by hand and save on cleanup.
- A microwave oven is handy for cooking foods quickly or thawing frozen foods in a snap. You can also use it to warm breads, cook frozen vegetables, or reheat leftovers. To prepare a recipe using your microwave oven, refer to the microwave directions that accompany some of the recipes throughout the book.
- When choosing pots and pans, opt for cookware with nonstick finishes. These surfaces require less fat for cooking, and cleanup is a breeze.
- Baking dishes (glass or ceramic) and baking pans (metal) of similar size can be used interchangeably in recipes. If a baked recipe, such as bread or cake, calls for a baking pan, you can substitute a glass or ceramic baking dish. However, be sure to lower the oven temperature 25 degrees to prevent overbrowning.
- Using a wok is a fast and easy way to prepare vegetables and stir-fry recipes. Many woks now come with nonstick finishes, which allow you to use less oil.
- Electric crockery cookers (slow cookers) are the perfect way to prepare a make-ahead meal that can cook all day. This method may not be quick, but it sure is easy! Look for crockery-cooker directions with some of the recipes throughout the book.
- Pressure cookers can cook a typical long-simmering supper in less than an hour. Although the recipes in this book do not use a pressure cooker, some of them could be easily adapted to one. Refer to the manufacturer's directions that come with your pressure cooker.

Cooking for a Healthy Heart

Now for the fun part—cooking! If you follow the recipes in this book, you'll be on your way to heart-healthful eating. Here are some preparation tips that will help keep your healthful foods healthful until they reach your table:

- Broiling meats and poultry lets the fat drip away from the food as it cooks.
- Poaching in a nonfat or low-fat liquid is a great way to cook chicken, fish, or eggs. It keeps the food moist and flavorful and doesn't add fat.
- Baking is a fat-free form of cooking that's excellent for meat, poultry, and fish.
- Braising or stewing is a slow-cooking method that tenderizes tough cuts of meat. Since the fat usually cooks out of the food, it's best to cook it a day ahead and chill it overnight, which will make the fat rise to the top. Then you can remove the chilled fat before reheating.
- Steaming is a perfect way to cook food without fat while retaining the food's natural flavor, vitamins, and minerals. Try it with fish or vegetables.
- Sautéing or stir-frying allows you to cook meat or vegetables quickly over high heat with little or no fat. Here's where a nonstick finish on your skillet or wok comes in handy.
- Grilling adds a new flavor dimension to cooked meats and allows the fat to drip away from the meat as it cooks. Vegetables are also delicious when cooked on the grill.

- Microwave cooking is a snap, and it dries food less than conventional cooking, so it requires little or no added fat.

About the Recipe Timings

Each recipe in this book provides you with a preparation time and cooking time. Since everyone works at different speeds in the kitchen, the preparation time is only an estimate. Use it as an indicator of approximately how much time it will take you to prepare the recipe once all the ingredients are assembled on the counter.

Fresh Is Best

Here are some easy ways to keep food as fresh and flavorful as possible during storage:

- Always cover food to be refrigerated. Otherwise, bacteria can attack it, changing its flavor and composition.
- Store milk in its original container in the refrigerator, and close the carton after each use.
- Store eggs in the refrigerator the same way they were purchased—in their cartons with the large end of the egg up.
- Refrigerate meat at the lowest temperature possible without freezing it. Use within a few days after buying.
- Refrigerate poultry in its original wrapping and use it within one to two days after purchasing. Freeze it for longer storage.
- Let bananas ripen at room temperature and then refrigerate them. The cold will darken the skin, but the flavor will be fine.
- For best flavor, store cantaloupe at room temperature for two to four days.
- Store all-purpose flour and cereals at room temperature in a dry place in tightly covered containers. This keeps out dust, moisture, and insects. Store whole-wheat flour in your refrigerator to keep it from becoming rancid.
- Keep vegetable oils tightly sealed, and store them at room temperature. For longer storage, place them in the refrigerator. Most oils stay clear when chilled, but olive oil becomes thick and cloudy.
- Refrigerate homemade salad dressings in a jar with a tight-fitting lid for up to two weeks.

Freeze-Ahead Tips

Freezing prepared foods to eat later is a smart way to ease the dinner rush hour. Here are a few hints to help you.

To freeze casseroles, line the baking container with heavy-duty foil three times the length of the dish. Add prepared food to the container and cool. Seal foil over food and place in the freezer. When the food is frozen, lift it out of the dish and store just the wrapped food, without the container, in the freezer. To serve, remove the foil and place the frozen food back in its original dish. If you did not cook the casserole before freezing it, bake it according to recipe directions, allowing more time. If the casserole has been baked, you need only to reheat it before serving. To shorten the baking or reheating time, remove the foil and place the frozen food in its original dish, then thaw it for several hours or overnight in the refrigerator before baking or reheating according to recipe directions.

Soups and stews freeze well. Thaw them quickly by freezing them in one-serving portions. This also allows you to use only what you need for a meal.

Season the food lightly, since freezing intensifies some flavors. You can always add more seasonings after the food is cooked, if necessary.

If a casserole contains vegetables, undercook them just a bit, since they will cook more when reheated.

Freeze casseroles without toppers such as bread crumbs or shredded cheese. Just before reheating a casserole, sprinkle with desired topping.

Substitution List

To help you convert some of your own favorite recipes to more heart-healthful fare, look to this list for heart-smart substitutions.

Food	Substitution
Whole milk (1 cup)	1 cup skim milk in most recipes. For added richness, stir in 1 tablespoon unsaturated oil.
Heavy cream (1 cup)	1 cup evaporated skim milk or a combination of ½ cup low-fat or nonfat yogurt and ½ cup low-fat or nonfat cottage cheese.

Food	Substitution
Sour cream	Nonfat or light sour cream; blended low-fat or nonfat cottage cheese or ricotta cheese made with partially skimmed milk (thinned with a little skim milk or buttermilk, if necessary).
Cream cheese	Light cream cheese, Neufchâtel cheese, or nonfat cream cheese; 1 cup blended dry low-fat cottage cheese and ¼ cup acceptable margarine. Thin with skim milk, if necessary. Season with herbs and seasonings, if desired.
Butter (1 tablespoon)	1 tablespoon acceptable margarine or ¾ tablespoon polyunsaturated oil.
Shortening (1 cup)	1 cup (2 sticks) acceptable margarine.
Eggs (1 egg)	1 egg white plus 2 teaspoons unsaturated oil; cholesterol-free egg substitute used according to package directions; 3 egg whites for 2 whole eggs; 2 egg whites for 1 whole egg in baking.
Unsweetened baking chocolate (1 ounce)	3 tablespoons unsweetened cocoa powder or baking carob powder plus 1 tablespoon polyunsaturated oil or margarine.

How to Use These Recipes

$\mathbf{I}$f you're interested in eating healthful, delicious foods that don't require a lot of kitchen time, these recipes are for you. They were not created for people on a strict sodium- or fat-restricted diet, but many of these recipes are low enough in sodium and fat to fit into such diets.

Nutrient Analysis

Take a look at the nutrition breakdown at the bottom of each recipe. This analysis will help you determine whether the recipe fits into your specific eating plan. Expect to see a large variation in the amount of each nutrient from one recipe to another. So if you're on a restricted diet, read these carefully and choose recipes according to your needs.

Here is some helpful information to keep in mind when reviewing the nutrient analyses for the recipes:

- Garnishes and optional ingredients were not included in the nutrient analysis.
- Ingredients with a weight range (a 2½- to 3-pound chicken, for example) were analyzed at the lower weight.
- Statistics on meat were based on cooked lean meat trimmed of all visible fat.

- When a recipe lists two ingredient options to pick from (1 cup non-fat or low-fat yogurt, for example), the first was used in the nutrient analysis.
- Each analysis is based on a single serving, unless otherwise indicated.
- When a recipe calls for low-fat cheese, it was analyzed using cheese that has 33 percent less fat than regular cheese. If you would like to cut down on fat even further, choose cheese that has 50 percent less fat than regular cheese. For cold dishes, you may wish to use nonfat cheese products. If you're watching your sodium intake, be aware that the nonfat cheeses are typically higher in sodium than the low-fat cheeses.
- The values for saturated, monounsaturated, and polyunsaturated fatty acids may not add up precisely to the total fat in the recipe. That's because the total fat includes not only the fatty acids but other fatty substances and glycerol as well.
- When the recipe calls for *acceptable margarine*, we used corn-oil margarine for the analysis. Remember to choose a margarine that lists liquid vegetable oil as the first ingredient. It should contain no more than 2 grams of saturated fat per tablespoon.
- When a recipe calls for *acceptable vegetable oil*, we used corn oil. Other examples of acceptable vegetable oils are safflower, soybean, sunflower, sesame, canola, and olive oil. Peanut oil is recommended for occasional use only.
- The listing for "kcal" (an abbreviation for "kilocalorie") in the nutrient analysis is the scientific notation for what most people refer to simply as "calorie."
- The abbreviation for "gram" is "g"; the abbreviation for milligram is "mg."
- If a meat marinade was used, the nutrient analysis includes only the amount absorbed by the meat, based on USDA data on absorption.
- For vegetable marinades, no absorption data exists, so we added in the total amount of marinade used in the recipe.
- Feel free to make substitutions that will not affect the nutrition profile of the recipe. For example, use reconstituted lemon juice instead of fresh, or try tarragon vinegar instead of white wine vinegar.

Breakfast Dishes

Don't underestimate the importance of a good morning meal. Breakfast is the time to get your engine up and running for a full day of activity. Choose the proper fuel to start your day right by filling up with the eye-opening low-fat foods you'll find in this chapter. Take your pick from recipes that are fast to fix first thing in the morning or ones that are made ahead and waiting for you when you rise.

You don't have to give up pancakes, French toast, or egg sandwiches if you use the heart-healthful recipes in this chapter. You can even splurge and eat a few cookies for breakfast as long as they're our Rise-and-Shine Cookies. These crunchy little morsels will remind you of big chunks of granola without the guilt. Make them ahead and enjoy them all week long.

Bran Muffin Breakfast Trifle

This recipe uses store-bought bran muffins. Be sure to buy muffins that are low in fat and high in fiber, or make your own if you have time. Choose a pretty variety of fresh fruits, such as kiwifruit, melons, berries, pineapple, bananas, and mangoes.

Serves 6; 1 cup per serving

Preparation time: 10 minutes

Chilling time: 6 hours or overnight

3 cups coarsely crumbled low-fat bran muffins (about 3 medium muffins)
4 cups assorted fresh fruit chunks
2 cups nonfat or low-fat vanilla or fruit-flavored yogurt

Place half the muffin crumbs in a 2½-quart glass bowl or airtight container. Arrange 3½ cups of fruit on top. Cover with remaining muffin crumbs. Spoon yogurt evenly over the top. Top with remaining fruit, cover, and refrigerate for at least 6 hours or overnight.

Nutrient Analysis (per serving)

Calories 177 kcal
Protein 6 g
Carbohydrate 38 g
Cholesterol 2 mg
Sodium 98 mg
Total fat 2 g
  Saturated 0 g
  Polyunsaturated 1 g
  Monounsaturated 0 g

Pineapple Breakfast Parfaits

This is a quick and pretty way to serve fruit, yogurt, and cereal for breakfast or a snack. Don't make it ahead or the granola will lose its crunchiness.

Serves 3; ½ cup per serving

Preparation time: 5 minutes

15¼-ounce can pineapple chunks, canned in fruit juice, drained
8-ounce container nonfat or low-fat vanilla or fruit-flavored yogurt
½ cup low-fat granola

Layer half the fruit, half the yogurt, and half the granola in three parfait glasses or drinking glasses. Repeat layers. Serve immediately.

Nutrient Analysis (per serving)

Calories 184 kcal
Protein 6 g
Carbohydrate 39 g
Cholesterol 2 mg
Sodium 33 mg
Total fat 2 g
  Saturated 0 g
  Polyunsaturated 1 g
  Monounsaturated 1 g

Stuffed French Toast

This recipe only tastes rich and sinful. Actually, it is low in fat, cholesterol, and calories compared with classic French toast. Serve with fresh berries and light maple syrup.

Serves 3; 2 slices per serving

Preparation time: 10 minutes

Cooking time: 6 to 8 minutes

6 slices French bread, 1 inch thick
¼ cup nonfat or light cream cheese
½ teaspoon finely shredded orange peel
1 teaspoon orange juice
Egg substitute equivalent to 3 eggs
2 tablespoons skim milk
Vegetable oil spray

Cut a pocket horizontally into each slice of French bread, being careful not to cut all the way through. Set aside.

In a small bowl, stir together cream cheese, orange peel, and orange juice. Spoon about 1 heaping teaspoon cream cheese mixture into each bread pocket. Spread evenly with a knife.

In a shallow bowl, beat together egg substitute and milk. Place a slice of stuffed bread in the egg mixture. Let it soak about 30 seconds. Turn bread over and let it soak another 30 seconds. Repeat with remaining pieces of bread.

Spray a griddle or large skillet with vegetable oil. Place over medium heat. Cook bread slices 3 to 4 minutes on each side or until golden brown. Serve warm.

NUTRIENT ANALYSIS (PER SERVING)

Calories 242 kcal
Protein 15 g
Carbohydrate 42 g
Cholesterol 2 mg
Sodium 646 mg
Total fat 1 g
  Saturated 0 g
  Polyunsaturated 0 g
  Monounsaturated 0 g

Cook's Tip

There's no need to give up eggs when you're on a heart-healthful diet. Egg substitutes make a great stand-in for the real thing. They are made with egg whites and contain no fat and cholesterol, or less fat and cholesterol than whole eggs. When recipes in this book call for egg substitute, we used the kind with no fat and no cholesterol. Besides using them in egg dishes, try them in breads, muffins,

cakes, cookies, casseroles, sauces, and puddings. Don't use egg substitutes in cream puffs or pop-overs, because they won't puff or pop.

Instead of using egg substitutes, you can also use egg whites in place of whole eggs. Use 2 egg whites for each whole egg called for in a recipe. If the recipe requires a large number of eggs, then use 2 egg whites and 1 whole egg for every 2 whole eggs.

Cinnamon-Bran Pancakes

For a really quick breakfast or snack, prepare these pancakes in advance and store them in an airtight container in your refrigerator for up to one week. To reheat them in your microwave oven before serving, cook on 100% power (high) for 15 to 20 seconds for one pancake and 20 to 25 seconds for two pancakes.

Serves 6; 2 pancakes per serving

Preparation time: 5 minutes

Cooking time: 6 to 9 minutes total (2 to 3 minutes per 4 pancakes)

1½ cups reduced-fat baking and pancake mix
½ cup unprocessed wheat bran
1 teaspoon ground cinnamon
1 cup skim milk
Egg substitute equivalent to 2 eggs or 3 egg whites
Vegetable oil spray

In a medium mixing bowl, combine baking and pancake mix, bran, and cinnamon. Add milk and egg substitute. Beat with a wire whisk or rotary beater until well blended.

Spray griddle or heavy skillet with vegetable oil. Preheat griddle or skillet. Pour about ¼ cup batter for each pancake onto hot griddle or skillet. Cook each pancake until it is golden brown, turning to cook second side when pancake has a bubbly surface and slightly dry edges.

Top with fresh fruit or syrup.

NUTRIENT ANALYSIS*
(PER SERVING)

Calories 147 kcal
Protein 6 g
Carbohydrate 25 g
Cholesterol 1 mg
Sodium 389 mg
Total fat 2 g
 Saturated 1 g
 Polyunsaturated 1 g
 Monounsaturated 1 g

*Analyzed without toppings

Egg, Spinach, and Bacon Sandwiches

Don't limit these handy pocket sandwiches to the morning. They're also great at lunchtime.

Serves 4; 1 sandwich per serving

Preparation time: 5 minutes

Cooking time: 5 minutes

Egg substitute equivalent to 4 eggs
¼ cup skim milk
1 tablespoon imitation bacon bits
⅛ teaspoon black pepper
Vegetable oil spray
2 6-inch white or whole-wheat pita bread rounds, split crosswise
8 fresh spinach leaves, rinsed and patted dry
4 1-ounce slices low-fat American or Swiss cheese

In a small bowl, stir together egg substitute, milk, bacon bits, and pepper.

Spray a medium skillet with vegetable oil, place over medium heat, and add egg mixture. Cook, without stirring, until mixture begins to set on the bottom and around the edges. Using a large spoon or spatula, lift and fold partially cooked eggs so uncooked portion flows underneath. Continue cooking 2 to 3 minutes or until eggs are cooked throughout but are still glossy and moist.

Line each pita pocket with spinach and 1 slice of cheese. Spoon warm egg mixture into pita pockets.

NUTRIENT ANALYSIS (PER SERVING)

Calories 185 kcal
Protein 16 g
Carbohydrate 18 g
Cholesterol 15 mg
Sodium 701 mg
Total fat 5 g
  Saturated 3 g
  Polyunsaturated 0 g
  Monounsaturated 1 g

Cook's Tip

This book relies on vegetable oil spray to keep foods from sticking without much fat. Keep these tips in mind when you use it.

- Do not spray near an open flame or other heat source. Vegetable oil sprays are flammable.
- Spray only onto cold cooking surfaces, because vegetable oil sprays can burn or smoke if they are sprayed onto hot surfaces.
- Don't overspray. A one-second spray coats about as well as 1 tablespoon of vegetable oil.

- Hold the pan you are spraying over the sink so you don't make the floor or counter slippery.
- Always read and follow the manufacturer's directions before using.

Rise-and-Shine Cookies

Cookies for breakfast? Sure—when they are rich in fiber and low in fat and taste like big chunks of granola. Make these ahead of time for a quick breakfast treat.

Serves 15; 2 cookies per serving

Preparation time: 10 minutes

Cooking time: 10 minutes

½ cup all-purpose flour
¼ cup whole-wheat flour
½ teaspoon baking soda
¼ teaspoon salt
¼ teaspoon ground cinnamon
⅛ teaspoon ground nutmeg
½ cup firmly packed brown sugar
Egg substitute equivalent to 1 egg
3 tablespoons acceptable vegetable oil
1¼ cups quick-cooking or regular rolled oats
½ cup wheat germ

Preheat oven to 350° F.

In a small bowl, stir together flours, baking soda, salt, cinnamon, and nutmeg. Set aside.

In a large bowl, combine brown sugar, egg substitute, and vegetable oil. Stir until well combined. Stir in flour mixture, oats, and wheat germ.

Drop dough by tablespoons about 1 inch apart on a baking sheet. Flatten slightly to a 2-inch diameter with your hand or the bottom of a glass. Bake 10 minutes or until light brown. Cool on wire racks. Store cooled cookies in an airtight container for one week or in the freezer for several weeks.

NUTRIENT ANALYSIS (PER SERVING)

Calories 116 kcal
Protein 3 g
Carbohydrate 18 g
Cholesterol 0 mg
Sodium 74 mg
Total fat 4 g
  Saturated 1 g
  Polyunsaturated 2 g
  Monounsaturated 1 g

Cook's Tip

When a recipe calls for acceptable vegetable oil, we used corn oil. Other examples of acceptable vegetable oils are safflower, soybean, sunflower, sesame, canola, and olive oil.

Homemade Muesli

To give this European-inspired cereal a nuttier flavor, place the almonds on a baking sheet and toast them in a preheated 350° F oven for a few minutes or until light brown. Let cool and add to cereal mixture.

Serves 9; ½ cup per serving

Preparation time: 5 minutes

Standing time: 5 minutes

1 cup mixed-grain rolled oats or quick-cooking rolled oats
1 cup whole-grain flakes or bran cereal
1 cup dried cranberries or mixed dried fruit bits
⅓ cup slivered almonds
¼ cup firmly packed brown sugar
½ teaspoon ground cinnamon
3 cups skim milk

NUTRIENT ANALYSIS (PER SERVING)

Calories 161 kcal
Protein 6 g
Carbohydrate 30 g
Cholesterol 1 mg
Sodium 88 mg
Total fat 3 g
  Saturated 0 g
  Polyunsaturated 1 g
  Monounsaturated 2 g

In a large bowl, combine all ingredients except milk. Transfer to an airtight container.

For each serving, place about ⅓ cup oat mixture in a cereal bowl. Stir in ⅓ cup skim milk; let stand 5 minutes to allow oats to soften before serving.

Overnight Mixed-Grain Cereal

This whole-grain cereal must soak overnight so it will be ready to cook in just a few minutes the next morning. If you prefer, serve it like oatmeal by adding some skim milk and a little sugar to the cooked mixture.

1 cup steel-cut oats
1 cup pearl barley
1 cup whole-wheat berries or triticale berries
1 cup dried cranberries, dried blueberries, or
   chopped dates
⅔ cup millet
Water

Serves 14; ⅓ cup per serving

Preparation time:
5 minutes

Standing time:
Overnight

Cooking time:
6 to 12 minutes

NUTRIENT ANALYSIS
(PER SERVING)

Calories 182 kcal
Protein 5 g
Carbohydrate 40 g
Cholesterol 0 mg
Sodium 5 mg
Total fat 1 g
 Saturated 0 g
 Polyunsaturated 0 g
 Monounsaturated 0 g

Combine all ingredients except water in a large bowl. Transfer to an airtight container.

For each serving, combine ⅓ cup cereal mixture and ⅔ cup water in a saucepan. Cover and let stand overnight. In the morning, bring cereal mixture to a boil over high heat. Reduce heat and simmer, uncovered, 5 to 10 minutes, stirring occasionally.

Chunky Cranberry Whip

Serve this breakfast drink with a bowl of whole-grain cereal and skim milk.

1 cup canned whole cranberry sauce
1 cup orange juice
4 to 6 ice cubes
1 tablespoon powdered lemonade drink mix or
   granulated sugar

Serves 2; ¾ cup per serving

Preparation time:
5 minutes

NUTRIENT ANALYSIS
(PER SERVING)

Calories 298 kcal
Protein 1 g
Carbohydrate 73 g
Cholesterol 0 mg
Sodium 39 mg
Total fat 0 g
 Saturated 0 g
 Polyunsaturated 0 g
 Monounsaturated 0 g

Combine all ingredients in a blender or the work bowl of a food processor fitted with a metal blade. Cover and process until well combined. Pour into glasses and serve immediately.

Banana-Kiwi Breakfast Shake

Depending on the sweetness of the fruit, you may want to add one or two tablespoons of sugar to this smooth morning drink.

Serves 2; 1 cup per serving

Preparation time: 5 minutes

1 medium banana, peeled and quartered
1 medium kiwifruit, peeled and halved
1 cup low-fat buttermilk
6-ounce container nonfat or low-fat fruit-flavored yogurt
1 to 2 tablespoons sugar (optional)

Combine all ingredients in a blender or the work bowl of a food processor fitted with a metal blade. Cover and process until smooth. Pour into glasses to serve.

NUTRIENT ANALYSIS
(PER SERVING)

Calories 181 kcal
Protein 8 g
Carbohydrate 36 g
Cholesterol 6 mg
Sodium 167 mg
Total fat 2 g
  Saturated 1 g
  Polyunsaturated 0 g
  Monounsaturated 0 g

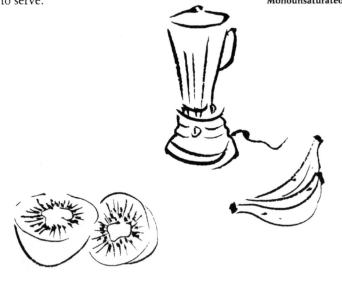

Appetizers, Spreads, and Snacks

Here's a simple fat-fighting philosophy: If you can't beat the munchies, then join them! Just be sure you choose from one of the easy appetizer recipes on the next few pages that keep fat and calories in check. Treat yourself to a couple of smart snack mixes, Southwest quesadillas, a hot vegetable dip, a fruity spread, and lots more.

All these recipes take little time to prepare yet reap big flavor rewards. Just watch the serving sizes so you can keep your nibbling within your daily meal plan.

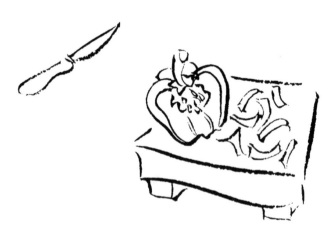

Savory Snack Mix

This five-ingredient nibble mix goes together in a snap, ready to bake in your oven or microwave.

6 4-inch rice or popcorn cakes, broken into bite-size pieces
2 cups bite-size low-salt cheese-flavored or low-salt plain fish-shaped or other bite-size crackers
2 tablespoons acceptable margarine, melted
½ teaspoon chili powder
½ teaspoon garlic powder

Makes 5 cups

Serves 10; ½ cup per serving

Preparation time: 10 minutes

Cooking time: 25 minutes

Microwave cooking time: 2 minutes

Preheat oven to 325° F.

In a large plastic bag with a tight-fitting seal, combine the rice-cake pieces and crackers. In a small bowl, stir together the melted margarine, chili powder, and garlic powder. Pour over cracker mixture. Seal bag and gently shake mixture until well coated. Transfer to a baking sheet.

Bake, uncovered, for 25 minutes, stirring once or twice during baking.

Spread mixture onto paper towels to cool.

The mix can be stored at room temperature in an airtight container for up to 2 weeks.

NUTRIENT ANALYSIS (PER SERVING)

Calories 81 kcal
Protein 1 g
Carbohydrate 11 g
Cholesterol 1 mg
Sodium 89 mg
Total fat 4 g
 Saturated 1 g
 Polyunsaturated 1 g
 Monounsaturated 2 g

Microwave Method

Prepare recipe as directed above, but place cracker mixture in a microwave-safe bowl or casserole dish. Microwave on 100% power (high) for 2 minutes, stirring after 1 minute.

Cook's Tip

All of our recipes use margarine instead of butter. When choosing margarine, look for one that lists liquid vegetable oil as the first ingredient. Diet margarine contains water, so it's not suitable as a cooking substitute for butter or margarine.

Sugar-and-Spice Snack Mix

How's this for time saving? This mix cooks in your microwave oven in three minutes, and it's crisp and crunchy after it cools.

Makes 7 cups

Serves 14; ½ cup per serving

Preparation time: 10 minutes

Cooking time: 25 minutes

Microwave cooking time: 3 minutes

3 cups lightly sweetened toasted oat squares cereal
3 cups miniature no-salt-added pretzels
2 tablespoons acceptable margarine, melted
1 tablespoon firmly packed brown sugar
½ teaspoon ground cinnamon
1 cup miniature marshmallows or dried fruit bits

Preheat oven to 325° F.

In a large plastic bag with a tight-fitting seal, combine oat squares and pretzels. In a small bowl, stir together melted margarine, brown sugar, and cinnamon. Pour over cereal mixture. Seal bag and gently shake mixture until well coated. Transfer to a baking sheet.

Bake, uncovered, for 25 minutes, stirring once or twice. Spread mixture onto paper towels to cool. Add marshmallows and stir to mix.

Store at room temperature in an airtight container for up to 2 weeks.

NUTRIENT ANALYSIS (PER SERVING)

Calories 107 kcal
Protein 3 g
Carbohydrate 20 g
Cholesterol 0 mg
Sodium 89 mg
Total fat 3 g
 Saturated 1 g
 Polyunsaturated 1 g
 Monounsaturated 1 g

Microwave Method

Prepare recipe as directed above, but place cereal mixture in a microwave-safe bowl or casserole dish. Microwave on 100% power (high) for 3 minutes, stirring once every minute.

Cook's Tip

You can quickly melt the 2 tablespoons of margarine in your microwave oven by placing the margarine in a custard cup or other small microwave-safe container, covering it with wax paper, and heating it on 100% power (high) for 40 to 50 seconds.

Cauliflower and Mushroom Nibbles

Now you can enjoy the taste of fried cauliflower and mushrooms without the grease. These oven-baked morsels are low in fat and high in flavor.

Serves 8; approximately 4 pieces per serving

Preparation time: 15 minutes

Cooking time: 8 to 10 minutes

⅔ cup plain bread crumbs
¼ cup grated Parmesan cheese
1 egg white
1 teaspoon water
2 cups bite-size cauliflower florets
8 ounces bite-size whole fresh mushrooms, cleaned and trimmed
Low-fat meatless spaghetti sauce (optional)

Preheat oven to 400° F.

In a plastic bag with a tight-fitting seal, combine bread crumbs and Parmesan cheese.

In a small bowl, stir together egg white and water.

Dip a few cauliflower florets in egg-white mixture. Place in the plastic bag with the bread crumbs and Parmesan mixture. Seal bag and shake gently until vegetables are evenly coated. Place in a single layer on a baking sheet. Repeat with remaining cauliflower florets and mushrooms.

Bake for 8 to 10 minutes or until lightly browned. Serve warm with hot spaghetti sauce for dipping if desired.

NUTRIENT ANALYSIS (PER SERVING)

Calories 57 kcal
Protein 3 g
Carbohydrate 8 g
Cholesterol 2 mg
Sodium 121 mg
Total fat 1 g
Saturated 1 g
Polyunsaturated 0 g
Monounsaturated 0 g

Cook's Tip

To clean fresh mushrooms, wipe them with a clean, damp cloth or rinse them briefly in a colander under running water and dry gently with a paper towel. Never soak fresh mushrooms, since they absorb water like a sponge, which will ruin their texture and taste.

Mushroom Quesadillas

What makes these finger foods so easy to make? You just sauté a few ingredients, assemble the quesadillas, and bake them in the oven. Team them with Fresh and Chunky Salsa (see page 48) or commercial salsa.

Serves 6; 2 wedges per serving

Preparation time: 10 minutes

Cooking time: 5 minutes

Microwave cooking time: 1 to 2 minutes

Vegetable oil spray
8 ounces sliced fresh mushrooms
½ medium onion, thinly sliced and separated into rings
1 teaspoon bottled minced garlic
3 tablespoons chopped fresh cilantro
3 8-inch whole-wheat flour tortillas
6 tablespoons shredded low-fat Monterey Jack cheese with jalapeño peppers or low-fat cheddar cheese
Commercial salsa or Fresh and Chunky Salsa (page 48) (optional)

Preheat oven to 350° F.

Spray a large skillet with vegetable oil. Cook mushrooms, onion, and garlic in skillet over medium heat until onion is tender, about 5 to 7 minutes. Stir in cilantro and remove from heat.

Arrange one-third of the mushroom mixture on half of one tortilla. Sprinkle with 2 tablespoons of the cheese. Fold the other half of the tortilla over cheese. Place on a baking sheet. Repeat with remaining ingredients to make 3 quesadillas total.

Bake quesadillas about 5 minutes or until filling is hot and cheese melts. Cut each quesadilla into 4 wedges.

Serve warm—with salsa, if desired.

NUTRIENT ANALYSIS (PER SERVING)

Calories 67 kcal
Protein 4 g
Carbohydrate 10 g
Cholesterol 4 mg
Sodium 115 mg
Total fat 2 g
  Saturated 1 g
  Polyunsaturated 0 g
  Monounsaturated 0 g

Microwave Method

Spray a microwave-safe casserole with vegetable oil. Add mushrooms, onion, and garlic. Cook, uncovered, on 100% power (high) for 5 to 7 minutes or until onion is tender, stirring twice. Stir in cilantro. Assemble quesadillas as directed above and arrange them on a microwave-safe plate or platter. Cook, uncovered, on 100% power (high), rotating plate once, for 1 to 2 minutes or until filling is hot and cheese melts.

Bite-Size Pizzas

These beat-the-clock snacks are just right for hungry kids after school.

8 garlic or onion melba toast rounds
3 tablespoons low-fat meatless spaghetti sauce
⅓ cup shredded part-skim mozzarella cheese

Preheat broiler. Place melba toast rounds on a baking sheet. Spoon about 1 teaspoon spaghetti sauce over each round. Sprinkle with cheese. Broil 4 inches from the heat for 1 to 2 minutes or just until cheese melts.

Microwave Method

Prepare recipe as directed above, but arrange assembled melba toast rounds in a circle on a microwave-safe plate. Cook on 100% power (high) for 15 to 30 seconds. Rotate plate a half turn and cook an additional 15 to 30 seconds or just until cheese melts.

Serves 4; 2 pizzas per serving

Preparation time: 5 minutes

Cooking time: 1 to 2 minutes

Microwave cooking time: 30 to 60 seconds

NUTRIENT ANALYSIS (PER SERVING)

Calories 60 kcal
Protein 3 g
Carbohydrate 7 g
Cholesterol 5 mg
Sodium 63 mg
Total fat 2 g
  Saturated 1 g
  Polyunsaturated 0 g
  Monounsaturated 1 g

Homemade Corn Tortilla Chips

These crisp chips are full of natural flavor and low in fat and sodium.

10 5-inch corn tortillas

Preheat oven to 400° F.

Place 3 or 4 tortillas in a stack and cut them into 4 wedges. Repeat with remaining tortillas, making 40 wedges total.

Arrange wedges in a single layer on baking sheets. Bake for 8 to 10 minutes or until crisp. Cool before serving. Store in an airtight container for up to 2 weeks.

Serve with Fresh and Chunky Salsa (see below) or commercial salsa.

Makes 40 tortilla chips

Serves 8; 5 chips per serving

Preparation time: Less than 5 minutes

Cooking time: 8 to 10 minutes

NUTRIENT ANALYSIS (PER SERVING)

Calories 49 kcal
Protein 2 g
Carbohydrate 9 g
Cholesterol 0 mg
Sodium 39 mg
Total fat 1 g
  Saturated 0 g
  Polyunsaturated 0 g
  Monounsaturated 0 g

Fresh and Chunky Salsa

Start with canned chopped tomatoes and embellish them with a harvest of fresh vegetables and seasonings. Green onions are also called scallions.

14½-ounce can chopped tomatoes
½ cup chopped green or yellow bell pepper
2 green onions, sliced
2 tablespoons snipped fresh cilantro or parsley
1 tablespoon white wine vinegar
½ teaspoon ground cumin
½ teaspoon bottled minced garlic
Few dashes bottled red hot pepper sauce

In a bowl, stir together all ingredients.

Serve with Homemade Corn Tortilla Chips (see above) or commercial tortilla chips with no added fat. Can be covered and stored in the refrigerator for up to 1 week.

Makes 2 cups

Serves 8; ¼ cup per serving

Preparation time: 5 to 10 minutes

NUTRIENT ANALYSIS (PER SERVING)

Calories 15 kcal
Protein 1 g
Carbohydrate 3 g
Cholesterol 0 mg
Sodium 85 mg
Total fat 0 g
  Saturated 0 g
  Polyunsaturated 0 g
  Monounsaturated 0 g

Layered Pesto Spread

Pesto is an aromatic blend of fresh basil, parsley, Parmesan cheese, garlic, nuts, and oil. Although it is relatively high in fat, a little bit goes a long way in this flavorful spread. Making homemade pesto will add a few minutes to the preparation time, but it will also reduce the amount of fat in this recipe. Look for pesto in the specialty-cheese section of your supermarket. If there is a layer of oil on top of the pesto, spoon or pour it off before using. This makes a great take-along appetizer. To make more servings, just double the recipe and layer the ingredients in a two-cup mold.

Makes ¾ cup

Serves 6; 2 tablespoons per serving

Preparation time: 10 minutes

Chilling time: At least 1 hour

1 cup nonfat or low-fat cottage cheese
2 tablespoons purchased pesto or Homemade
  Pesto (see page 229)
Paprika (optional)
Fresh basil leaves (optional)

Place cottage cheese in a colander; rinse under cold running water. Drain, pressing out as much liquid as possible with the back of a large spoon. Place drained cottage cheese in a blender or the work bowl of a food processor fitted with a metal blade. Cover and process until smooth (there should be about ¾ cup).

Line a 1-cup custard cup or mold with plastic wrap. Spread ¼ cup of the blended cottage cheese in the bottom of the cup. Spread 1 tablespoon of pesto over cheese. Repeat cheese and pesto layers, ending with cheese. Cover and chill for several hours or overnight before serving.

Before serving, uncover and invert custard cup or mold onto a serving plate. Remove cup and carefully peel plastic wrap from mold. Sprinkle with paprika and garnish with fresh basil leaves if desired.

Serve with light crackers or thin slices of French bread.

NUTRIENT ANALYSIS
(PER SERVING)

Calories 38 kcal
Protein 4 g
Carbohydrate 1 g
Cholesterol 2 mg
Sodium 36 mg
Total fat 2 g
  Saturated 0 g
  Polyunsaturated 1 g
  Monounsaturated 1 g

Appetizers, Spreads, and Snacks

Hot Broccoli Dip

Serve this surprisingly low-fat dip with fresh vegetables—such as cauliflower, carrots, and zucchini—or crispy breadsticks. Or use it as a tasty topping for baked potatoes.

Makes 1½ cups

Serves 12; 2 tablespoons per serving

Preparation time: 5 minutes

Cooking time: 5 to 8 minutes

Reheating time: 5 minutes

Microwave reheating time: 1 to 3 minutes

10-ounce package frozen no-salt-added cut broccoli or broccoli florets
2 ounces light processed cheese
¼ cup warm skim milk
½ teaspoon bottled minced garlic
½ teaspoon dried thyme

Prepare broccoli according to package directions. Place hot, cooked broccoli in a blender or the work bowl of a food processor fitted with a metal blade. Immediately add remaining ingredients. Cover and process until smooth.

Transfer to a serving bowl and serve immediately with fresh vegetables and breadsticks, or refrigerate to reheat and serve later.

Reheating Directions

To serve later, place dip in a covered bowl and refrigerate. When ready to reheat, place mixture in a saucepan over low heat and heat just until hot, about 5 minutes, stirring occasionally. Or place in a microwave-safe bowl and cover loosely with wax paper. Cook on 100% power (high) for 1 to 3 minutes or until heated through, stirring once.

NUTRIENT ANALYSIS
(PER SERVING)

Calories 21 kcal
Protein 2 g
Carbohydrate 2 g
Cholesterol 3 mg
Sodium 80 mg
Total fat 1 g
  Saturated 1 g
  Polyunsaturated 0 g
  Monounsaturated 0 g

Cranberry Fruit Dip

This refreshing fruit dip comes together in 5 minutes or less. Serve it with a variety of fresh fruit, such as apple slices, orange sections, melon spears, and pineapple chunks.

Makes 1 cup

Serves 8; 2 tablespoons per serving

Preparation time: Less than 5 minutes

½ cup nonfat or low-fat vanilla, lemon, or peach yogurt
½ cup whole-berry cranberry sauce
¼ teaspoon ground cinnamon
⅛ teaspoon ground ginger

In a medium bowl, stir together all ingredients. Serve with fruit. This dip can be stored in an airtight container in the refrigerator for up to 3 days.

NUTRIENT ANALYSIS
(PER SERVING)

Calories 37 kcal
Protein 1 g
Carbohydrate 9 g
Cholesterol 0 mg
Sodium 11 mg
Total fat 0 g
  Saturated 0 g
  Polyunsaturated 0 g
  Monounsaturated 0 g

Parsley-Mustard Spread

This is a spicy spread for bread or crackers. Don't forget to read labels when you buy margarine. Choose a brand with no more than 2 grams of saturated fat per tablespoon.

Makes about ½ cup

Serves 24; 1 teaspoon per serving

Preparation time: 7 minutes

½ cup acceptable margarine
2 tablespoons snipped fresh parsley
1 tablespoon Dijon or spicy brown mustard

In a medium mixing bowl, combine all ingredients. Beat with an electric mixer on medium to high speed until well combined.

This can be stored in an airtight container in the refrigerator for several weeks.

NUTRIENT ANALYSIS
(PER SERVING)

Calories 34 kcal
Protein 0 g
Carbohydrate 0 g
Cholesterol 0 mg
Sodium 52 mg
Total fat 4 g
  Saturated 1 g
  Polyunsaturated 1 g
  Monounsaturated 2 g

Appetizers, Spreads, and Snacks

Easy Peach Spread

Team this mild peach-flavored spread with Pecan-Topped Pumpkin Bread (page 235) or your favorite quick bread.

Makes about ½ cup

Serves 24; 1 teaspoon per serving

Preparation time: 5 minutes

4 ounces light cream cheese, softened
3 tablespoons strained baby food peaches
2 tablespoons firmly packed brown sugar

NUTRIENT ANALYSIS
(PER SERVING)

Calories 17 kcal
Protein 0 g
Carbohydrate 2 g
Cholesterol 4 mg
Sodium 19 mg
Total fat 1 g
  Saturated 1 g
  Polyunsaturated 0 g
  Monounsaturated 0 g

In a medium mixing bowl, combine all ingredients. Beat with an electric mixer on medium-high speed until well combined.

Use as a spread for bread. This can be stored in an airtight container in the refrigerator for a few weeks.

Soups and Stews

Hooray for soups and stews! Just turn the page and you'll see why there's a lot to cheer about in this chapter. We've developed a potful of delicious and nourishing soups and stews that you don't have to fuss with all day. In fact, many of the recipes can be made in thirty minutes or less. Try Broccoli–Lima Bean Soup, Macaroni-and-Cheese Soup, or Thirty-Minute Minestrone.

There are also a few long-simmering but easy-to-prepare stews, such as Easy Oven Beef Stew and Hearty Pork and Onion Stew. Whichever you choose, you're in for some mighty good sippin' spoonfuls.

Thirty-Minute Minestrone

You can make this classic Italian soup in about a half hour from start to finish.

4 cups water
2 cups miniature peeled carrots
15-ounce can Great Northern beans, rinsed and drained
14-ounce can peeled Italian plum tomatoes, cut up
1 cup chopped onion
4 teaspoons low-sodium beef bouillon granules or 2 teaspoons regular beef bouillon granules
1 teaspoon bottled minced garlic
½ teaspoon dried basil, crushed
½ teaspoon dried oregano, crushed
¼ teaspoon black pepper
9-ounce package frozen no-salt-added Italian green beans
1 small zucchini, halved lengthwise and sliced
½ cup elbow macaroni, alphabet macaroni, or broken spaghetti, uncooked
¼ cup grated or shredded Parmesan cheese

In a large saucepan, combine water, carrots, beans, tomatoes, onion, bouillon granules, garlic, basil, oregano, and pepper. Bring to a boil over high heat. Add green beans, zucchini, and pasta. Return to a boil. Reduce heat, cover, and simmer for 10 minutes or until pasta is done.

Spoon into bowls and sprinkle each serving with Parmesan cheese.

Serves 6 as a main dish; 1⅔ cups per serving

Preparation time: 15 minutes

Cooking time: 15 minutes

NUTRIENT ANALYSIS (PER SERVING)

Calories 204 kcal
Protein 11 g
Carbohydrate 37 g
Cholesterol 3 mg
Sodium 278 mg
Total fat 3 g
 Saturated 1 g
 Polyunsaturated 1 g
 Monounsaturated 1 g

Three-Bean Chili

The key to a thick consistency is simmering the chili, uncovered, for 15 minutes. For thinner chili, reduce the cooking time to 10 minutes.

Serves 4 as a main dish; 1¾ cups per serving

Preparation time: 10 minutes

Cooking time: 10 to 15 minutes

28-ounce can no-salt-added tomatoes, cut up
15½-ounce can red kidney beans, rinsed and drained
15-ounce can garbanzo beans, rinsed and drained
15-ounce can no-salt-added pinto beans, rinsed and drained
12-ounce can light beer or nonalcoholic beer
2 tablespoons chili powder
2 teaspoons ground cumin
½ cup plain nonfat yogurt
Chopped fresh parsley (optional)

In a large saucepan, combine tomatoes, beans, beer, chili powder, and cumin. Bring to a boil over high heat. Reduce heat and simmer, uncovered, for 10 to 15 minutes, depending on desired consistency.

Pour chili into 4 bowls. Top each serving with a dollop of yogurt and sprinkle with parsley if desired.

NUTRIENT ANALYSIS
(PER SERVING)

Calories 411 kcal
Protein 23 g
Carbohydrate 70 g
Cholesterol 1 mg
Sodium 275 mg
Total fat 4 g
  Saturated 1 g
  Polyunsaturated 2 g
  Monounsaturated 1 g

Light Chicken Chili

You can shave a few more minutes off the preparation time if you buy boneless, skinless chicken breast chunks. The toppings for this chili add flavor and texture, but they also add sodium. So if you're trying to cut down on sodium, skip the toppings or use them sparingly.

Serves 6 as a main dish;
¾ cup per serving

Preparation time:
15 minutes

Cooking time:
15 minutes

Vegetable oil spray
1 pound boneless, skinless chicken breasts, cut
  into bite-size pieces
1 medium onion, chopped
1 teaspoon bottled minced garlic
2 cups low-sodium chicken broth
4-ounce can chopped green chili peppers
1 teaspoon ground cumin
½ teaspoon ground white pepper
2 16-ounce cans navy beans, rinsed and drained
4 5-inch whole-wheat tortillas
4-ounce can sliced ripe olives, drained (optional)
½ cup shredded low-fat cheddar cheese (optional)

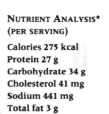

Lightly spray a Dutch oven with vegetable oil. Add chicken, onion, and garlic. Cook over medium-high heat until chicken is just tender, about 5 minutes. Stir in broth, chili peppers, cumin, and white pepper. Bring to a boil. Reduce heat and simmer 5 minutes, uncovered.

Meanwhile, place half of the drained beans in a medium bowl and mash thoroughly. Stir mashed beans and remaining whole beans into chicken mixture. Simmer 5 minutes.

Line each of 4 soup bowls with a whole-wheat tortilla. Spoon in chili and top with olives and cheese if desired. Serve immediately.

Nutrient Analysis*
(per serving)

Calories 275 kcal
Protein 27 g
Carbohydrate 34 g
Cholesterol 41 mg
Sodium 441 mg
Total fat 3 g
  Saturated 1 g
  Polyunsaturated 1 g
  Monounsaturated 1 g

*Analyzed without optional toppings

Soups and Stews

Southwestern Turkey Stew

If you want to save ten minutes of cooking time, halve the recipe and make this full-flavored stew in your microwave oven.

Serves 8 as a main dish;
1¼ cups per serving

Preparation time:
15 minutes

Cooking time:
25 minutes

Microwave cooking
time: 15 minutes

¼ cup all-purpose flour
¼ teaspoon salt
⅛ teaspoon black pepper
1½ pounds boneless, skinless turkey breast, cut into ½-inch cubes
2 14½-ounce cans no-salt-added tomatoes, chopped
10½-ounce can low-sodium chicken broth
10-ounce package frozen no-salt-added corn
1 cup chopped onion
4-ounce can chopped green chili peppers
2 teaspoons bottled minced garlic
1½ teaspoons ground cumin
1½ teaspoons dried oregano, crushed
¼ cup chopped fresh cilantro

In a large plastic bag with a tight-fitting seal, combine flour, salt, and black pepper. Add turkey cubes and shake until well coated. Shake off excess flour.

In a Dutch oven, combine coated turkey with remaining ingredients except cilantro. Place over high heat and bring to a boil. Reduce heat, cover, and simmer for 25 minutes or until turkey is done, stirring occasionally. Stir in cilantro.

NUTRIENT ANALYSIS (PER SERVING)

Calories 189 kcal
Protein 23 g
Carbohydrate 18 g
Cholesterol 50 mg
Sodium 305 mg
Total fat 3 g
  Saturated 1 g
  Polyunsaturated 1 g
  Monounsaturated 1 g

Microwave Method

Halve ingredients listed above (will serve 4 as a main dish). Prepare turkey cubes as directed. Combine coated turkey and remaining ingredients except cilantro in a 2-quart microwave-safe casserole. Cover and cook on 100% power (high) for 15 minutes or until turkey is done, stirring twice. Stir in cilantro.

Easy Oven Beef Stew

What makes this so easy? Simply toss all the ingredients together in a Dutch oven, place it in the oven, and forget about it for two hours, or cook it all day in your electric crockery cooker.

Serves 6 as a main dish; 1 cup per serving

Preparation time: 15 minutes

Cooking time: 2 hours

Crockery cooker time: 4½ to 5½ hours on high or 9 to 11 hours on low

¼ cup all-purpose flour
¼ teaspoon black pepper
1½ pounds lean boneless round steak, trimmed of fat and cut into ½-inch cubes
3 cups water
2 medium potatoes, scrubbed and cut into bite-size pieces
9-ounce package frozen no-salt-added whole baby carrots
8 ounces sliced fresh mushrooms
1 cup frozen no-salt-added pearl onions
4 teaspoons low-sodium beef bouillon granules
1 teaspoon dried savory or thyme, crushed
½ teaspoon garlic powder

Preheat oven to 350° F.

In a large plastic bag with a tight-fitting seal, combine flour and pepper. Add meat and shake until well coated. Shake off excess flour.

In an ovenproof Dutch oven, combine coated meat and remaining ingredients. Cover and bake for 2 hours or until meat is tender, stirring once or twice.

NUTRIENT ANALYSIS (PER SERVING)

Calories 248 kcal
Protein 27 g
Carbohydrate 23 g
Cholesterol 63 mg
Sodium 81 mg
Total fat 5 g
  Saturated 2 g
  Polyunsaturated 1 g
  Monounsaturated 2 g

Crockery Cooker Method

Prepare beef cubes as directed above. Combine coated meat and remaining ingredients in a 3½- to 4-quart electric slow cooker. Cover and cook on high for 4½ to 5½ hours or on low for 9 to 11 hours or until meat is tender.

Hearty Pork and Onion Stew

This is an ideal recipe to start in the morning and let cook all day in your electric crockery cooker. Simply follow the crockery cooker directions below.

Serves 6 as a main dish; 1¼ cups per serving

Preparation time: 15 minutes

Cooking time: 1½ hours

Crockery cooker time: 4 to 5 hours on high or 8 to 10 hours on low

⅓ cup all-purpose flour
¼ teaspoon salt
⅛ teaspoon black pepper
1½ pounds lean boneless pork loin roast, trimmed of fat and cut into ½-inch cubes
16-ounce package frozen no-salt-added pearl onions
12-ounce can light beer or nonalcoholic beer
10½-ounce can low-sodium chicken broth
10-ounce package frozen no-salt-added chopped spinach
2 tablespoons red wine vinegar
1 tablespoon firmly packed brown sugar
1 teaspoon caraway seeds
1 teaspoon bottled minced garlic
1 bay leaf

Preheat oven to 350° F.

In a large plastic bag with a tight-fitting seal, combine flour, salt, and pepper. Add pork and shake until well coated. Shake off excess flour.

In an ovenproof Dutch oven or 3-quart casserole, combine coated pork and remaining ingredients. Cover and bake for 1½ hours or until meat is tender, stirring occasionally. Remove bay leaf before serving.

NUTRIENT ANALYSIS (PER SERVING)

Calories 285 kcal
Protein 25 g
Carbohydrate 17 g
Cholesterol 71 mg
Sodium 187 mg
Total fat 11 g
  Saturated 4 g
  Polyunsaturated 1 g
  Monounsaturated 5 g

Crockery Cooker Method

Prepare pork cubes as directed above. Combine coated pork and remaining ingredients in a 3½- to 4-quart electric slow cooker. Cover and cook on high for 4 to 5 hours or on low for 8 to 10 hours or until meat is tender, stirring occasionally. Remove bay leaf before serving.

Curried Shrimp Bisque

This company-special soup can be made ahead and refrigerated right after blending. Just before serving, bring soup to a boil, add shrimp, and finish cooking as directed.

Serves 4 as a main dish; 1½ cups per serving

Preparation time: 20 minutes

Cooking time: 20 minutes

Vegetable oil spray
2 medium apples, peeled, cored, and chopped
1 cup chopped onion
½ cup shredded carrot
½ cup sliced celery
2 10½-ounce cans low-sodium chicken broth
2 medium potatoes, peeled and diced
2 tablespoons curry powder
¼ teaspoon ground cardamom
¼ teaspoon ground allspice
½ cup instant nonfat dry milk powder
¼ cup no-salt-added tomato sauce
1 pound frozen uncooked shelled and deveined
    medium shrimp
Popcorn (optional)
Chopped fresh cilantro (optional)

Spray a large saucepan with vegetable oil. Add apples, onion, carrot, and celery to saucepan and cook over medium-high heat until apples are tender, about 5 minutes. Stir in broth, potatoes, curry powder, cardamom, and allspice. Bring to a boil. Reduce heat, cover, and simmer for 10 minutes or until potatoes are tender.

Meanwhile, stir together nonfat dry milk and tomato sauce in a small bowl.

Transfer hot broth mixture to a blender or the work bowl of a food processor fitted with a metal blade. Cover and process until smooth.

Add tomato sauce mixture to blended mixture. Cover and process until well combined.

Return mixture to saucepan and bring to a boil over high heat. Add shrimp and simmer for 3 to 5 minutes or until shrimp are done.

Garnish each serving with popcorn and cilantro if desired.

NUTRIENT ANALYSIS
(PER SERVING)
Calories 255 kcal
Protein 24 g
Carbohydrate 35 g
Cholesterol 163 mg
Sodium 298 mg
Total fat 3 g
  Saturated 1 g
  Polyunsaturated 1 g
  Monounsaturated 0 g

Broccoli-Lima Bean Soup

Toasting sesame seeds brings out their nutty flavor. Simply place seeds in a small skillet and cook over medium heat about 5 minutes or until light brown, stirring occasionally.

Serves 6 as a side dish;
1 cup per serving

Preparation time:
10 minutes

Cooking time:
15 minutes

4 cups low-sodium chicken broth
10-ounce package frozen lima beans (with trace of salt necessary for processing)
10-ounce package frozen no-salt-added chopped broccoli
1 cup sliced carrots
½ cup chopped onion
2 tablespoons light soy sauce
1 teaspoon bottled minced garlic
1 teaspoon grated gingerroot
2 tablespoons sesame seeds, toasted
2 tablespoons dry sherry (optional)

In a large saucepan, bring broth to a boil over high heat. Add lima beans, broccoli, carrots, onion, soy sauce, garlic, and gingerroot. Return to a boil. Reduce heat, cover, and simmer for 15 minutes or until beans are just tender. Stir in sesame seeds and, if desired, sherry.

Nutrient Analysis
(per serving)

Calories 113 kcal
Protein 8 g
Carbohydrate 17 g
Cholesterol 0 mg
Sodium 287 mg
Total fat 3 g
Saturated 0 g
Polyunsaturated 1 g
Monounsaturated 1 g

Cook's Tip

You can keep any unused gingerroot fresh for several months. How? Just submerge it in a jar of dry sherry. Cover the jar tightly and store it in the refrigerator. Or wrap the gingerroot in plastic wrap and store it in the freezer.

Potato-Vegetable Chowder

Use your family's favorite frozen vegetable blend in this hearty side-dish soup. Serve it with a main-dish salad and whole-grain rolls for a complete meal.

Serves 4 as a side dish;
1¼ cups per serving

Preparation time:
5 minutes

Cooking time:
15 minutes

3 cups low-sodium chicken broth
½ teaspoon salt
¼ teaspoon ground nutmeg
⅛ teaspoon black pepper
2 medium potatoes, scrubbed and chopped
2 cups frozen no-salt-added mixed vegetables
12-ounce can evaporated skim milk
¼ cup all-purpose flour

In a large saucepan, combine broth, salt, nutmeg, and pepper. Bring to a boil over high heat. Add potatoes and frozen vegetables. Return to a boil. Reduce heat, cover, and simmer for 10 minutes or until potatoes are tender.

Meanwhile, in a small bowl, combine evaporated skim milk and flour. Stir to mix well. Set aside.

When potatoes are tender, add milk mixture to potato mixture. Cook and stir over medium heat until thickened and bubbly, about 5 minutes. Cook 1 minute more, stirring constantly.

NUTRIENT ANALYSIS
(PER SERVING)

Calories 238 kcal
Protein 14 g
Carbohydrate 44 g
Cholesterol 3 mg
Sodium 455 mg
Total fat 1 g
  Saturated 0 g
  Polyunsaturated 0 g
  Monounsaturated 0 g

Mushroom-Asparagus Chowder

Prepare recipe as directed above, but omit potatoes and frozen vegetables and use 8 ounces sliced fresh mushrooms and 1 pound fresh asparagus, trimmed and cut into 1-inch pieces. Cook only 5 minutes or until asparagus is just tender. For a pretty presentation, slice the asparagus spears diagonally when you prepare this creamy soup.

NUTRIENT ANALYSIS
(PER SERVING)

Calories 158 kcal
Protein 14 g
Carbohydrate 24 g
Cholesterol 3 mg
Sodium 423 mg
Total fat 2 g
  Saturated 0 g
  Polyunsaturated 0 g
  Monounsaturated 0 g

Macaroni-and-Cheese Soup

If your kids like macaroni and cheese, they'll like this easy-on-the-cook soup.

2½ cups water

7¼-ounce package macaroni-and-cheese mix

10-ounce package frozen no-salt-added peas and carrots

¼ teaspoon dried dill weed

2 cups skim milk

Serves 4 as a side dish;
1¼ cups per serving

Preparation time:
5 minutes

Cooking time:
15 minutes

In a large saucepan, combine water and dry cheese-sauce mix from the macaroni-and-cheese mix. Bring to a boil over high heat. Stir in macaroni, peas and carrots, and dill weed. Return to a boil. Reduce heat, cover, and simmer for 7 to 10 minutes or until macaroni is tender, stirring occasionally. Stir in milk; simmer for 2 to 3 minutes more.

**NUTRIENT ANALYSIS
(PER SERVING)**

Calories 267 kcal

Protein 14 g

Carbohydrate 45 g

Cholesterol 6 mg

Sodium 333 mg

Total fat 3 g

Saturated 1 g

Polyunsaturated 0 g

Monounsaturated 1 g

Peppery Pumpkin Soup

You don't need to wait until pumpkin harvest to try this first-course soup. Since it's made with canned pumpkin, you can enjoy it all year. For a less peppery soup, reduce the pepper to ⅛ teaspoon.

Serves 4 as a side dish;
1 cup per serving

Preparation time:
5 minutes

Cooking time:
15 minutes

16-ounce can pumpkin (*not* pumpkin-pie filling)
10½-ounce can low-sodium chicken broth
¼ teaspoon salt
¼ teaspoon onion powder
¼ teaspoon black pepper
⅛ teaspoon ground nutmeg
12-ounce can evaporated skim milk
¼ cup nonfat or low-fat sour cream
1 tablespoon unsalted pumpkin seeds (optional)

In a medium saucepan, combine pumpkin, broth, salt, onion powder, pepper, and nutmeg. Cook over medium-high heat until bubbly, about 10 minutes, stirring occasionally. Stir in evaporated skim milk. Heat through, about 5 minutes, but do not boil.

Spoon into 4 bowls and top each serving with a dollop of sour cream. Garnish with pumpkin seeds if desired.

NUTRIENT ANALYSIS (PER SERVING)

Calories 130 kcal
Protein 10 g
Carbohydrate 22 g
Cholesterol 4 mg
Sodium 278 mg
Total fat 1 g
  Saturated 0 g
  Polyunsaturated 0 g
  Monounsaturated 0 g

Cook's Tip

Here's an easy way to defat chicken broth for this recipe or any other recipe calling for canned broth: Store the can of broth in the refrigerator. When you're ready to use it, open the top of the can and skim the solidified fat off the top.

Strawberry-Cantaloupe Soup

This soup makes a delicious addition to breakfast or brunch. Just make it the day before and chill overnight.

Serves 3 as a side dish;
1 cup per serving

Preparation time:
10 minutes

½ medium cantaloupe, peeled, seeded, and cut into chunks (about 2 cups)
1 cup fresh strawberries, rinsed and hulled, or raspberries, rinsed
1 small ripe banana, peeled and cut into chunks
½ cup unsweetened pineapple juice
½ cup nonfat vanilla yogurt

Place all ingredients except yogurt in a blender or the work bowl of a food processor fitted with a metal blade. Cover and process until smooth. Add yogurt. Cover and process until well combined. Serve immediately, or cover and chill until serving time.

NUTRIENT ANALYSIS
(PER SERVING)

Calories 147 kcal
Protein 4 g
Carbohydrate 34 g
Cholesterol 1 mg
Sodium 32 mg
Total fat 1 g
    Saturated 0 g
    Polyunsaturated 0 g
    Monounsaturated 0 g

Cook's Tip

Save chopping time by buying chunks of peeled fresh cantaloupe and fresh strawberries at your supermarket's salad bar or in the produce section. For the fullest fruit flavor, prepare this in the summer, when melons and berries are at their peak.

Salads and Salad Dressings

Salads never had it so good, thanks to the bountiful selection of fresh produce available in supermarkets. The best part is, much of the work has been done for you. When shopping for your salad fixin's, take advantage of ready-to-eat salad greens, sliced mushrooms, shredded cabbage and carrots, and in-store salad bar selections. These products will save you time in the kitchen without skimping on quality.

When it comes to salad dressings, here's a simple guideline for reducing the fat in homemade vinaigrette: replace half of the oil with low-sodium chicken broth. That's what we did in the Honey-Lime Vinaigrette and the Strawberry-Spinach Salad with Champagne Dressing. The chicken broth makes a great-tasting, low-fat substitute for olive oil or vegetable oil.

Don't miss your chance to sample some of the freshest-tasting and quick-to-fix salads around. You'll find them right here in this chapter. Choose from updated classics, such as Light and Lemony Caesar Salad or Fresh Herb Potato Salad. Or try something new, such as Warm Chicken and Papaya Salad or Mediterranean Black Bean Salad. No matter what your menu, you'll find a salad to fit it.

Layered Southwestern Salad

This colorful salad gets its inspiration from the special flavors of the Southwest, such as beans, corn, and cilantro. Make it ahead and bring it to your next potluck party.

Serves 8 as a main dish; 1¼ cups per serving

Preparation time: 15 to 20 minutes

Chilling time: 1 to 24 hours

3 cups torn lettuce
15-ounce can red kidney beans, rinsed and drained
15-ounce can black beans, rinsed and drained
8 ounces sliced fresh mushrooms
12-ounce can no-salt-added corn, drained
¼ cup chopped red onion
1 cup nonfat or low-fat sour cream
¼ cup snipped fresh cilantro or parsley
2 tablespoons white wine vinegar
¼ teaspoon salt
⅛ teaspoon black pepper
1 cup shredded low-fat cheddar cheese

Place lettuce in the bottom of a large, shallow clear glass bowl or baking dish. Add the following layers in the order listed: beans, mushrooms, corn, and onion. Set aside.

In a small bowl, stir together sour cream, cilantro, vinegar, salt, and pepper. Spread evenly over top of salad. Sprinkle with cheese. Cover and chill for 1 to 24 hours.

NUTRIENT ANALYSIS (PER SERVING)

Calories 187 kcal
Protein 13 g
Carbohydrate 30 g
Cholesterol 8 mg
Sodium 389 mg
Total fat 3 g
  Saturated 2 g
  Polyunsaturated 0 g
  Monounsaturated 1 g

Cook's Tip

Nonfat sour cream can vary in flavor and texture among the different brands available on the market. For this recipe, choose one that has a soft texture so it will spread easily.

Warm Chicken and Papaya Salad

The warm chicken, refreshing papaya, and tart lime dressing make a delightful combination in this leaf lettuce and radicchio salad. You can save a few minutes by using chicken or turkey breast tenderloin strips.

Serves 4 as a main dish; 1¼ cups per serving

Preparation time: 20 minutes

Cooking time: 3 to 5 minutes

12 ounces boneless, skinless chicken or turkey breast tenderloins
2 tablespoons lime juice
4 cups torn leaf lettuce
1 cup torn radicchio or red leaf lettuce
1 medium papaya, halved, seeded, peeled, and cubed (1½ cups)
¼ cup sliced green onions
2 tablespoons lime juice
2 tablespoons olive oil
2 tablespoons low-sodium chicken broth
½ teaspoon Dijon mustard
½ teaspoon bottled minced garlic
⅛ teaspoon black pepper
Vegetable oil spray

Cut chicken into 2-inch strips. Place in a shallow glass dish. Pour 2 tablespoons lime juice over chicken, turning to coat. Set aside.

In a large bowl, toss together leaf lettuce, radicchio, papaya, and green onions. Set aside.

In a small jar with a tight-fitting lid, combine 2 tablespoons lime juice, oil, broth, mustard, garlic, and pepper. Cover and shake until ingredients are well combined. Set aside.

Spray a large skillet with vegetable oil and place over medium-high heat. Drain chicken and place in hot skillet. Cook for 3 to 5 minutes or until tender and no longer pink, turning once.

Shake dressing and pour over lettuce mixture. Toss to coat. Top with warm chicken and serve immediately.

NUTRIENT ANALYSIS
(PER SERVING)

Calories 204 kcal
Protein 20 g
Carbohydrate 10 g
Cholesterol 47 mg
Sodium 63 mg
Total fat 9 g
  Saturated 2 g
  Polyunsaturated 1 g
  Monounsaturated 6 g

Melon-Chicken Salad

You can cut the preparation time of this fruity chicken salad by using two cups of leftover chopped cooked chicken and buying three cups of chopped cantaloupe at your supermarket salad bar.

Serves 4 as a main dish; 1¼ cups per serving

Preparation time: 15 to 20 minutes

Cooking time: 6 minutes

Water
12 ounces boneless, skinless chicken breast strips or turkey breast tenderloin strips
2 small cantaloupes or 1 large cantaloupe
1 cup sliced celery
2 tablespoons sliced green onions
¼ cup nonfat or low-fat peach or vanilla yogurt
¼ cup fat-free, cholesterol-free mayonnaise
4 large lettuce leaves

Place water in a large skillet to a depth of 1 inch and bring to a boil over high heat. Carefully add chicken strips. Reduce heat, cover, and simmer for 5 minutes or until tender and no longer pink. Drain and set strips aside to cool slightly.

Meanwhile, halve cantaloupes and remove the seeds and rind. Cut cantaloupes into bite-size pieces. There should be about 3 cups.

In a large bowl, combine cantaloupe, celery, and green onions.

Cut cooked chicken or turkey into bite-size pieces (there should be about 2 cups) and add to bowl with cantaloupe mixture.

Add yogurt and mayonnaise to mixture. Stir until well combined. Serve immediately or cover and chill until serving time. Serve on lettuce leaves.

NUTRIENT ANALYSIS (PER SERVING)

Calories 223 kcal
Protein 22 g
Carbohydrate 29 g
Cholesterol 47 mg
Sodium 292 mg
Total fat 3 g
    Saturated 1 g
    Polyunsaturated 1 g
    Monounsaturated 1 g

Salads and Salad Dressings

Speedy Taco Salad

For added crunch, serve this south-of-the-border salad with Homemade Corn Tortilla Chips (see page 48) or store-bought tortilla chips made without added fat.

Serves 4 as a main dish; 2 cups per serving

Preparation time: 20 minutes

Cooking time: 7 to 10 minutes

5 cups torn lettuce

12 ounces ground turkey or chicken, ground without skin

15-ounce can red kidney beans, rinsed and drained

14½-ounce can no-salt-added tomatoes, drained and chopped

1 tablespoon chili powder

1 teaspoon ground cumin

¼ teaspoon salt

4-ounce can chopped green chili peppers, drained (optional)

½ cup shredded low-fat cheddar cheese

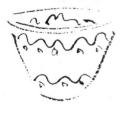

Arrange lettuce on 4 individual salad plates. Set aside.

In a large skillet over medium-high heat, cook turkey about 5 minutes or until no longer pink, stirring occasionally. Place turkey in a colander and rinse under hot water. Drain well. Wipe skillet with a paper towel. Return turkey to skillet. Stir in remaining ingredients except cheese. Cook and stir over medium heat for 2 minutes.

Spoon turkey mixture onto prepared plates. Sprinkle with cheese.

NUTRIENT ANALYSIS
(PER SERVING)

Calories 273 kcal
Protein 31 g
Carbohydrate 25 g
Cholesterol 57 mg
Sodium 513 mg
Total fat 6 g
 Saturated 2 g
 Polyunsaturated 1 g
 Monounsaturated 1 g

Salmon Salad Bundles with Lemon and Dill

Use the outer leaves from a head of romaine lettuce when making this rolled-up "salad sandwich." The outer leaves are larger and more flexible than the smaller, inner leaves of the head.

Serves 4 as a main dish; 2 bundles per serving

Preparation time: 10 to 15 minutes

2 6⅛-ounce cans boneless, skinless pink salmon
1 cup nonfat or low-fat cottage cheese
¼ cup sliced green onions
2 tablespoons freshly snipped dill or ¾ teaspoon
  dried dill weed
1 teaspoon finely shredded lemon peel
1 tablespoon lemon juice
¼ teaspoon lemon pepper
⅛ teaspoon black pepper
8 large romaine lettuce leaves

If desired, place salmon in a colander and rinse under cold running water (this reduces the saltiness). Drain well. In a medium bowl, stir together salmon and remaining ingredients except romaine. Cover and chill until serving time or proceed as directed.

To assemble bundles, cut off the heavy base from each lettuce leaf. Place about ⅓ cup of the salmon mixture in the center, near the base of each leaf. Turn in the side edges of the lettuce and roll up jelly-roll style, starting at the base.

NUTRIENT ANALYSIS
(PER SERVING)

Calories 130 kcal
Protein 20 g
Carbohydrate 2 g
Cholesterol 39 mg
Sodium 396 mg
Total fat 4 g
  Saturated 1 g
  Polyunsaturated 1 g
  Monounsaturated 1 g

Tuna Salad Bundles with Lemon and Dill

Use water-packed low-salt tuna in place of the salmon.

Cook's Tip

Canned salmon is now as easy to use as canned tuna. Look for cans of boneless, skinless pink salmon at your supermarket with other canned fish and seafood.

NUTRIENT ANALYSIS
(PER SERVING)

Calories 147 kcal
Protein 31 g
Carbohydrate 2 g
Cholesterol 17 mg
Sodium 198 mg
Total fat 1 g
  Saturated 0 g
  Polyunsaturated 0 g
  Monounsaturated 0 g

Salads and Salad Dressings

Curried Shrimp Salad

Look for cooked shrimp at your grocer's fish counter or buy 12 ounces of frozen cooked shrimp and thaw and drain them before beginning this recipe.

Serves 4 as a main dish; 1½ cups per serving

Preparation time: 15 minutes

2 tablespoons tarragon vinegar or white wine vinegar
1 tablespoon low-sodium chicken broth
1 tablespoon acceptable vegetable oil
1 tablespoon honey
1 teaspoon curry powder
5 cups torn leaf or romaine lettuce
12 ounces cooked shelled and deveined medium shrimp
1 medium zucchini or yellow summer squash, halved lengthwise and sliced crosswise
¼ cup raisins
¼ cup chopped unsalted, dry-roasted peanuts

In a small jar with a tight-fitting lid, combine vinegar, broth, oil, honey, and curry powder. Cover and shake until ingredients are well combined. Set aside.

In a large bowl, combine lettuce, shrimp, and zucchini.

Shake dressing and pour over lettuce mixture. Toss to coat. Sprinkle each serving with raisins and peanuts.

NUTRIENT ANALYSIS
(PER SERVING)

Calories 228 kcal
Protein 22 g
Carbohydrate 17 g
Cholesterol 166 mg
Sodium 202 mg
Total fat 9 g
  Saturated 1 g
  Polyunsaturated 4 g
  Monounsaturated 3 g

Cook's Tip

Using a variety of vinegars is an easy way to add flavor to salads and other foods without adding fat, calories, or sodium. Here are some tasty choices.

- Balsamic vinegar is made from high-sugar grapes and aged in wooden barrels for at least six years. The result is an intense, dark vinegar that is sweeter than most.
- Rice wine vinegar is made with Japanese rice wine and has a clean, mild taste. Look for it at

your supermarket with other vinegars or in the Asian-foods section.

- Fruit and herb vinegars are mild-flavored vinegars infused with such fresh flavors as raspberry and tarragon.
- Wine vinegars are made from wine, sherry, or champagne and can range in taste from mild (champagne vinegar) to strong (red wine vinegar).

Fresh Herb Potato Salad

The secret to this speedy, fresh-tasting potato salad is canned whole potatoes.

Serves 6; 1 cup per serving

Preparation time: 15 to 20 minutes

Chilling time: 2 to 24 hours

2 16-ounce cans whole potatoes, rinsed, drained, and patted dry
1 cup sliced fresh carrots
1 cup sliced celery
1 cup frozen no-salt-added tiny or regular peas
2 tablespoons chopped shallots or green onions
½ cup fat-free, cholesterol-free mayonnaise
1 tablespoon snipped fresh dill or ½ teaspoon dried dill weed
1 tablespoon snipped fresh basil or ½ teaspoon dried basil
2 teaspoons white wine vinegar
2 teaspoons Dijon mustard
⅛ teaspoon black pepper

Cut potatoes into bite-size pieces. Place in a large bowl. Add carrots, celery, peas, and shallots. Set aside.

In a small bowl, stir together remaining ingredients. Pour over potato mixture; stir until well combined. Cover and chill for 2 to 24 hours. Stir before serving.

NUTRIENT ANALYSIS (PER SERVING)

Calories 136 kcal
Protein 3 g
Carbohydrate 31 g
Cholesterol 0 mg
Sodium 324 mg
Total fat 0 g
  Saturated 0 g
  Polyunsaturated 0 g
  Monounsaturated 0 g

Mustard-Marinated Vegetable Salad

If you love marinated vegetables but don't have time to chop them, this recipe is for you. It uses frozen chopped vegetables that thaw as they marinate in a tangy dressing.

Serves 5; 1 cup per serving

Preparation time: 10 minutes

Thawing time: 3 to 4 hours at room temperature or overnight in the refrigerator

Chilling time: At least 30 minutes

2 cups frozen no-salt-added cauliflower florets
10-ounce package frozen no-salt-added brussels sprouts
10-ounce package frozen no-salt-added broccoli florets
1 medium yellow summer squash, sliced
½ cup bottled nonfat Italian salad dressing
1 tablespoon Dijon mustard

In a large container or plastic bag with a tight-fitting seal, combine cauliflower, brussels sprouts, broccoli, and squash. Set aside.

In a small bowl, stir together salad dressing and mustard. Pour over vegetable mixture. Seal container or bag and gently shake until vegetables are well coated. Let stand at room temperature for 3 to 4 hours or until vegetables are thawed, gently shaking container or bag occasionally, or place container or bag of frozen vegetable mixture in the refrigerator and thaw overnight. Chill in the refrigerator at least 30 minutes or until serving time, gently shaking container or bag occasionally. Serve with a slotted spoon.

NUTRIENT ANALYSIS
(PER SERVING)

Calories 64 kcal
Protein 5 g
Carbohydrate 13 g
Cholesterol 0 mg
Sodium 408 mg
Total fat 1 g
  Saturated 0 g
  Polyunsaturated 0 g
  Monounsaturated 0 g

No-Chop Cajun Coleslaw

This spicy salad comes together in just 5 minutes. How? By using preshredded cabbage and carrots, which are available in your grocer's produce department.

Serves 6; ½ cup per serving

Preparation time: 5 minutes

Chilling time: 2 to 24 hours

3 cups preshredded cabbage
2 cups preshredded carrots
½ cup fat-free, cholesterol-free mayonnaise
1 tablespoon white wine vinegar or cider vinegar
2 teaspoons prepared horseradish
¼ teaspoon onion powder
⅛ teaspoon ground red pepper

NUTRIENT ANALYSIS (PER SERVING)

Calories 41 kcal
Protein 1 g
Carbohydrate 10 g
Cholesterol 0 mg
Sodium 275 mg
Total fat 0 g
  Saturated 0 g
  Polyunsaturated 0 g
  Monounsaturated 0 g

In a large bowl, combine cabbage and carrots. Set aside.

In a small bowl, stir together remaining ingredients. Pour over cabbage mixture and stir until well combined. Cover and chill for 2 to 24 hours. Stir before serving.

Mediterranean Black Bean Salad

Balsamic vinegar gives this salad a slightly sweet-tart flavor. This unique Italian vinegar has a rich brown hue and is less acidic than other types of vinegar.

Serves 4; ¾ cup per serving

Preparation time: 15 to 20 minutes

Chilling time: 2 to 24 hours

16-ounce can black beans, rinsed and drained
1 medium red, yellow, or orange bell pepper, seeded and chopped
1 medium green bell pepper, seeded and chopped
2 tablespoons chopped onion
1 tablespoon balsamic vinegar or red wine vinegar
2 tablespoons low-sodium chicken broth
1 teaspoon olive oil
½ teaspoon bottled minced garlic
¼ teaspoon dried thyme, crushed
¼ teaspoon dried rosemary, crushed
⅛ teaspoon black pepper
¼ cup snipped fresh parsley

In a medium bowl, combine beans, bell peppers, and onion. Set aside.

In a small jar with a tight-fitting lid, combine remaining ingredients except parsley. Cover and shake until ingredients are well combined. Pour over bean mixture, stirring to coat. Stir in parsley, cover, and chill for 2 to 24 hours. Stir before serving.

NUTRIENT ANALYSIS
(PER SERVING)

Calories 135 kcal
Protein 7 g
Carbohydrate 24 g
Cholesterol 0 mg
Sodium 97 mg
Total fat 2 g
 Saturated 0 g
 Polyunsaturated 0 g
 Monounsaturated 1 g

Warm Brown Rice Salad with Feta Cheese

For a burst of flavor, treat yourself to flavored feta cheeses, such as tomato-basil and black pepper.

Serves 4; ⅔ cup per serving

Preparation time: 10 minutes

Cooking time: 15 minutes

1½ cups uncooked quick-cooking brown rice
1¾ cups low-sodium chicken broth
2 tablespoons low-sodium chicken broth
1 tablespoon white wine vinegar
1 teaspoon olive oil
½ teaspoon dried oregano, crushed
½ teaspoon bottled minced garlic
⅛ teaspoon black pepper
2 tablespoons chopped ripe olives
4 large red leaf lettuce leaves
¼ cup crumbled feta cheese (1 ounce)

Cook the rice according to package directions, but omit butter and salt and substitute 1¾ cups low-sodium chicken broth for the water.

Meanwhile, in a small jar with a tight-fitting lid, combine 2 tablespoons broth, vinegar, oil, oregano, garlic, and pepper. Cover and shake until ingredients are well combined. Set aside.

In a medium bowl, combine rice and olives. Pour dressing over rice mixture, tossing to coat.

Arrange lettuce leaves on 4 individual salad plates. Spoon rice mixture over lettuce leaves. Sprinkle each serving with feta cheese. Serve warm or at room temperature.

Nutrient Analysis
(per serving)
Calories 307 kcal
Protein 9 g
Carbohydrate 55 g
Cholesterol 6 mg
Sodium 154 mg
Total fat 6 g
  Saturated 2 g
  Polyunsaturated 1 g
  Monounsaturated 2 g

Cook's Tip

Feta is a soft, white crumbly cheese with a sharp flavor. It is often used in Greek cooking. When it is packaged in liquid, simply drain off the liquid and pat the cheese dry with a paper towel before using. Feta has a relatively high fat content, so use it only occasionally and in small amounts.

Time-Saving Tabbouleh

This bulgur salad with Middle Eastern roots goes well with grilled meats or sandwiches. It takes a little time to clean and chop the fresh parsley and mint, but the fresh flavor makes it worthwhile.

Serves 8; ½ cup per serving

Preparation time: 20 minutes

Chilling time: 2 to 24 hours

5¼-ounce package (¾ cup) wheat salad mix or ¾ cup fine bulgur
¾ cup boiling water
14-ounce can Italian-style chopped stewed tomatoes
1 cup snipped fresh parsley
½ cup snipped fresh mint
½ cup currants or raisins
¼ cup low-sodium chicken broth
¼ cup lemon juice
2 tablespoons olive oil
½ teaspoon curry powder
½ teaspoon ground cumin
½ teaspoon ground cinnamon
½ teaspoon bottled minced garlic

Remove seasoning packet from wheat salad mix. Save for another use or discard. In a small bowl, combine wheat salad mix and boiling water. Set aside.

In a large bowl, stir together undrained tomatoes, parsley, mint, and currants. Set aside.

Combine remaining ingredients in a jar with a tight-fitting lid. Cover and shake until ingredients are well combined.

Stir wheat salad mix into tomato mixture. Pour dressing over mixture and stir. Cover and chill for 2 to 24 hours (liquid is absorbed by wheat during chilling). Stir before serving.

NUTRIENT ANALYSIS
(PER SERVING)

Calories 118 kcal
Protein 3 g
Carbohydrate 20 g
Cholesterol 0 mg
Sodium 94 mg
Total fat 4 g
 Saturated 1 g
 Polyunsaturated 0 g
 Monounsaturated 3 g

Cook's Tip

Bulgur is a quick-cooking grain, also called precooked cracked wheat. You can find it at health-food stores or with other grains or pastas at your supermarket. Sometimes it is sold in boxes and called wheat salad mix. You can use the boxed product, but discard the enclosed seasoning packet.

Light and Lemony Caesar Salad

This classic salad went on a diet and ended up with less fat, no eggs, and easy-to-use anchovy paste instead of canned anchovies. Look for anchovy paste next to the canned anchovies and sardines at your supermarket.

Serves 4; 1¼ cups per serving

Preparation time: 15 to 20 minutes

¼ teaspoon finely shredded lemon peel
2 tablespoons lemon juice
1 tablespoon low-sodium chicken broth
2 teaspoons olive oil
1 teaspoon anchovy paste
½ teaspoon Dijon mustard
5 cups torn romaine lettuce
½ cup shredded or grated Parmesan cheese
Freshly ground black pepper
Heart-Healthful Croutons (page 240) (optional)

In a small jar with a tight-fitting lid, combine lemon peel, lemon juice, broth, oil, anchovy paste, and mustard. Cover and shake until ingredients are well combined. Set aside.

Place lettuce in a large bowl. Pour dressing over lettuce, tossing to coat. Sprinkle with Parmesan cheese, tossing to coat. Season to taste with pepper. If desired, sprinkle with Heart-Healthful Croutons.

NUTRIENT ANALYSIS
(PER SERVING)
Calories 89 kcal
Protein 6 g
Carbohydrate 2 g
Cholesterol 11 mg
Sodium 266 mg
Total fat 6 g
 Saturated 3 g
 Polyunsaturated 0 g
 Monounsaturated 3 g

Strawberry-Spinach Salad with Champagne Dressing

Serve this vibrantly colored dish with dinner on a very special occasion.

Serves 4; 1¼ cups per serving

Preparation time: 15 minutes

3 tablespoons brut champagne, champagne vinegar, or white wine vinegar
1 tablespoon strawberry spreadable fruit or reduced-sugar preserves
1 teaspoon acceptable vegetable oil
5 cups rinsed and trimmed fresh spinach
2 cups halved fresh strawberries, hulled
¼ cup sliced unsalted, dry-roasted almonds

NUTRIENT ANALYSIS
(PER SERVING)

Calories 113 kcal
Protein 4 g
Carbohydrate 11 g
Cholesterol 0 mg
Sodium 58 mg
Total fat 6 g
  Saturated 1 g
  Polyunsaturated 2 g
  Monounsaturated 3 g

In a small jar with a tight-fitting lid, combine champagne, strawberry spreadable fruit, and oil. Cover and shake until ingredients are well combined. Place in the refrigerator until serving time.

Tear spinach into bite-size pieces. Place in a large salad bowl and add strawberries. Shake dressing, pour over spinach mixture, and toss to coat. Sprinkle with almonds.

Cook's Tip

If you have the time to toast the sliced almonds, place them on a baking sheet in a single layer and bake in a preheated 350° F oven for 5 to 10 minutes or until lightly browned, stirring once. This will give them an even nuttier taste and more crunch.

Honey-Lime Vinaigrette

Chicken broth replaces part of the oil in this fresh citrus salad dressing. Toss this with a salad such as romaine with mandarin oranges and toasted almonds.

¼ cup lime juice
2 tablespoons low-sodium chicken broth
2 tablespoons olive oil, acceptable vegetable oil, or combination
2 tablespoons honey
¼ teaspoon bottled minced garlic

Combine all ingredients in a jar with a tight-fitting lid. Cover and shake until ingredients are well combined. This dressing can be stored, refrigerated, for up to 1 week.

Makes about ½ cup
Serves 4: 2 tablespoons per serving
Preparation time: 5 minutes

NUTRIENT ANALYSIS
(PER SERVING)
Calories 96 kcal
Protein 0 g
Carbohydrate 10 g
Cholesterol 0 mg
Sodium 5 mg
Total fat 7 g
  Saturated 1 g
  Polyunsaturated 1 g
  Monounsaturated 5 g

Jalapeño Salad Dressing

This chili-pepper dressing is a terrific accompaniment for shredded jícama, a taco salad, or a fajita salad.

1 cup plain nonfat yogurt
3 tablespoons skim milk
1 tablespoon bottled minced jalapeño peppers
¼ teaspoon bottled minced garlic
¼ teaspoon ground cumin
⅛ teaspoon salt

Stir all ingredients together in a small bowl. Cover and chill until serving time.

Cook's Tip

The bottled minced jalapeño peppers used in this recipe are a real time-saver. Look for them at your supermarket near the bottled minced garlic or with other Mexican foods.

Makes about 1 cup
Serves 8; 2 tablespoons per serving
Preparation time: 5 minutes

NUTRIENT ANALYSIS
(PER SERVING)
Calories 20 kcal
Protein 2 g
Carbohydrate 3 g
Cholesterol 1 mg
Sodium 72 mg
Total fat 0 g
  Saturated 0 g
  Polyunsaturated 0 g
  Monounsaturated 0 g

Salads and Salad Dressings

Orange-Chèvre Salad Dressing

Chèvre is a distinct-tasting, tangy cheese made from goat's milk. It's relatively low in fat and sodium, making it a good choice in this recipe. Try this creamy salad dressing drizzled over a mixture of leaf lettuce and mandarin oranges.

4 ounces soft chèvre
½ cup skim milk
1 tablespoon honey
1 teaspoon finely shredded orange peel
1 tablespoon fresh orange juice
½ teaspoon poppy seeds

In a blender or the work bowl of a food processor fitted with a metal blade, combine all ingredients except poppy seeds. Cover and process until smooth. Stir in poppy seeds. Cover and chill at least 30 minutes. (Dressing will thicken slightly as it chills.) Stir before serving.

Makes about 1 cup
Serves 8; 2 tablespoons per serving
Preparation time: 5 minutes
Chilling time: At least 30 minutes

NUTRIENT ANALYSIS (PER SERVING)

Calories 53 kcal
Protein 3 g
Carbohydrate 4 g
Cholesterol 13 mg
Sodium 166 mg
Total fat 3 g
Saturated 2 g
Polyunsaturated 0 g
Monounsaturated 1 g

Sandwiches

In this chapter we've wrapped up a selection of savory sandwiches that are sure to take the ho-hum out of lunchtime without taking many minutes out of your busy day. Need a sandwich for a take-along lunch? Try Cornmeal Chicken Muffinwiches or No-Cholesterol Egg Salad Sandwiches. Want a sandwich to go with your cup of soup? Make Grilled Cheese and Cilantro Sandwiches or Cucumber and Herbed Cream Cheese Sandwiches. How about a sandwich for the day of the big game? Try our Make-Ahead Tuna Hoagie.

These sandwiches all have something in common: they're quick, healthful, and delicious. And don't limit them to lunchtime, either. They make a nice light dinner—just serve them along with a salad or soup for a great-tasting, heart-healthful meal.

Make-Ahead Tuna Hoagie

Need a terrific-tasting sandwich for the big game? Try this unique hoagie featuring the fresh flavors of the Mediterranean. Make the sandwich up to two hours in advance so that the flavors will soak into the bread.

Serves 8

Preparation time: 15 minutes

Chilling time: 2 to 24 hours

16-ounce loaf sourdough French bread
12¼-ounce can water-packed low-salt tuna, drained and flaked
2 tablespoons balsamic or red wine vinegar
¼ cup fat-free, cholesterol-free mayonnaise or salad dressing
1 teaspoon anchovy paste
1 large ripe tomato, thinly sliced
Freshly ground black pepper
½ medium red onion, thinly sliced
¼ cup loosely packed chopped fresh parsley leaves

Cut the bread in half horizontally. Using your fingers, hollow out each half of the bread, leaving a ½-inch shell. Save bread from inside loaf for another use.

In a small bowl, combine tuna and vinegar; set aside.

In another small bowl, stir together mayonnaise and anchovy paste. Spread the inside of each half of loaf with mayonnaise mixture.

Spoon tuna mixture into the bottom half of bread. Arrange tomato slices over tuna and season with pepper. Arrange onions over tomatoes and sprinkle with parsley. Top with remaining bread half.

Wrap loaf in foil and store in the refrigerator for 2 to 24 hours. To serve, cut into 8 slices.

NUTRIENT ANALYSIS (PER SERVING)

Calories 223 kcal
Protein 17 g
Carbohydrate 35 g
Cholesterol 8 mg
Sodium 519 mg
Total fat 1 g
Saturated 0 g
Polyunsaturated 0 g
Monounsaturated 0 g

Cook's Tip

To make good use of the leftover bread from this recipe, place it in the work bowl of a food processor fitted with a metal blade. Cover and process until ground into fine crumbs. Transfer the crumbs to a freezer container and freeze for up to several months. Use the crumbs anytime a recipe calls for soft bread crumbs, such as for meatloaf or crumb-topped casseroles.

Cornmeal Chicken Muffinwiches

This handy sandwich in a muffin can be made in advance and stored in an airtight plastic bag in the freezer for up to two months. Simply pop a frozen muffinwich into a lunch bag in the morning, and it will be thawed by noon.

Serves 6; 1 muffin per serving

Preparation time: 10 minutes

Cooking time: 15 to 20 minutes

8½-ounce package corn muffin mix
Egg substitute equivalent to 1 egg or 2 egg whites
⅓ cup skim milk
2 cups (8 ounces) coarsely chopped cooked chicken (cooked without skin)
4 green onions, sliced
¼ teaspoon dried sage
Vegetable oil spray (optional)

Preheat oven to 400° F.

Prepare corn muffin mix according to package directions, but use egg substitute or egg whites for the egg and skim milk for the milk. Fold chicken, green onions, and sage into batter.

Spray 6 muffin cups with vegetable oil or line with paper bake cups. Spoon batter into cups. Bake 15 to 20 minutes or until a toothpick inserted near the center comes out clean. Cool. Serve warm or chilled.

NUTRIENT ANALYSIS
(PER SERVING)

Calories 205 kcal
Protein 15 g
Carbohydrate 27 g
Cholesterol 29 mg
Sodium 307 mg
Total fat 4 g
  Saturated 1 g
  Polyunsaturated 1 g
  Monounsaturated 1 g

Cook's Tip

When cooked chicken is called for in a recipe, use leftover grilled or baked chicken breast meat or choose lean, low-sodium cooked chicken breast from your grocery-store delicatessen.

Heart-Healthful Turkey Reubens

This classic sandwich is made lighter by using nonfat dressing, lean cooked turkey, and low-fat Swiss cheese. Don't forget to rinse the sauerkraut to remove some of the sodium. Also, try to select low-sodium foods for the rest of the day's meals so your sodium intake does not exceed 3000 milligrams.

Serves 4; 1 sandwich per serving

Preparation time: 5 minutes

Cooking time: 8 to 12 minutes

¼ cup nonfat Thousand Island salad dressing
8 slices dark rye or pumpernickel bread
8 ounces thinly sliced low-fat, low-sodium cooked
  turkey or chicken
½ cup sauerkraut, rinsed and well drained
4 slices low-fat Swiss cheese (1½ ounces)
Vegetable oil spray

Spread salad dressing on one side of each slice of bread. Top 4 slices of the bread with turkey, sauerkraut, and cheese. Top with remaining bread slices, dressing side down.

Spray a large skillet with vegetable oil. Cook 2 sandwiches over medium heat for 4 to 6 minutes or until bread toasts and cheese melts, turning once. Repeat with remaining sandwiches.

NUTRIENT ANALYSIS (PER SERVING)

Calories 273 kcal
Protein 24 g
Carbohydrate 31 g
Cholesterol 48 mg
Sodium 780 mg
Total fat 5 g
  Saturated 1 g
  Polyunsaturated 2 g
  Monounsaturated 1 g

Double-Bean Lunch Burritos

The green chili peppers and Southwest seasoning give these fiber-rich burritos a wonderful flavor.

Serves 4; 1 sandwich per serving

Preparation time: 5 minutes

1 cup nonfat refried beans
1 cup canned black beans, rinsed and drained
4-ounce can chopped green chili peppers, drained
1 teaspoon ground cumin
4 to 8 lettuce leaves
4 8-inch flour tortillas
Commercial salsa or Fresh and Chunky Salsa
  (page 48)

In a medium bowl, stir together beans, chilies, and cumin. Arrange lettuce over tortillas. Spoon about ½ cup bean mixture near one edge of each tortilla. Top with salsa if desired. Roll tortilla around filling. Serve immediately for a refreshing cold lunch. Or, if you want to serve these warm, place one or more burritos on a microwave-safe plate. Cook, uncovered, on 100% power (high) for 35 to 40 seconds for one burrito, 1 to 1¼ minutes for two, 1½ to 2 minutes for three, or 2 to 2½ minutes for four burritos.

NUTRIENT ANALYSIS
(PER SERVING)

Calories 269 kcal
Protein 12 g
Carbohydrate 50 g
Cholesterol 3 mg
Sodium 565 mg
Total fat 4 g
  Saturated 1 g
  Polyunsaturated 1 g
  Monounsaturated 2 g

Cook's Tip

Canned green chili peppers are mild compared with other chili peppers, such as jalapeños or serranos. To save time in the kitchen, buy the green chili peppers that are already chopped.

Open-Face Vegetable Sandwiches

You'll think you're eating a salad when you bite into this English muffin heaped with fresh, crunchy vegetables. The melted cheese on top makes the sandwich taste rich and helps hold the ingredients together.

Serves 2; 2 muffin halves per serving

Preparation time: 10 minutes

Cooking time: 2 to 3 minutes

2 to 4 teaspoons Dijon mustard
2 whole-grain English muffins, split and toasted
½ cup small broccoli florets
¼ cup chopped red, yellow, or green bell pepper
¼ cup shredded carrot
½ cup shredded low-fat Monterey Jack cheese

Preheat broiler.

Spread mustard over the cut side of each English muffin half. Arrange broccoli, bell pepper, and carrot over mustard. Sprinkle with cheese.

Place English muffin halves on the unheated rack of a broiler pan. Broil about 4 inches from the heat for 2 to 3 minutes or until cheese melts.

NUTRIENT ANALYSIS (PER SERVING)

Calories 246 kcal
Protein 14 g
Carbohydrate 34 g
Cholesterol 17 mg
Sodium 352 mg
Total fat 6 g
Saturated 4 g
Polyunsaturated 0 g
Monounsaturated 2 g

Tomato and Mozzarella Sandwiches with Pesto Mayonnaise

If you like, substitute fresh mozzarella cheese for the part-skim mozzarella cheese in this recipe. Look for it at large supermarkets, health-food stores, or specialty-food stores.

Serves 2; 1 sandwich per serving

Preparation time: 5 minutes

2 tablespoons fat-free, cholesterol-free mayonnaise
  or salad dressing
1 teaspoon purchased pesto or Homemade Pesto
  (see page 229)
⅛ teaspoon black pepper
4 slices whole-grain bread
4 ounces part-skim mozzarella cheese, sliced
1 medium ripe tomato, sliced

In a small bowl, stir together mayonnaise, pesto, and pepper. Spread mayonnaise mixture on one side of each piece of bread. Evenly divide cheese and tomato slices between two slices of the bread. Top with remaining bread slices.

NUTRIENT ANALYSIS
(PER SERVING)

Calories 332 kcal
Protein 22 g
Carbohydrate 35 g
Cholesterol 33 mg
Sodium 813 mg
Total fat 13 g
  Saturated 7 g
  Polyunsaturated 1 g
  Monounsaturated 4 g

Grilled Cheese and Cilantro Sandwiches

You don't need to spread your bread with butter or margarine to make a golden grilled cheese sandwich. The heat of the skillet browns the bread, and a light coating of vegetable oil spray keeps it from sticking. You'll get more even browning by using bread with a soft texture. For best results, use a nonstick skillet.

Serves 2; 1 sandwich per serving

Preparation time: 5 minutes

Cooking time: 7 to 9 minutes

4 ounces sliced low-fat Monterey Jack cheese or part-skim mozzarella cheese
4 slices soft-textured whole-grain bread
¼ cup loosely packed fresh cilantro leaves
Freshly ground black pepper (optional)
Vegetable oil spray

Divide the cheese between 2 slices of the bread. Top with cilantro, and season with pepper if desired. Cover with remaining bread slices.

Spray a large skillet with vegetable oil. Place sandwiches in skillet over medium heat. Cook 5 to 7 minutes or until bread is golden brown. Flip sandwiches and cook 2 minutes more or until bread is golden brown and cheese is melted.

NUTRIENT ANALYSIS (PER SERVING)

Calories 295 kcal
Protein 21 g
Carbohydrate 28 g
Cholesterol 32 mg
Sodium 572 mg
Total fat 11 g
Saturated 7 g
Polyunsaturated 1 g
Monounsaturated 3 g

Sandwiches

Fruity Cheese Pockets

You can enjoy this easy pita filling right away, but for the best flavor, let it chill a few hours before serving.

1 cup nonfat or low-fat cottage cheese
1 cup drained juice-pack fruit cocktail
½ cup shredded nonfat or low-fat cheddar cheese
2 6-inch pita bread rounds, split crosswise
4 lettuce leaves

In a medium bowl, stir together cottage cheese, fruit cocktail, and cheddar cheese. If desired, cover and chill mixture until serving time.

To serve, line each pita pocket half with a lettuce leaf and spoon in fruit and cheese mixture.

Serves 4; ½ pita per serving

Preparation time: 5 minutes

Chilling time: Several hours (optional)

NUTRIENT ANALYSIS (PER SERVING)
Calories 146 kcal
Protein 12 g
Carbohydrate 22 g
Cholesterol 3 mg
Sodium 339 mg
Total fat 1 g
  Saturated 0 g
  Polyunsaturated 0 g
  Monounsaturated 0 g

Cucumber and Herbed Cream Cheese Sandwiches

For easier mixing, bring the cream cheese to room temperature or soften it in your microwave before combining it with the seasonings.

Serves 4; 1 sandwich per serving

Preparation time: 5 minutes

8 ounces nonfat or light cream cheese
1 teaspoon dried basil or oregano, crushed
½ teaspoon bottled minced garlic
½ teaspoon dried thyme, crushed
¼ teaspoon dried tarragon, crushed
Dash ground red pepper
Skim milk
8 slices rye or whole-grain bread
1 large cucumber, thinly sliced

In a small bowl, blend together cream cheese, basil, garlic, thyme, tarragon, and pepper until well combined. If necessary, add milk, 1 teaspoon at a time, until mixture is spreadable. Serve immediately or cover and chill until serving time.

To serve, spread about 2 tablespoons mixture onto one side of each slice of bread. Arrange cucumber slices on half of the bread slices. Top with remaining bread slices.

NUTRIENT ANALYSIS (PER SERVING)

Calories 197 kcal
Protein 14 g
Carbohydrate 30 g
Cholesterol 4 mg
Sodium 704 mg
Total fat 2 g
 Saturated 0 g
 Polyunsaturated 1 g
 Monounsaturated 0 g

Cook's Tip

It's easy to soften cream cheese in your microwave. Just unwrap the cream cheese and place it in a small microwave-safe bowl. Cook on 30% power (low) for about 1 minute or until soft.

No-Cholesterol Egg Salad Sandwiches

This yolk-free sandwich filling is deceptive. It looks as if it's full of egg yolks, but it gets its rich yellow color from mustard and turmeric.

Serves 3; 1 sandwich per serving

Preparation time: 10 minutes

Cooking time: 20 minutes

6 eggs
Water
¼ cup fat-free, cholesterol-free mayonnaise or salad dressing
2 tablespoons finely chopped green onion or shallots
2 tablespoons finely chopped red bell pepper
1 tablespoon prepared mustard
¼ teaspoon ground turmeric
¼ teaspoon paprika
⅛ teaspoon black pepper
6 slices whole-grain bread
3 lettuce leaves

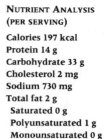

Place eggs in a large saucepan; cover with cold water. Cover pan and bring to a boil over high heat. Remove from heat and let stand, covered, for 15 minutes. Drain and rinse with cold water.

Peel eggs and remove and discard yolks. Chop egg whites.

In a small bowl, combine egg whites, mayonnaise, green onion, bell pepper, mustard, turmeric, paprika, and black pepper. Serve immediately or cover and chill until serving time.

To serve, spread egg mixture on 3 slices of bread. Top with lettuce and remaining bread slices.

NUTRIENT ANALYSIS
(PER SERVING)

Calories 197 kcal
Protein 14 g
Carbohydrate 33 g
Cholesterol 2 mg
Sodium 730 mg
Total fat 2 g
 Saturated 0 g
 Polyunsaturated 1 g
 Monounsaturated 0 g

Fish and Shellfish

Fish is a great catch, since it's low in saturated fat and cholesterol. The little fat you find in fish is the good kind: polyunsaturated omega-3 fatty acids.

Another plus for fish is that it's so easy to cook. You can poach, bake, broil, grill, or sauté it. Fish cooks fast, so be careful not to overcook it. It's a cinch if you follow the timings in our recipes, or figure about five minutes of cooking time for every half-inch thickness of fish. When measuring the thickness of your fish, you'll want to measure the fish at the thickest part to determine the cooking time. To see how to tell when fish is done, see the Cook's Tip on page 101.

When buying fresh fish, make sure the fish is displayed on a bed of ice. It should have a mild smell, not a fishy one. Avoid fish that is dry around the edges. Once you get your fish home, store it in the coldest part of your refrigerator for no more than one to two days before using.

Fish farming, also called aquaculture, is the business of raising fish and seafood in a controlled environment. The fish hatch, feed, and live in disease-free, unpolluted pens, tanks, or ponds until they are ready to harvest. Common farm-raised fish include catfish, tilapia, salmon, and trout. Expect farm-raised fish to be milder-tasting than their wild counterparts.

We've netted you some family-style favorites in this chapter. Try our Crunchy Fish Nuggets with Lemon Tartar Sauce or Dilled Albacore Cakes. We've also snagged you a few elegant entrées, such as Pan-Seared Tuna with Mandarin Orange Pico de Gallo and Greek Scallops with Feta Cheese. Delight your family with one tonight.

Pasta-Crusted Fish with Marinara Sauce

You don't have to cook the fresh pasta before putting it on the fish. It bakes to form a crisp coating on the fillets.

Serves 4; ¼-pound fillet per serving

Preparation time: 5 minutes

Cooking time: 10 minutes

Vegetable oil spray
1 pound boneless, skinless fish fillets
1 cup finely chopped fresh refrigerated angel-hair pasta
¼ teaspoon dried dill weed
Freshly ground black pepper
1 cup low-fat meatless spaghetti sauce or refrigerated marinara sauce

Preheat oven to 450° F. Spray a baking sheet with vegetable oil.

Rinse fish and pat dry. If necessary, cut fish into 4 serving-size pieces. Set aside.

Place chopped pasta in a glass pie plate or shallow bowl. Press one side of the fillets into pasta until well coated. Place fillets, pasta side up, in a single layer on baking sheet. Sprinkle with dill weed and pepper. Spray fillets lightly with more vegetable oil.

Bake fillets, uncovered, 8 to 10 minutes or until fish flakes easily when tested with a fork.

Meanwhile, place spaghetti sauce in a small saucepan. Cook over medium-low heat until heated through, about 5 minutes. Spoon ¼ cup sauce over each serving of cooked fish.

NUTRIENT ANALYSIS (PER SERVING)

Calories 199 kcal
Protein 25 g
Carbohydrate 20 g
Cholesterol 60 mg
Sodium 300 mg
Total fat 2 g
Saturated 0 g
Polyunsaturated 1 g
Monounsaturated 0 g

Cook's Tip

When a recipe calls for a boneless, skinless fish fillet, you can customize the recipe to your individual taste. Just choose fillets that you like best. For this recipe, try flounder, haddock, cod, or orange roughy.

Fish and Shellfish

Peanut-Coated Fillets with Corn Salsa

This pretty lime-and-corn salsa uses no-salt-added canned corn, which is much crisper and juicier than the salt-added variety. You'll find them next to each other on your supermarket shelf.

Serves 4; ¼-pound fillet and ⅓ cup corn salsa per serving

Preparation time: 15 minutes

Cooking time: 10 to 15 minutes

Vegetable oil spray
1 pound boneless, skinless fish fillets, cut into 4 pieces
½ of a 17-ounce can no-salt-added whole-kernel corn, drained
½ cup chopped green bell pepper
¼ cup chopped red onion
2 tablespoons lime juice
½ teaspoon bottled minced garlic
⅛ teaspoon ground red pepper
⅛ teaspoon salt (optional)
2 tablespoons chopped fresh cilantro or parsley
2 tablespoons fat-free, cholesterol-free mayonnaise
Freshly ground black pepper
⅓ cup chopped unsalted dry-roasted peanuts

Preheat oven to 450° F. Spray a shallow glass baking dish with vegetable oil.

Rinse fillets and pat dry. Set aside.

In a medium bowl, stir together corn, green pepper, onion, lime juice, garlic, red pepper, and, if desired, salt. Stir in cilantro. Set aside.

Place fillets in prepared dish, tucking under any thin edges. Lightly brush the top of each fillet with mayonnaise. Season with black pepper. Sprinkle with chopped nuts. Bake 10 to 15 minutes or until fish flakes easily with a fork. Serve with corn mixture.

**NUTRIENT ANALYSIS
(PER SERVING)**

Calories 246 kcal
Protein 32 g
Carbohydrate 14 g
Cholesterol 77 mg
Sodium 220 mg
Total fat 7 g
  Saturated 1 g
  Polyunsaturated 2 g
  Monounsaturated 3 g

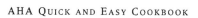

Spicy Sole and Tomatoes

You can adjust the level of spiciness in this recipe to suit your taste. Just increase or reduce the amount of bottled hot pepper sauce you use.

Serves 4; ¼-pound fillet per serving

Preparation time: 10 minutes

Cooking time: 4 to 6 minutes

1 pound boneless, skinless sole, flounder, or whitefish fillets, about ½ inch thick, cut into 4 pieces
Vegetable oil spray
½ cup chopped onion
½ teaspoon bottled minced garlic
14½-ounce can diced tomatoes
1 teaspoon drained capers
4 peppercorns
4 to 6 dashes bottled red hot pepper sauce

Rinse fish and pat dry. Set aside.

Spray a large skillet with vegetable oil. Place over medium-high heat.

Add onion and garlic to hot skillet and cook until tender, about 5 minutes. Stir in remaining ingredients and bring to a boil. Arrange fish on top. Return to a boil. Reduce heat, cover, and simmer for 4 to 6 minutes or until fish flakes easily with a fork. Remove peppercorns before serving.

NUTRIENT ANALYSIS (PER SERVING)

Calories 121 kcal
Protein 20 g
Carbohydrate 6 g
Cholesterol 53 mg
Sodium 254 mg
Total fat 1 g
  Saturated 0 g
  Polyunsaturated 1 g
  Monounsaturated 0 g

Cook's Tip

Remember that fish is done when it becomes opaque, begins to flake easily when tested with a fork, and comes away from the bone readily.

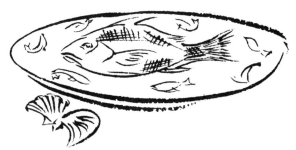

Tilapia with Black Bean Relish

You can make the black bean relish up to 24 hours in advance and reheat it over low heat or serve it at room temperature with the broiled fish.

Serves 4; ¼-pound fillet and ⅓ cup black bean relish per serving

Preparation time: 15 minutes

Cooking time: 8 to 10 minutes

15-ounce can black beans
¼ cup diced low-fat, low-sodium ham
4 green onions, sliced
1 medium stalk celery, chopped
1 medium carrot, peeled and chopped
1 teaspoon ground cumin
½ teaspoon bottled minced garlic
¼ teaspoon bottled minced jalapeño pepper
Vegetable oil spray
1 pound tilapia fillets, cut into 4 pieces
1 lime, cut in half
¼ cup snipped fresh cilantro or parsley (optional)

Drain some of the liquid from the black beans (about 1 inch off the top of the can). In a medium saucepan, combine partially drained beans, ham, green onions, celery, carrot, cumin, garlic, and jalapeño pepper. Cook, uncovered, over medium-low heat while preparing fish, stirring occasionally.

Meanwhile, preheat broiler and spray the rack of a broiler pan with vegetable oil. Rinse fish and pat dry. Place fish on prepared rack of unheated broiler pan. Squeeze one half of the lime over fish. Broil 4 inches from the heat for 4 minutes. Turn fish over and squeeze remaining lime half over fish. Broil for 2 to 4 minutes more or until fish flakes easily with a fork.

Stir cilantro into black bean mixture if desired. Serve fish with black bean mixture.

NUTRIENT ANALYSIS (PER SERVING)

Calories 262 kcal
Protein 31 g
Carbohydrate 28 g
Cholesterol 64 mg
Sodium 438 mg
Total fat 3 g
  Saturated 1 g
  Polyunsaturated 1 g
  Monounsaturated 1 g

Cook's Tip

Tilapia is a lean farm-raised fish with white, firm flesh and a mild flavor.

Crunchy Fish Nuggets with Lemon Tartar Sauce

The cornflake coating keeps these bite-size pieces of fish crunchy on the outside and oh-so-moist on the inside.

Serves 4; 6 nuggets and 2 tablespoons tartar sauce per serving

Preparation time: 10 minutes

Cooking time: 5 minutes

1 pound skinless halibut fillets or other white fish fillets
Egg substitute equivalent to 1 egg
2 tablespoons skim milk
¼ cup grated Parmesan cheese
¼ cup cornflake crumbs or plain dry bread crumbs
½ teaspoon paprika
½ cup fat-free, cholesterol-free mayonnaise
2 tablespoons finely chopped dill pickle
1 teaspoon finely shredded lemon peel
1 teaspoon lemon juice

Preheat oven to 450° F.

Rinse fish and pat dry. Cut fish into 24 bite-size pieces. Set aside.

In a medium bowl, combine egg substitute and skim milk. In a large plastic bag with a tight-fitting seal, combine Parmesan cheese, cornflake crumbs, and paprika.

Add fish chunks to egg mixture, stirring until well coated. Using a slotted spoon, remove fish from egg mixture and place several in bag with crumb mixture. Seal bag and toss until fish is well coated with crumbs. Repeat until all fish is coated.

Arrange fish in a single layer on a baking sheet or in a shallow baking pan. Bake about 5 minutes or until fish flakes easily with a fork.

Meanwhile, in a small bowl, stir together remaining ingredients. Serve the lemon tartar sauce with fish.

NUTRIENT ANALYSIS (PER SERVING)

Calories 191 kcal
Protein 26 g
Carbohydrate 14 g
Cholesterol 64 mg
Sodium 739 mg
Total fat 3 g
  Saturated 1 g
  Polyunsaturated 1 g
  Monounsaturated 1 g

Broiled Halibut with Chunky Tomato-Cream Sauce

This versatile tomato sauce can double as an easy pasta sauce.

Serves 4; ¼-pound fillet and ⅓ cup sauce per serving

Preparation time: 10 minutes

Cooking time: 8 to 12 minutes

Vegetable oil spray
2 halibut or swordfish steaks, cut about 1 inch thick (about 1 pound total)
1 teaspoon olive oil
Freshly ground black pepper
14½-ounce can Italian-style, pasta-style, or Cajun-style stewed tomatoes
¼ cup nonfat or low-fat sour cream
1 tablespoon all-purpose flour

Remove the rack of the broiler pan and spray it with vegetable oil. Preheat the broiler.

Rinse fish and pat dry. Place fish on prepared rack of unheated broiler pan. Brush fish lightly with olive oil and season to taste with pepper. Broil 4 inches from the heat for 5 minutes. Turn fish over and broil 3 to 7 minutes more or until fish flakes easily with a fork. Cut each fish steak in half.

Meanwhile, use a slotted spoon to remove tomatoes from liquid in can. Pour liquid into a medium saucepan. Coarsely chop tomatoes and place them in the saucepan with their liquid. Cook over medium-high heat until bubbly, about 5 minutes.

In a small bowl, stir together sour cream and flour. Add to tomatoes. Cook and stir until thickened and bubbly, about 3 to 4 minutes. Cook 1 minute more, stirring constantly, and serve with the broiled fish.

NUTRIENT ANALYSIS (PER SERVING)

Calories 150 kcal
Protein 23 g
Carbohydrate 7 g
Cholesterol 60 mg
Sodium 272 mg
Total fat 3 g
Saturated 1 g
Polyunsaturated 1 g
Monounsaturated 1 g

Poached Salmon with Spinach

Place the unwrapped block of spinach on a microwave-safe plate and cook on 30% power (medium-low) for 2 minutes, or until just soft enough to cut through with a sharp knife. Rewrap and return half the spinach to the freezer. Use the rest as directed in the recipe.

Serves 4; ¼-pound fillet and ¼ cup spinach mixture per serving

Preparation time: 10 minutes

Cooking time: 10 to 15 minutes

1 pound salmon fillets
1½ cups water
½ cup dry white wine or water
2 green onions, sliced
1 bay leaf
½ of a 10-ounce package frozen no-salt-added chopped spinach
⅛ teaspoon ground nutmeg
¼ cup shredded part-skim mozzarella cheese
Freshly ground black pepper
Lemon slices (optional)

Cut salmon into 4 pieces, rinse, and pat dry. Set aside.

In a large skillet, combine water, wine, green onions, and bay leaf. Over high heat, bring just to a boil. Carefully add salmon and return to a boil. Reduce heat, cover, and simmer 8 to 10 minutes or until fish flakes easily with a fork. Remove fish and pat it dry with paper towels.

Meanwhile, cook spinach according to package directions. Drain well, squeezing out moisture. Stir in nutmeg.

Preheat broiler. Place fish on a broiler-proof serving platter or on the rack of an unheated broiler pan. Top with spinach mixture, sprinkle with cheese, and season with pepper. Broil 4 inches from the heat for 1 to 2 minutes or until cheese melts. Garnish with lemon slices if desired.

NUTRIENT ANALYSIS (PER SERVING)

Calories 190 kcal
Protein 27 g
Carbohydrate 2 g
Cholesterol 47 mg
Sodium 110 mg
Total fat 8 g
Saturated 2 g
Polyunsaturated 2 g
Monounsaturated 3 g

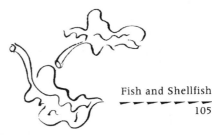

Fish and Shellfish

Pan-Seared Tuna with Mandarin Orange Pico de Gallo

Pico de gallo is traditionally made with tomatoes, onions, and peppers. The mandarin oranges and avocado in this recipe turn the classic mixture into a fresh-tasting hot and spicy orange mixture. It gives tuna steaks a new flavor twist.

Try this hot and spicy orange mixture with other varieties of fish, such as swordfish, shark, and mahimahi.

Serves 4; ¼-pound fillet and ⅓ cup orange mixture per serving

Preparation time: 10 minutes

Cooking time: 10 minutes

Vegetable oil spray
½ cup chopped red or yellow onion
½ teaspoon bottled minced garlic
1 tablespoon balsamic vinegar or red wine vinegar
1 teaspoon firmly packed brown sugar
⅛ to ¼ teaspoon crushed red pepper flakes
11-ounce can mandarin orange sections in light
   syrup, drained
⅓ cup chopped tomato
⅓ cup chopped avocado
1 tablespoon lime juice
2 tuna steaks (about 1 pound total)

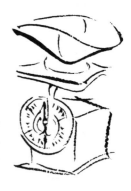

Spray a medium saucepan with vegetable oil. Place over medium-high heat. Add onion and garlic and cook until onion is tender, about 5 minutes. Stir in vinegar, brown sugar, and pepper flakes. Cook and stir until sugar dissolves, about 2 to 3 minutes. Remove from heat and stir in remaining ingredients except tuna. Set aside.

Rinse fish and pat dry. Set aside.

Spray a large skillet with vegetable oil. Place over medium-high heat. Add fish to hot skillet and cook about 5 minutes per side or until fish flakes easily when tested with a fork. Cut each steak in half to make 4 portions. Serve fish with mandarin orange mixture.

Nutrient Analysis
(per serving)

Calories 205 kcal
Protein 24 g
Carbohydrate 13 g
Cholesterol 58 mg
Sodium 73 mg
Total fat 7 g
  Saturated 2 g
  Polyunsaturated 1 g
  Monounsaturated 2 g

Dilled Albacore Cakes

Chunk white tuna is also called albacore tuna and has the mildest flavor of all types of tuna. Be sure the canned tuna you buy is the low-salt version that's packed in water, not oil.

Serves 6; 1 patty per serving

Preparation time: 15 minutes

Cooking time: 15 minutes

Vegetable oil spray
2 6⅛-ounce cans water-packed low-salt chunk white tuna, drained
Egg substitute equivalent to 2 eggs
¼ cup plain dry bread crumbs or cornflake crumbs
¼ cup grated or shredded Parmesan cheese
2 green onions, sliced
1 tablespoon snipped fresh dill or ½ teaspoon dried dill weed
½ teaspoon coarsely cracked black pepper
⅓ cup fat-free, cholesterol-free mayonnaise
Fresh dill sprigs (optional)

Preheat oven to 400° F. Spray a shallow baking pan with vegetable oil.

In a medium bowl, combine tuna, egg substitute, bread crumbs, Parmesan cheese, green onions, dill, and pepper. Stir until well combined.

Using your hands, shape tuna mixture into 6 patties. Place patties in a single layer in prepared baking pan. Bake, uncovered, about 15 minutes or until lightly golden brown. Top each patty with a dollop of mayonnaise. If desired, garnish with fresh dill.

NUTRIENT ANALYSIS
(PER SERVING)
Calories 125 kcal
Protein 20 g
Carbohydrate 7 g
Cholesterol 13 mg
Sodium 414 mg
Total fat 1 g
  Saturated 1 g
  Polyunsaturated 0 g
  Monounsaturated 0 g

Fish and Shellfish

Sherried Seafood Sauté

This easy recipe uses fresh shrimp and lump crabmeat, which is cooked nuggets of white meat from the body of the crab. You can substitute less expensive imitation crab, but beware of higher sodium. Serve this easy, elegant dish over hot cooked spinach fettuccine or rice.

Serves 4; ½ cup per serving

Preparation time: 10 minutes

Cooking time: 5 minutes

8 ounces uncooked shelled and deveined medium or large shrimp
Vegetable oil spray
1 tablespoon acceptable margarine
½ cup shredded carrot
3 green onions, sliced
1 teaspoon bottled minced garlic
6 ounces lump crabmeat, flaked, cartilage removed
2 tablespoons dry sherry, dry white wine, or non-alcoholic white wine

Rinse shrimp and pat dry. Set aside.

Spray a large skillet with vegetable oil. Place over medium-high heat and add margarine. When margarine has melted, add shrimp, carrot, green onions, and garlic to hot skillet. Cook about 3 minutes, or until shrimp turns pink, stirring often. Add crabmeat and sherry. Cook and stir until heated through, about 2 to 3 minutes.

NUTRIENT ANALYSIS
(PER SERVING, NOT INCLUDING PASTA)

Calories 121 kcal
Protein 17 g
Carbohydrate 3 g
Cholesterol 120 mg
Sodium 246 mg
Total fat 4 g
 Saturated 1 g
 Polyunsaturated 1 g
 Monounsaturated 1 g

Cook's Tip

There are some good options available for those who don't care to cook with alcohol. Try nonalcoholic wine—it's fermented just like regular wine, then processed to remove the alcohol. Alcohol-free beer is another good choice. It's made without traditional fermentation and instead gets its beer taste from added flavorings. But beware of nonalcoholic beer. It may sound as though it's alcohol-free, but it's not. By law, nonalcoholic beers must contain less than 0.5 percent alcohol. The brewers call them malt beverage, cereal beverage, or near beer.

Dijon Mussels

Serve these tender saltwater shellfish with French bread or whole-grain rolls to soak up every bit of the creamy sauce.

Serves 4; 6 mussels per serving

Preparation time: 15 minutes

Cooking time: 3 to 5 minutes

24 mussels (approximately 2 pounds)
½ cup dry white wine or nonalcoholic white wine
4 green onions, sliced
¼ teaspoon black pepper
½ cup evaporated skim milk
2 tablespoons Dijon mustard
1 tablespoon all-purpose flour

Scrub mussels and remove beards. (Do this just before cooking, because the mussels will die once they are debearded.) Set aside.

In a Dutch oven, combine wine, green onions, and pepper. Bring to a boil over high heat. Add mussels. Cover and steam for 3 to 5 minutes or until mussels open. Discard any mussels that do not open. Turn off heat.

With a slotted spoon, transfer mussels to a dish or bowl. Retain liquid.

In a small bowl, stir together milk, mustard, and flour. Add to liquid in Dutch oven. Over high heat, cook and stir until sauce is thickened, about 5 minutes. Cook 1 minute more, stirring constantly. Return mussels to Dutch oven; stir to coat with sauce.

NUTRIENT ANALYSIS
(PER SERVING)
Calories 126 kcal
Protein 16 g
Carbohydrate 10 g
Cholesterol 36 mg
Sodium 193 mg
Total fat 1 g
  Saturated 0 g
  Polyunsaturated 0 g
  Monounsaturated 0 g

Cook's Tip

To debeard mussels, use your fingers to grasp the mossy-looking beards that stick out of the shells. Pull them firmly until they dislodge from the shell. Discard the beards.

Fish and Shellfish

Greek Scallops with Feta Cheese

If you're concerned about sodium, replace the pasta-style stewed tomatoes with no-salt-added stewed tomatoes and 1 teaspoon dried oregano, crushed. Serve this easy dish over the hot cooked pasta of your choice.

Serves 4; 1 cup per serving

Preparation time: 5 minutes

Cooking time: 8 to 10 minutes

1 pound bay scallops
Vegetable oil spray
14½-ounce can pasta-style, Italian-style, or Cajun-style stewed tomatoes
⅛ teaspoon black pepper
½ cup crumbled feta cheese (2 ounces)

Rinse scallops and pat dry. Set aside.

Spray a large skillet with vegetable oil. Place over medium-high heat. Add scallops to hot skillet and cook 3 to 5 minutes, or until scallops are opaque, stirring often. Add undrained tomatoes and pepper to skillet. Heat through, about 5 minutes. Spoon mixture evenly onto four plates. Sprinkle each serving with feta cheese.

NUTRIENT ANALYSIS
(PER SERVING, NOT INCLUDING PASTA)

Calories 188 kcal
Protein 28 g
Carbohydrate 9 g
Cholesterol 49 mg
Sodium 626 mg
Total fat 5 g
  Saturated 2 g
  Polyunsaturated 1 g
  Monounsaturated 1 g

Poultry

There are a few very good reasons why this chapter boasts so many great recipes. One of poultry's greatest attributes is that it's so versatile. Maybe that's why we're all eating more chicken and turkey than our grandparents did. Poultry has a well-rounded flavor that appeals to a wide range of tastes. And it's a real blessing for low-fat food fanciers as long as the skin and cleverly hidden pockets of fat are removed. Don't forget that poultry is quick to fix and economical, too.

Poultry's popularity has caught the attention of our nation's food manufacturers. Look for all kinds of chicken and turkey products, ranging from marinated chicken breasts to turkey breakfast sausages. Some of these products are real kitchen time savers. Just be sure to read the label to determine if the poultry product you choose fits within your healthful-eating guidelines. When buying ground chicken or turkey, be sure to choose the kind ground without skin.

In this chapter you'll find tasteful simplicity in recipes such as Baked Dijon Chicken and Cheesy Oven-Fried Chicken. For an elegant dinner, try Velvet Turkey and Herbs or Lemon-Sauced Chicken with Asparagus. We think you'll agree that we've put together some of the tastiest poultry recipes around.

Seven-Spice Chicken

Although this Moroccan-spiced chicken takes about an hour to bake, you can put it together in a snap.

2½- to 3-pound whole chicken
1 teaspoon garlic powder
½ teaspoon ground cumin
½ teaspoon ground ginger
¼ teaspoon salt
¼ teaspoon ground turmeric
¼ teaspoon paprika
¼ teaspoon ground cinnamon

Serves 4; ¼ chicken per serving

Preparation time: 10 minutes

Cooking time: 1 to 1¼ hours

Preheat oven to 375° F.

Rinse chicken and pat dry. Remove giblets and neck and save for other use or discard. Twist wings under back. Place chicken, breast side up, on a rack in a shallow roasting pan.

In a small bowl, stir together remaining ingredients. Set aside.

Using your fingers and beginning at the neck of the chicken, gently separate the skin from the body across the breast and down the legs. Do not separate the skin near the tail. Reach under the skin and rub the spice mixture over the flesh of the chicken. If necessary, secure any loose skin to the chicken with toothpicks.

Roast in oven 1 to 1¼ hours or until chicken is tender and no longer pink and drumsticks move easily in their sockets. Before serving, remove skin from chicken, leaving the spice mixture on the meat.

NUTRIENT ANALYSIS (PER SERVING)

Calories 202 kcal
Protein 32 g
Carbohydrate 1 g
Cholesterol 90 mg
Sodium 219 mg
Total fat 7 g
Saturated 2 g
Polyunsaturated 2 g
Monounsaturated 2 g

Cook's Tip

At the grocery store, pay attention to the date stamped on poultry products, dairy foods, meats, and some packaged products. These are "sell by" or "use by" dates that indicate that these products are fresh up to the date shown on the package.

Pesto "Fried" Chicken

The aromatic pesto keeps the chicken moist during baking and helps the crumbs stick, too. You can also use the pesto-and-crumb coating on boneless, skinless chicken breasts or thighs, but be sure to reduce the baking time to 20 to 30 minutes.

Serves 6; 1 to 2 pieces chicken per serving

Preparation time: 10 minutes

Cooking time: 45 to 55 minutes

2 to 2½ pounds chicken pieces (breasts, thighs, and drumsticks), skinned, all visible fat removed

3 tablespoons purchased pesto or Homemade Pesto (see page 229)

¼ cup cornflake crumbs

Fresh lemon or lime wedges (optional)

Preheat oven to 375° F.

Rinse chicken and pat dry. Place breasts and thighs bone side down in a shallow baking pan. Add drumsticks and brush top of chicken with pesto and sprinkle with cornflake crumbs.

Bake, uncovered, 45 to 55 minutes or until chicken is tender and no longer pink. Serve with lemon or lime wedges if desired.

NUTRIENT ANALYSIS (PER SERVING)

Calories 188 kcal
Protein 25 g
Carbohydrate 5 g
Cholesterol 66 mg
Sodium 163 mg
Total fat 7 g
  Saturated 2 g
  Polyunsaturated 2 g
  Monounsaturated 2 g

Cook's Tip

Skinning chicken, especially drumsticks and wings, can be tricky, since they are so slippery. An easy way around this problem is to grasp the skin with a dry paper towel as you pull it away from the meat.

Honey-Roasted Chicken

This simple recipe uses a tangy sauce that is bursting with flavor. You may need to use a wire whisk to blend the mustard into the other sauce ingredients.

Serves 6; 1 to 2 pieces chicken per serving

Preparation time: 10 minutes

Cooking time: 45 minutes

Microwave cooking time: 20 minutes

2 pounds chicken pieces (breasts, thighs, and drumsticks), skinned, all visible fat removed
1 cup honey
½ cup reduced-sodium teriyaki sauce
¼ cup orange juice
1 tablespoon Dijon mustard

Preheat oven to 375° F.

Rinse chicken and pat dry. Place in a single layer in a shallow baking pan.

In a medium bowl, stir together remaining ingredients. Pour over chicken pieces.

Bake, uncovered, basting with the honey mixture occasionally, about 45 minutes or until chicken is tender and no longer pink.

Microwave Method

Prepare recipe as directed above, but place chicken in a deep microwave-safe baking dish and pour honey mixture over chicken. Cover with vented plastic wrap and cook on 100% power (high) about 10 minutes. Rotate dish a half turn and baste with honey mixture. Re-cover and cook on high about 10 minutes more or until chicken is tender and no longer pink.

NUTRIENT ANALYSIS (PER SERVING)

Calories 321 kcal
Protein 23 g
Carbohydrate 52 g
Cholesterol 58 mg
Sodium 625 mg
Total fat 4 g
 Saturated 1 g
 Polyunsaturated 1 g
 Monounsaturated 1 g

Marinated Hoisin Chicken

Hoisin sauce, sometimes called Chinese ketchup, is a tongue-tingling mixture of fermented soybeans and seasonings. Look for jars of hoisin sauce in your grocery store alongside other Asian ingredients. Although hoisin sauce has no real substitute, in a pinch you can substitute 1 tablespoon of dark molasses and 1 tablespoon of ketchup for 2 tablespoons hoisin sauce.

Serves 4; 1 to 2 pieces chicken per serving

Preparation time: 10 minutes

Marinating time: 1 to 24 hours

Cooking time: 45 to 55 minutes

1½ pounds chicken pieces (breasts, thighs, and drumsticks), skinned, all visible fat removed
2 tablespoons hoisin sauce
2 tablespoons rice wine vinegar or cider vinegar
1 tablespoon sesame seeds

Rinse chicken and pat dry. Place in a plastic bag with a tight-fitting seal.

In a small bowl, stir together remaining ingredients. Pour over chicken in bag. Seal and marinate in the refrigerator for 1 to 24 hours, turning bag occasionally to distribute marinade.

Preheat oven to 375° F.

Drain chicken and discard marinade. Arrange chicken in a single layer in a glass baking dish. Bake, uncovered, 45 to 55 minutes or until chicken is tender and no longer pink.

NUTRIENT ANALYSIS (PER SERVING)

Calories 141 kcal
Protein 24 g
Carbohydrate 0 g
Cholesterol 65 mg
Sodium 61 mg
Total fat 4 g
  Saturated 1 g
  Polyunsaturated 1 g
  Monounsaturated 1 g

Garlic Baked Chicken Breasts

Serve this garlic lover's special with your favorite steamed vegetables and warm whole-grain bread.

2 whole medium chicken breasts (1½ pounds), halved lengthwise and skinned, all visible fat removed
2 teaspoons bottled minced garlic

Preheat oven to 375° F.

Rinse chicken and pat dry. Arrange on a baking sheet or in a shallow baking pan. Spread ½ teaspoon garlic over each piece of chicken.

Bake, uncovered, about 30 minutes or until chicken is tender and no longer pink.

Serves 4; one-half breast per serving

Preparation time:
5 minutes

Cooking time:
30 minutes

NUTRIENT ANALYSIS
(PER SERVING)

Calories 144 kcal
Protein 26 g
Carbohydrate 1 g
Cholesterol 66 mg
Sodium 61 mg
Total fat 3 g
  Saturated 1 g
  Polyunsaturated 1 g
  Monounsaturated 1 g

Chinese-Style Chicken Thighs

You can also prepare this Asian-inspired dish with chicken breasts. Whichever you choose, serve the chicken and sauce alongside ramen noodles or brown rice.

Serves 4; 1 thigh and 1 tablespoon sauce per serving

Preparation time: 5 minutes

Cooking time: 35 minutes

Microwave cooking time: 13 to 17 minutes

4 chicken thighs (1½ pounds), skinned, all visible fat removed
2 tablespoons light soy sauce
2 tablespoons rice wine vinegar or cider vinegar
2 tablespoons dry sherry or orange juice
1 teaspoon toasted sesame oil
1 teaspoon honey
½ teaspoon bottled minced garlic
1 tablespoon orange juice or water
1 teaspoon cornstarch

Preheat oven to 375° F.

Rinse chicken and pat dry. Arrange in a single layer in a glass baking dish. Set aside.

In a small bowl, stir together soy sauce, vinegar, sherry, sesame oil, honey, and garlic. Pour over chicken. Bake, uncovered, 30 minutes or until chicken is tender and no longer pink. Remove chicken from baking dish and keep warm.

Transfer sauce to a small saucepan. In a small bowl, stir together orange juice and cornstarch. Add to sauce. Cook and stir over medium heat until thickened and bubbly, about 3 minutes. Cook 2 minutes more, stirring constantly. Serve chicken with sauce.

NUTRIENT ANALYSIS
(PER SERVING)
Calories 133 kcal
Protein 15 g
Carbohydrate 5 g
Cholesterol 46 mg
Sodium 346 mg
Total fat 6 g
  Saturated 1 g
  Polyunsaturated 2 g
  Monounsaturated 2 g

Microwave Method

Prepare recipe as directed above, but cover baking dish with vented plastic wrap and cook on 100% power (high) 6 to 7 minutes. Rotate dish a half turn. Re-cover and cook on high for 6 to 8 minutes or until chicken is tender and no longer pink. Remove chicken from baking dish and keep warm.

Transfer sauce to a 2-cup glass measuring cup. In a small bowl, stir together orange juice and cornstarch. Add to sauce. Cook, uncovered, on 100% power (high) for 1 to 2 minutes or until thick and bubbly, stirring every 30 seconds. Serve chicken with sauce.

Cook's Tip

When a recipe calls for wine or dry sherry, don't use cooking sherry or wine. These bottled cooking liquids are very salty and have little resemblance to wine or sherry. You're better off using the real thing or substituting water or fruit juice.

Skillet Chicken Thighs with Dried Berries

You'll get a rich sauce with a robust flavor if you choose red wine, and you'll get a slightly sweet and fruity sauce with cranberry juice cocktail.

Serves 4; ¼ pound chicken and ¼ cup sauce per serving

Preparation time:
10 minutes

Cooking time:
10 minutes

1 pound boneless, skinless chicken thighs, all visible fat removed
Vegetable oil spray
⅔ cup dry red wine or cranberry juice cocktail
¼ cup dried cranberries, dried blueberries, dried cherries, or mixed dried fruit bits
½ teaspoon dried thyme, crushed
1 tablespoon water
1 teaspoon cornstarch

Rinse chicken and pat dry.

Spray a large skillet with vegetable oil. Place over medium-high heat. Place chicken in hot skillet and brown for 1 minute on each side. Remove chicken from skillet.

Stir wine, dried fruit, and thyme into the skillet. Bring to a boil over high heat; reduce heat. Arrange chicken over liquid mixture. Cover and simmer for 5 minutes or until chicken is tender and no longer pink. Remove chicken to a serving platter and keep warm.

In a small bowl, stir together water and cornstarch. Add to liquid in skillet. Cook and stir over medium heat until thickened and bubbly, about 3 minutes. Cook 2 minutes more, stirring constantly. Serve sauce with chicken.

NUTRIENT ANALYSIS
(PER SERVING)

Calories 203 kcal
Protein 24 g
Carbohydrate 7 g
Cholesterol 77 mg
Sodium 79 mg
Total fat 7 g
 Saturated 2 g
 Polyunsaturated 2 g
 Monounsaturated 2 g

Chicken with Fresh Fruit Salsa

The Fresh Fruit Salsa can be made up to twenty-four hours in advance and stored in a tightly covered container in the refrigerator. For the best flavor, bring it to room temperature before serving it with the chicken.

½ cup chopped fresh apricots, peaches, or nectarines (see Note)
1 small tomato, chopped
¼ cup chopped red onion
2 tablespoons lemon juice
¼ teaspoon finely shredded gingerroot
¼ teaspoon bottled minced garlic
1 pound boneless, skinless chicken breasts, all visible fat removed

Serves 4; ¼ pound chicken and ¼ cup salsa per person

Preparation time: 10 minutes

Cooking time: 10 minutes

Preheat broiler.

In a medium bowl, combine all ingredients except chicken breasts. Set aside.

Rinse chicken and pat dry. Place chicken on grill or on an unheated broiler rack. Grill or broil 4 to 5 inches from the heat about 5 minutes or until lightly browned. Turn and grill or broil about 5 minutes more, or until chicken is tender and no longer pink. Serve with fruit salsa.

Note: If fresh fruit is not available, use canned and drained apricots or peaches canned in fruit juice.

NUTRIENT ANALYSIS (PER SERVING)

Calories 153 kcal
Protein 25 g
Carbohydrate 5 g
Cholesterol 62 mg
Sodium 61 mg
Total fat 3 g
  Saturated 1 g
  Polyunsaturated 1 g
  Monounsaturated 1 g

Cheesy Oven-Fried Chicken

These crispy chicken strips are just right for little hands and big appetites. Serve them with Crispy Skin-On Oven Fries (see page 208) and a salad or fresh fruit.

Serves 4; 4 chicken strips per serving

Preparation time: 15 minutes

Cooking time: 5 to 7 minutes

Vegetable oil spray
2 cups bite-size, low-fat cheddar-cheese-flavored crackers
½ to ¾ teaspoon dried basil
⅛ teaspoon black pepper
1 pound boneless, skinless chicken breasts or turkey breast tenderloins, all visible fat removed
2 tablespoons skim milk

Preheat oven to 400° F. Spray a shallow baking pan with vegetable oil.

Place crackers, basil, and pepper in a large plastic bag with a tight-fitting seal (leave end open so air can escape) and use a rolling pin to crush the crackers. Or place crackers, basil, and pepper in the work bowl of a food processor fitted with a metal blade and process until finely crushed; transfer to large plastic bag. Set aside.

Rinse chicken and pat dry. Cut into 16 strips, about 1×3 inches each. Dip chicken in milk. Add chicken strips, a few pieces at a time, to bag with cracker mixture. Seal bag and shake until chicken is coated. Place coated chicken in a single layer on prepared baking pan.

Bake, uncovered, 5 to 7 minutes or until chicken is tender and no longer pink.

NUTRIENT ANALYSIS
(PER SERVING)

Calories 212 kcal
Protein 27 g
Carbohydrate 14 g
Cholesterol 62 mg
Sodium 292 mg
Total fat 5 g
  Saturated 1 g
  Polyunsaturated 1 g
  Monounsaturated 2 g

Cheesy Chicken Nuggets

Prepare recipe as above except cut chicken into bite-size pieces. Bake, uncovered, in a preheated 400° F oven about 5 minutes or until tender and no longer pink.

Lemon-Pepper Chicken over Pasta

For a pretty presentation, use green spinach linguine or fettuccine. If you choose fresh refrigerated pasta, be sure to buy the reduced-fat variety.

Serves 4; ¼ pound chicken and ½ cup pasta per serving

Preparation time: 10 minutes

Cooking time: 15 to 20 minutes

Microwave cooking time: 9 to 12 minutes

1 pound boneless, skinless chicken breasts, all visible fat removed
½ lemon
Freshly ground black pepper
8 or 9 ounces dried linguine or fettuccine
1 cup low-fat meatless spaghetti sauce
2 tablespoons snipped fresh basil or parsley

Preheat oven to 375° F.

Rinse chicken and pat dry. Arrange in a single layer in a glass baking dish. Squeeze juice from lemon half over chicken. Season generously with pepper. Cover and bake for 15 to 20 minutes or until chicken is tender and no longer pink.

Meanwhile, in a large saucepan, cook linguine according to package directions but omit oil and salt. Drain and return pasta to saucepan. Add spaghetti sauce and basil. Toss to mix well. Serve chicken over pasta mixture.

Microwave Method

Prepare recipe as directed above, but cover baking dish with vented plastic wrap and cook on 100% power (high) for 4 to 5 minutes. Rotate dish a half turn. Re-cover and cook on high for 4 to 5 minutes or until chicken is tender and no longer pink. To warm spaghetti sauce, place sauce in a 2-cup glass measuring cup. Cover with wax paper and cook on 100% power (high) for 1 to 2 minutes or until warm, stirring once.

NUTRIENT ANALYSIS (PER SERVING)

Calories 395 kcal
Protein 34 g
Carbohydrate 54 g
Cholesterol 62 mg
Sodium 267 mg
Total fat 4 g
  Saturated 1 g
  Polyunsaturated 1 g
  Monounsaturated 1 g

Coriander-Coated Chicken

Serve this spicy honeyed chicken with a wedge of Easy Mexican Cornbread (see page 234).

Serves 4; ¼ pound per serving

Preparation time: 10 minutes

Cooking time: 12 minutes

1 pound boneless, skinless chicken breasts, all
   visible fat removed
Vegetable oil spray
2 tablespoons honey
2 teaspoons ground coriander
1 to 2 teaspoons ground cumin
1 teaspoon sesame seeds
1 teaspoon snipped fresh thyme or ¼ teaspoon
   dried thyme, crushed
¼ to ½ teaspoon coarsely cracked black pepper

Preheat oven to 350° F.

Rinse chicken and pat dry.

Spray a large ovenproof skillet with vegetable oil. (If you don't have an ovenproof skillet, brown the chicken in a skillet and transfer chicken pieces to a shallow baking pan.) Place over medium-high heat. Add chicken to hot skillet and cook about 1 minute on each side or until chicken is brown. Remove skillet from heat.

Brush honey over browned chicken in skillet.

In a small bowl, stir together remaining ingredients. Sprinkle mixture over honey-brushed chicken. Bake, uncovered, about 10 minutes or until chicken is tender and no longer pink.

NUTRIENT ANALYSIS
(PER SERVING)

Calories 174 kcal
Protein 25 g
Carbohydrate 9 g
Cholesterol 62 mg
Sodium 59 mg
Total fat 4 g
  Saturated 1 g
  Polyunsaturated 1 g
  Monounsaturated 1 g

Mexican Chicken in Tortillas

We used flour tortillas in this recipe because they are easier to roll up than corn tortillas.

8 6-inch whole-wheat or regular flour tortillas
1 pound boneless, skinless chicken breasts or turkey breast tenderloins, all visible fat removed
8-ounce can no-salt-added tomato sauce
½ cup commercial salsa or Fresh and Chunky Salsa (page 48)
1 cup shredded low-fat cheddar cheese
Nonfat or low-fat sour cream (optional)

Serves 4; 2 tortillas per serving

Preparation time: 10 minutes

Cooking time: 5 to 7 minutes

Preheat oven to 250° F.

Wrap tortillas in foil and place in oven. Meanwhile, rinse chicken and pat dry. Cut into bite-size pieces. In a large skillet combine chicken, tomato sauce, and salsa. Bring to a boil over high heat. Reduce heat, cover, and simmer 5 to 7 minutes or until chicken is tender and no longer pink.

Remove tortillas from oven. Spoon one-eighth of chicken and salsa mixture down center of each tortilla. Sprinkle each tortilla with 2 tablespoons cheese. Place a dollop of sour cream on top of cheese if desired. Roll tortillas around filling.

NUTRIENT ANALYSIS (PER SERVING)

Calories 321 kcal
Protein 36 g
Carbohydrate 24 g
Cholesterol 77 mg
Sodium 705 mg
Total fat 9 g
  Saturated 4 g
  Polyunsaturated 1 g
  Monounsaturated 2 g

Spicy Peanut Chicken

Make this Thai-flavored dish as spicy as you like by using your favorite mild, medium, or hot salsa. Serve with rice or pasta.

Serves 4; ½ cup per serving

Preparation time: 10 minutes

Cooking time: 8 minutes

1 pound boneless, skinless chicken breasts or turkey breast tenderloins, all visible fat removed
Vegetable oil spray
1 medium green bell pepper, cut into bite-size pieces
½ cup commercial salsa or Fresh and Chunky Salsa (page 48)
1 tablespoon peanut butter
1 tablespoon light soy sauce
1 teaspoon finely shredded fresh gingerroot
1 teaspoon bottled minced garlic
¼ cup coarsely chopped, unsalted dry-roasted peanuts

Rinse chicken and pat dry. Cut into bite-size pieces.

Spray a large skillet with vegetable oil. Place over medium-high heat. Add chicken and bell pepper to hot skillet. Cook 5 minutes or until chicken is tender and no longer pink. Stir in remaining ingredients except peanuts. Cook and stir until thickened and bubbly, about 3 minutes. Sprinkle with peanuts.

NUTRIENT ANALYSIS (PER SERVING)

Calories 225 kcal
Protein 29 g
Carbohydrate 7 g
Cholesterol 62 mg
Sodium 540 mg
Total fat 9 g
 Saturated 2 g
 Polyunsaturated 3 g
 Monounsaturated 4 g

Lemon-Sauced Chicken with Asparagus

Before beginning the recipe, be sure to thaw the asparagus or broccoli in the refrigerator, or place the vegetable in a colander and run it under hot water for a few minutes. Pat dry before cooking.

Serves 4; 1 cup per serving

Preparation time: 10 minutes

Cooking time: 8 to 10 minutes

1 pound boneless, skinless chicken breasts or turkey breast tenderloins, all visible fat removed
½ cup low-sodium chicken broth
1 teaspoon finely shredded lemon peel
2 tablespoons lemon juice
1 tablespoon light soy sauce
1 tablespoon cornstarch
1 teaspoon sugar
¼ teaspoon black pepper
2 teaspoons cooking oil
10-ounce package frozen no-salt-added cut asparagus or broccoli florets, thawed
1 small red bell pepper, cut into bite-size pieces

Rinse chicken and pat dry. Cut into bite-size pieces.

In a small bowl, stir together broth, lemon peel, lemon juice, soy sauce, cornstarch, sugar, and black pepper. Set aside.

Preheat a wok or large skillet over high heat. Add 1 teaspoon of the oil. Stir-fry asparagus and bell pepper in the hot oil for 1 minute. Remove vegetables from wok or skillet. Add remaining oil and chicken. Stir-fry 3 minutes, or until chicken is tender and no longer pink.

Stir lemon mixture; add to center of wok or skillet. Cook and stir until thickened and bubbly, about 3 minutes. Cook 1 minute more, stirring constantly. Return vegetables to wok or skillet. Stir until coated with sauce.

NUTRIENT ANALYSIS (PER SERVING)

Calories 191 kcal
Protein 27 g
Carbohydrate 8 g
Cholesterol 62 mg
Sodium 218 mg
Total fat 6 g
Saturated 1 g
Polyunsaturated 2 g
Monounsaturated 1 g

Barbecue-Simmered Chicken Chunks

Combining bottled barbecue sauce with marmalade is a clever way to cut sodium and add flavor without adding fat. Serve the tangy poultry mixture in this recipe with hot cooked couscous or small shell pasta. Or cut the chicken or turkey into smaller pieces and serve it on a whole-grain bun or in pita bread as a barbecued chicken sandwich.

Serves 4; ½ cup per serving

Preparation time: 5 minutes

Cooking time: 6 to 7 minutes

1 pound boneless, skinless chicken breasts or turkey breast tenderloins, all visible fat removed
Vegetable oil spray
¼ cup barbecue sauce
¼ cup spreadable fruit or reduced-sugar marmalade, jelly, jam, or preserves

NUTRIENT ANALYSIS (PER SERVING)

Rinse chicken and pat dry. Cut into bite-size pieces. Spray a large skillet with vegetable oil. Place over medium-high heat. Add chicken pieces to hot skillet. Cook 3 to 4 minutes or until chicken is tender and no longer pink, stirring occasionally. Stir in remaining ingredients. Cook and stir until heated through, about 3 minutes.

Calories 174 kcal
Protein 25 g
Carbohydrate 10 g
Cholesterol 62 mg
Sodium 185 mg
Total fat 3 g
  Saturated 1 g
  Polyunsaturated 1 g
  Monounsaturated 1 g

Baked Dijon Chicken

Use this versatile lemon-mustard spread on other cuts of chicken, such as skinless breast halves, thighs, or drumsticks. Just be sure to bake a few extra minutes, or until chicken is no longer pink.

Serves 4; ¼ pound per serving

Preparation time: 5 minutes

Cooking time: 15 to 20 minutes

Microwave cooking time: 6 to 8 minutes

1 pound boneless, skinless chicken breasts or turkey breast tenderloins, all visible fat removed
1 tablespoon Dijon or coarse-grained mustard
2 teaspoons lemon or lime juice
½ teaspoon bottled minced garlic
⅛ teaspoon black pepper

Preheat oven to 375° F.

Rinse chicken and pat dry.

In a small bowl, stir together remaining ingredients. Arrange chicken in a single layer in a glass baking dish. Spread mustard mixture over the top of each piece.

Bake, uncovered, 15 to 20 minutes or until chicken is tender and no longer pink.

NUTRIENT ANALYSIS (PER SERVING)

Calories 137 kcal
Protein 25 g
Carbohydrate 1 g
Cholesterol 62 mg
Sodium 104 mg
Total fat 3 g
  Saturated 1 g
  Polyunsaturated 1 g
  Monounsaturated 1 g

Microwave Method

Prepare recipe as directed above, but arrange chicken in a single layer in a baking dish, placing thicker portions toward the outside edge of the dish. Cover with wax paper and cook on 100% power (high) 3 to 4 minutes. Give dish a half turn. Re-cover and cook on high 3 to 4 minutes or until chicken is tender and no longer pink.

Hawaiian Chicken

It's easy to escape to the islands when you concoct this pretty pineapple-topped chicken. Serve it with a crusty loaf of whole-grain bread.

Serves 4; ¼ pound chicken and ½ cup pineapple mixture per serving

Preparation time: 10 minutes

Cooking time: 10 minutes

1 pound boneless, skinless chicken breasts or turkey breast tenderloins, all visible fat removed
16-ounce can crushed pineapple, canned in fruit juice
¼ cup light soy sauce
1 kiwifruit, peeled and chopped
2 green onions, sliced
⅛ teaspoon ground ginger
Dash ground red pepper

Rinse chicken and pat dry. If necessary, cut chicken into 4 serving-size pieces.

Drain pineapple, reserving liquid (you should have about ½ cup).

Place pineapple liquid and soy sauce in a large skillet. Bring to a boil over high heat. Place chicken in soy sauce mixture. Return to a boil. Reduce heat, cover, and simmer about 10 minutes or until chicken is tender and no longer pink.

Meanwhile, in a small saucepan, combine drained pineapple, kiwifruit, green onions, ginger, and pepper. Cook over medium-low heat until warm, about 3 minutes.

To serve, remove chicken from soy sauce mixture. Spoon pineapple mixture over chicken or turkey.

NUTRIENT ANALYSIS
(PER SERVING)

Calories 221 kcal
Protein 26 g
Carbohydrate 22 g
Cholesterol 62 mg
Sodium 660 mg
Total fat 3 g
  Saturated 1 g
  Polyunsaturated 1 g
  Monounsaturated 1 g

Poultry and Mango Stir-Fry

You can save a lot of time by buying a jar of sliced mangoes in your grocer's produce department and using part of the fruit for this recipe. Store the remaining mangoes for up to 1 week in your refrigerator and enjoy them as a healthy snack.

Serves 4; ¾ cup per serving

Preparation time: 10 minutes

Cooking time: 8 to 10 minutes

1 pound boneless, skinless chicken breasts or
turkey breast tenderloins, all visible fat removed
1 cup mango or peach chunks
Vegetable oil spray
2 tablespoons Asian-style cooking sauce for
chicken, vegetables, and meat, or sweet-and-
sour sauce
¼ cup sliced almonds, toasted

Rinse chicken and pat dry. Cut into bite-size pieces. If using canned fruit, drain it and pat it dry. Set aside.

Spray a large skillet with vegetable oil. Place over medium-high heat. Add chicken to hot skillet. Cook 3 to 5 minutes or until tender and no longer pink. Remove from heat. Stir in sauce. Gently stir in mangoes or peaches. Return to heat; heat through, about 5 minutes. Sprinkle each serving with 1 tablespoon almonds.

NUTRIENT ANALYSIS
(PER SERVING)

Calories 224 kcal
Protein 26 g
Carbohydrate 11 g
Cholesterol 62 mg
Sodium 199 mg
Total fat 8 g
  Saturated 1 g
  Polyunsaturated 2 g
  Monounsaturated 4 g

Roast Turkey Breast with Mashed Sweet Potatoes and Fruit

These delightfully different mashed potatoes go great with the turkey in this recipe. You may also want to try them with another lean, roasted meat.

Serves 8; ¼ pound turkey and ½ cup potato mixture per serving

Preparation time: 15 minutes

Cooking time: 2½ to 3 hours

2½- to 3-pound turkey breast half with bone, skinned, all visible fat removed
2 pounds sweet potatoes
3 medium pears or apples
Water
2- to 3-inch stick cinnamon
1 tablespoon acceptable margarine
¼ teaspoon salt
⅛ teaspoon black pepper

Preheat oven to 325° F.

Rinse turkey and pat dry. Place turkey breast, bone side down, on a rack in a shallow roasting pan. Insert a meat thermometer into the thickest part of the breast. Cover loosely with foil. Roast in oven 2½ to 3 hours or until meat thermometer registers 165° F.

Meanwhile, peel sweet potatoes and cut into large chunks. Peel and core pears and cut into large chunks. In a medium saucepan, combine sweet potatoes and pears. Cover with water. Add cinnamon stick. Bring to a boil over high heat. Reduce heat, cover, and simmer 20 minutes or until tender. Drain liquid and discard cinnamon stick.

Mash potato mixture with a potato masher or beat with an electric mixer on low speed. Add margarine, salt, and pepper and mash or beat until well combined. Serve with slices of roast turkey.

NUTRIENT ANALYSIS (PER SERVING)

Calories 261 kcal
Protein 31 g
Carbohydrate 21 g
Cholesterol 75 mg
Sodium 159 mg
Total fat 5 g
  Saturated 1 g
  Polyunsaturated 1 g
  Monounsaturated 2 g

Cook's Tip

When it comes to cooking, all pears are not alike. The best varieties for cooking are Bartlett and Bosc. If you use apples in this recipe, choose Golden Delicious, Granny Smith, Jonathan, Rome Beauty, or Winesap.

Roast Turkey Breast with Cranberry-Jalapeño Sauce

An easy way to enjoy the flavor of fresh cranberry sauce without any effort is by using a container of cranberry-orange sauce. Look for it in your supermarket next to the canned fruits.

Serves 8; ¼ pound turkey and 2 tablespoons sauce per serving

Preparation time: 5 minutes

Cooking time: 2½ to 3 hours

2½- to 3-pound turkey breast half with bone, skinned, all visible fat removed
12-ounce container cranberry-orange sauce
1 tablespoon snipped fresh cilantro
1 teaspoon bottled minced jalapeño peppers

Preheat oven to 325° F.

Rinse turkey and pat dry. Place turkey breast, bone side down, on a rack in a shallow roasting pan. Insert a meat thermometer into the thickest part of the breast. Cover loosely with foil. Roast in oven 2 to 2½ hours.

Meanwhile, in a small saucepan, stir together remaining ingredients. Cook over low heat, stirring occasionally, until heated through, about 5 minutes. Keep warm.

Remove foil from turkey and baste with some of the cranberry mixture. Continue to cook turkey, basting frequently, for 30 minutes more or until the meat thermometer registers 165° F. Serve turkey with remaining warm cranberry mixture.

NUTRIENT ANALYSIS (PER SERVING)

Calories 236 kcal
Protein 30 g
Carbohydrate 20 g
Cholesterol 75 mg
Sodium 87 mg
Total fat 4 g
  Saturated 1 g
  Polyunsaturated 1 g
  Monounsaturated 1 g

Rosemary Turkey with Mushrooms

Chanterelle mushrooms give this dish a delicate, meaty flavor and richness.

Serves 4; ¼ pound turkey and 2 tablespoons sauce per serving

Preparation time:
10 minutes

Cooking time:
18 minutes

1 pound turkey breast tenderloin slices, all visible fat removed
½ cup low-sodium chicken broth
1 tablespoon cornstarch
⅛ teaspoon salt
⅛ teaspoon black pepper
Vegetable oil spray
2 tablespoons balsamic vinegar
1 teaspoon snipped fresh rosemary or ¼ teaspoon dried rosemary, crushed
8 ounces chanterelle or button mushrooms, cleaned, trimmed, and sliced
¼ cup chopped shallots or onion
Fresh rosemary (optional)

Rinse turkey and pat dry. Set aside.

In a small bowl, stir together broth, cornstarch, salt, and pepper. Set aside.

Spray a large skillet with vegetable oil. Place over medium-high heat. Add half the turkey to hot skillet. Cook about 2 minutes on each side or until turkey is tender and no longer pink. Repeat with remaining turkey. Remove skillet from heat; remove turkey from skillet and keep warm.

Add vinegar and rosemary to skillet, stirring to scrape up brown bits from bottom of pan. Return skillet to heat and add mushrooms and shallots. Over medium heat, cook and stir until mushrooms are tender, about 5 minutes. Stir broth mixture and add to skillet. Cook and stir until thickened and bubbly, about 3 minutes. Cook 2 minutes more, stirring constantly. Serve sauce with turkey. Serve on a bed of rosemary if desired.

NUTRIENT ANALYSIS
(PER SERVING)

Calories 169 kcal
Protein 28 g
Carbohydrate 5 g
Cholesterol 67 mg
Sodium 137 mg
Total fat 4 g
  Saturated 1 g
  Polyunsaturated 1 g
  Monounsaturated 1 g

Currant Turkey with Capers

The sweetness of the currants and the slight bitterness of the capers come together tastefully in this easy sauce.

Serves 4; ¼ pound turkey and 2 tablespoons sauce per serving

Preparation time: 15 minutes

Cooking time: 15 minutes

Vegetable oil spray
1 pound turkey breast tenderloin slices, all visible fat removed
½ cup plus 2 tablespoons dry white wine or unsweetened apple juice
¼ cup currants or raisins
2 tablespoons chopped onion
1 tablespoon drained capers
½ teaspoon bottled minced garlic
¼ teaspoon ground cinnamon
1 tablespoon cornstarch

Spray a large skillet with vegetable oil. Place over medium-high heat. Add half the turkey slices to hot skillet. Cook 1 minute on each side or until brown. Remove from skillet. Repeat with remaining turkey. Remove skillet from heat; remove turkey from skillet.

Slowly add ½ cup of the wine to skillet, scraping up brown bits from bottom of pan. Return skillet to heat. Add currants, onion, capers, garlic, and cinnamon. Bring to a boil and add turkey. Reduce heat, cover, and simmer 2 minutes or until turkey is tender and no longer pink.

Remove turkey from skillet; keep warm. In a small bowl, stir together the 2 tablespoons remaining wine and the cornstarch. Stir into liquid in skillet. Cook and stir until thickened and bubbly, about 3 minutes. Cook 2 minutes more, stirring constantly. Serve sauce with turkey.

NUTRIENT ANALYSIS (PER SERVING)

Calories 194 kcal
Protein 27 g
Carbohydrate 11 g
Cholesterol 67 mg
Sodium 78 mg
Total fat 3 g
  Saturated 1 g
  Polyunsaturated 1 g
  Monounsaturated 1 g

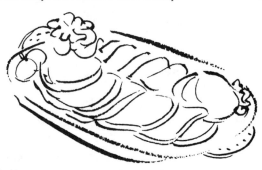

Turkey and Artichoke Fettuccine

Serve this for that special-occasion dinner when you want a bit of elegance without a lot of bother.

Serves 4; 1½ cups per serving

Preparation time: 15 minutes

Cooking time: 15 minutes

8 ounces dried fettuccine
9-ounce package frozen artichoke hearts
1 pound turkey breast tenderloins or boneless, skinless chicken breasts, all visible fat removed
Vegetable oil spray
½ teaspoon bottled minced garlic
1 tablespoon all-purpose flour
12-ounce can evaporated skim milk
¼ teaspoon salt
¼ teaspoon dried marjoram or basil, crushed
⅛ teaspoon black pepper
⅛ teaspoon ground nutmeg (optional)
½ cup shredded or grated Parmesan cheese

In a large saucepan, cook fettuccine according to package directions, but omit oil and salt. Add artichokes to boiling fettuccine water during the last 5 minutes of cooking. Drain. If necessary, halve any large artichoke hearts.

Meanwhile, rinse turkey and pat dry. Cut into bite-size pieces.

Spray a large skillet with vegetable oil. Place over medium-high heat. Add turkey pieces and garlic to hot skillet. Cook 3 minutes, or until turkey is tender and no longer pink. Stir in flour. Add remaining ingredients except Parmesan cheese. Cook and stir until thickened and bubbly, about 5 minutes. Cook 1 minute more, stirring constantly. Add turkey mixture to saucepan with drained fettuccine and artichokes. Add Parmesan cheese. Toss until well combined.

Turkey and Broccoli Fettuccine

Prepare recipe as directed above, except substitute a 10-ounce package frozen no-salt-added broccoli florets for the artichoke hearts.

NUTRIENT ANALYSIS
(PER SERVING)

Calories 534 kcal
Protein 49 g
Carbohydrate 64 g
Cholesterol 81 mg
Sodium 597 mg
Total fat 9 g
 Saturated 4 g
 Polyunsaturated 1 g
 Monounsaturated 2 g

NUTRIENT ANALYSIS
(PER SERVING)

Calories 520 kcal
Protein 49 g
Carbohydrate 60 g
Cholesterol 81 mg
Sodium 554 mg
Total fat 8 g
 Saturated 4 g
 Polyunsaturated 1 g
 Monounsaturated 2 g

Velvet Turkey and Herbs

The velvety cream sauce may taste rich, but don't worry. It's made with evaporated skim milk, which adds richness without fat. Serve over hot cooked orzo— small pasta shaped like rice—or brown rice.

Serves 4; ⅓ cup per serving

Preparation time: 10 minutes

Cooking time: 8 minutes

1 pound turkey breast tenderloins or boneless, skinless chicken breasts, all visible fat removed
Vegetable oil spray
¼ cup chopped shallots or onion
½ teaspoon bottled minced garlic
2 tablespoons all-purpose flour
1¼ cups evaporated skim milk
1 tablespoon snipped fresh oregano or ½ teaspoon dried oregano, crushed
1 tablespoon snipped fresh parsley
1 teaspoon snipped fresh basil or ¼ teaspoon dried basil, crushed

Rinse turkey and pat dry. Cut into bite-size pieces. Spray a skillet with vegetable oil. Place over medium-high heat. Add turkey, shallots, and garlic to hot skillet. Cook 3 to 4 minutes, or until turkey is tender and no longer pink.

Stir flour into mixture in skillet. Add remaining ingredients. Cook and stir until thickened and bubbly, about 3 minutes. Cook 1 minute more, stirring constantly.

NUTRIENT ANALYSIS (PER SERVING)

Calories 225 kcal
Protein 33 g
Carbohydrate 13 g
Cholesterol 70 mg
Sodium 155 mg
Total fat 4 g
Saturated 1 g
Polyunsaturated 1 g
Monounsaturated 1 g

Fresh Herb Turkey Loaf

Dress up this easy dish by spooning a half cup of warm no-salt-added tomato sauce over the top and garnishing with fresh herbs just before serving.

Serves 6; 1 slice per serving

Preparation time: 15 minutes

Cooking time: 40 to 45 minutes

2 egg whites or egg substitute equivalent to 1 egg
1 cup rolled oats
½ cup chopped red bell pepper
⅓ cup finely chopped celery
¼ cup chopped shallots or onion
2 tablespoons snipped fresh parsley
2 tablespoons snipped fresh basil or oregano or ½ teaspoon dried basil or oregano, crushed
¼ teaspoon salt
¼ teaspoon black pepper
1 pound ground turkey or chicken, ground without skin

Preheat oven to 350° F.

In a medium bowl, combine all ingredients except turkey. Add turkey and mix well.

Mold turkey mixture into a loaf pan. Bake 40 to 45 minutes or until no longer pink. Remove from oven, pat dry with paper towels, and cut into 6 slices.

NUTRIENT ANALYSIS (PER SERVING)

Calories 198 kcal
Protein 19 g
Carbohydrate 11 g
Cholesterol 51 mg
Sodium 161 mg
Total fat 9 g
 Saturated 2 g
 Polyunsaturated 2 g
 Monounsaturated 3 g

Cook's Tip

When selecting ground poultry for this or any other recipe, read the label to make sure no salt has been added to the mixture. Also, be sure the meat is not ground with skin, which adds fat to the meat. If you can't find this information on the label, then ask your butcher. Or purchase boneless, skinless turkey breast tenderloins or chicken breasts and ask your butcher to grind them for you.

Chicken and Black Bean Tacos

Ground chicken, black beans, and a handful of seasonings make these soft tacos a family favorite. If desired, serve them with chopped tomatoes, shredded lettuce, shredded nonfat or low-fat cheddar cheese, and your favorite salsa or taco sauce.

Serves 6; 2 tacos per serving

Preparation time: 10 minutes

Cooking time: 10 minutes

12 6-inch corn tortillas
1 pound ground chicken or turkey, ground without skin
½ cup chopped onion
½ teaspoon bottled minced garlic
15-ounce can low-sodium black beans, undrained
¼ cup chopped fresh cilantro or parsley
1 tablespoon chili powder
½ teaspoon ground cumin
¼ teaspoon salt
¼ teaspoon black pepper
¼ cup chopped tomatoes (optional)
¼ cup shredded lettuce (optional)
¼ cup shredded low-fat cheddar cheese (optional)
6 tablespoons commercial salsa or Fresh and Chunky Salsa (page 48) (optional)

Preheat oven to 250° F.

Wrap tortillas in foil. Place in oven while preparing chicken mixture.

In a large skillet, cook ground chicken, onion, and garlic over medium-high heat about 5 minutes or until chicken is no longer pink. Place mixture in a colander and rinse under hot water. Drain well. Wipe skillet with a paper towel. Return mixture to skillet.

Stir in beans, cilantro, chili powder, cumin, salt, and pepper. Cook and stir over medium-high heat until heated through, about 5 minutes. Spoon mixture over half of each corn tortilla; fold over. Add tomatoes, lettuce, cheese, and salsa if desired.

NUTRIENT ANALYSIS
(PER SERVING)

Calories 287 kcal
Protein 26 g
Carbohydrate 36 g
Cholesterol 44 mg
Sodium 235 mg
Total fat 5 g
  Saturated 1 g
  Polyunsaturated 2 g
  Monounsaturated 1 g

Turkey Tostadas

A tostada is the Mexican equivalent of an open-face sandwich. This version is lean and healthful, because the tortillas are crisped in the oven rather than fried in oil.

Serves 6; 1 tostada per serving

Preparation time: 15 minutes

Cooking time: 15 minutes

6 6-inch corn tortillas
Vegetable oil spray
1 pound ground turkey or chicken, ground without skin
8-ounce can no-salt-added tomato sauce
½ of a 1¼-ounce envelope (about 2 tablespoons) taco seasoning mix
Several dashes red hot pepper sauce, or to taste
2 cups shredded lettuce
2 medium tomatoes, chopped
1 cup shredded low-fat cheddar cheese
6 tablespoons commercial salsa or Fresh and Chunky Salsa (page 48) (optional)

Preheat oven to 350° F.

Arrange tortillas in a single layer on a large baking sheet. Spray lightly with vegetable oil. Bake 15 minutes or until tortillas are crisp.

Meanwhile, in a large skillet, cook turkey over medium-high heat about 5 minutes or until no longer pink. Place turkey in a colander and rinse under hot water. Drain well. Wipe skillet with a paper towel. Return turkey to skillet.

Stir tomato sauce, taco seasoning mix, and hot pepper sauce into skillet. Heat through, about 5 minutes.

Place tortillas on 6 dinner plates. Divide mixture equally among tortillas. Sprinkle with lettuce, tomatoes, and cheese. Top with salsa if desired.

NUTRIENT ANALYSIS (PER SERVING)

Calories 211 kcal
Protein 25 g
Carbohydrate 20 g
Cholesterol 45 mg
Sodium 515 mg
Total fat 4 g
  Saturated 1 g
  Polyunsaturated 1 g
  Monounsaturated 1 g

Cook's Tip

Red hot pepper sauce gets its kick from sun-ripened chili peppers. When using this sauce, you can adjust the amount to suit your taste preference. Use only a few dashes for a mild flavor and several more for a spicier taste.

Grilled Chicken Burgers

These sizzling burgers are as good as (or better than!) their ground beef cousins. Serve them on sesame seed buns or tucked inside pita bread with lettuce, tomatoes, and a spoonful of barbecue sauce.

Serves 6; 1 burger per serving

Preparation time: 10 minutes

Cooking time: 8 to 10 minutes

1 pound ground chicken or turkey, ground without skin
½ cup plain dry bread crumbs
2 green onions, chopped
2 tablespoons barbecue sauce
1 tablespoon lemon juice
2 teaspoons Worcestershire sauce
⅛ teaspoon salt
Vegetable oil spray (optional)

In a large bowl, combine all ingredients except vegetable oil spray. Use your hands to mix ingredients thoroughly. Shape mixture into 6 patties.

Grill over medium-hot coals 4 to 5 minutes per side or until no longer pink. Or preheat broiler and lightly spray the rack of an unheated broiler pan with vegetable oil. Place patties on rack. Broil 3 to 4 inches from heat for 4 to 5 minutes per side or until no longer pink.

NUTRIENT ANALYSIS (PER SERVING)
Calories 138 kcal
Protein 17 g
Carbohydrate 8 g
Cholesterol 46 mg
Sodium 208 mg
Total fat 4 g
  Saturated 1 g
  Polyunsaturated 1 g
  Monounsaturated 1 g

Jalapeño Hens

You can ask your butcher to split the hens for you before you take them home. If you do it yourself, use kitchen shears or a sharp knife and cut through the breastbone, just off center. Then cut through the center of the backbone.

2 1- to 1½-pound Cornish game hens, split
  lengthwise and skinned, all visible fat removed
½ cup jalapeño jelly
1 orange, cut into slices (optional)

Preheat oven to 375° F.

Rinse hens and pat dry.

In a small saucepan, heat jelly over low heat until warm. Place hen halves, cut side down, in a single layer in a shallow roasting pan. Spoon about half the warm jelly over the hens.

Roast, uncovered, for 30 minutes. Baste with jelly and cover loosely with foil to prevent over-browning. Continue roasting 15 minutes or until hens are tender and no longer pink. To serve, spoon remaining warm jelly over roasted hens and, if desired, garnish with orange slices.

Serves 4; ½ hen per serving

Preparation time:
5 minutes (if hens split by butcher)
10 minutes (if hens split at home)

Cooking time:
45 minutes

NUTRIENT ANALYSIS (PER SERVING)

Calories 282 kcal
Protein 37 g
Carbohydrate 14 g
Cholesterol 104 mg
Sodium 99 mg
Total fat 8 g
 Saturated 2 g
 Polyunsaturated 2 g
 Monounsaturated 2 g

Meats

It's no secret that you can enjoy meat and still maintain a low-fat eating plan. Just be sure to eat a moderate-size serving. A three-ounce serving of meat is about the size of a deck of cards. It's also important to choose the right grade and cut of meat (see Shopping for a Healthy Heart on page 11).

Cooking times for the ground beef recipes in this chapter are for a well-done product. Cooking times for whole cuts of beef are for medium doneness, which means the meat is light pink in the center and brown or gray on the edges.

Your meat choices don't have to be limited to beef. Whoever heard of a lean pig? We have! Pigs have been put on strict diets, and they are leaner today than ever before. (See Cook's Tip on page 157 for ways to tell when pork is done.)

For a tasty alternative to everyday foods, give low-fat lamb a try. Lamb is lean and tender, because it comes from sheep that are less than one year old.

Introduce yourself to veal and discover its subtle flavor, fine texture, and lean qualities. Veal is the meat from a young beef or dairy calf that has not yet put on adult fat. Veal's low-fat attributes make it a natural for quick cooking, since overcooking will toughen the young fibers.

This chapter is brimming with good-for-you recipes such as Pepper-Rubbed Beef Dijon, Cajun Meatloaf, Maple-Bourbon Pork Medallions, Double Apricot-Ham Kabobs, Rosemary Lamb Chops with Lemon Sauce, and Kiwi Veal.

Pepper-Rubbed Beef Dijon

Flank steak is very lean, and the Dijon sauce gives it a wonderful, rich flavor.

Serves 4; ¼ pound steak and ¼ cup sauce per serving

Preparation time: 10 minutes

Cooking time: 10 minutes

1-pound flank steak, all visible fat removed
2 teaspoons coarsely cracked black pepper
Vegetable oil spray
1 cup (about 3 ounces) sliced fresh mushrooms
2 green onions, sliced
½ teaspoon bottled minced garlic
1 tablespoon all-purpose flour
1 cup evaporated skim milk or skim milk
2 teaspoons Dijon mustard

Preheat broiler.

To prevent meat from curling as it cooks, make 6 shallow slashes on each side of the meat in a crisscross fashion (three slashes in each direction). Rub cracked pepper onto each side of the steak. Place steak on the unheated rack of a broiler pan. Broil 3 to 5 inches from the heat for 3 to 5 minutes. Turn and broil meat about 5 minutes more or until it reaches desired doneness.

Meanwhile, spray a medium saucepan with vegetable oil. Place over medium heat. Cook mushrooms, green onions, and garlic in skillet until mushrooms are just tender, about 5 minutes. Stir in flour. Add milk and mustard all at once. Cook and stir until thickened and bubbly, about 3 minutes. Cook 2 minutes more, stirring constantly.

To serve, thinly slice steak diagonally across the grain. Serve with the mustard sauce.

NUTRIENT ANALYSIS
(PER SERVING)

Calories 237 kcal
Protein 29 g
Carbohydrate 11 g
Cholesterol 64 mg
Sodium 162 mg
Total fat 8 g
  Saturated 3 g
  Polyunsaturated 0 g
  Monounsaturated 3 g

Sliced Sirloin with Leek Sauce

You'll love the robust leek sauce that tops this succulent sirloin.

Serves 4; ¼ pound sirloin and ¼ cup sauce per serving

Preparation time: 5 minutes

Cooking time: 22 minutes

Vegetable oil spray
1-pound sirloin steak, cut about 1½ inches thick, all visible fat removed
¾ cup water and ¼ cup dry red wine, or 1 cup water
½ cup sliced leeks
½ teaspoon low-sodium beef bouillon granules
½ teaspoon bottled minced garlic
4 teaspoons all-purpose flour
2 tablespoons water

Spray a 10-inch skillet with vegetable oil. Place over medium-high heat. Add steak to hot skillet and cook on one side for 8 minutes. Turn and cook 8 minutes more or until steak reaches desired doneness. Remove steak from skillet; cover tightly with foil to keep warm.

Add water-and-wine mixture, leeks, bouillon granules, and garlic to skillet. Reduce heat, cover, and simmer 3 minutes.

In a small bowl, stir together the flour and the 2 tablespoons water. Add to skillet. Cook and stir until thickened and bubbly, about 2 minutes. Cook 1 minute more, stirring constantly.

To serve, slice the steak crosswise into ½-inch-wide slices and serve with the leek sauce.

NUTRIENT ANALYSIS
(PER SERVING)

Calories 140 kcal
Protein 22 g
Carbohydrate 4 g
Cholesterol 56 mg
Sodium 43 mg
Total fat 3 g
  Saturated 1 g
  Polyunsaturated 0 g
  Monounsaturated 1 g

Cook's Tip

Leeks look like overgrown green onions and have a mild onion flavor. Cut off and discard the shaggy roots at the end of the bulb and the tough green leaves. The white stalk that remains is the part you use for cooking. Be sure to rinse leeks thoroughly to remove the sandy grit that collects in their stalks.

Molasses-Marinated Tenderloin

Molasses gives this marinade a unique and deliciously rich flavor. Since the molasses mixture tends to caramelize during cooking, be sure to use a nonstick skillet for easier cleanup.

⅓ cup molasses
1 shallot, chopped
2 tablespoons balsamic vinegar or red wine
  vinegar
½ teaspoon dried thyme, crushed
¼ teaspoon black pepper
1-pound beef tenderloin, all visible fat removed
Vegetable oil spray

Serves 4; ¼ pound tenderloin and 1½ tablespoons sauce per serving

Preparation time:
5 minutes

Marinating time:
24 hours or overnight

Cooking time:
10 minutes

In a large plastic bag with a tight-fitting seal, combine molasses, shallot, vinegar, thyme, and pepper. Add meat. Close bag tightly and place in the refrigerator for 24 hours or overnight, turning bag occasionally to distribute marinade.

Remove meat from marinade, reserving the marinade. Cut meat crosswise into 4 slices.

Spray a large skillet with vegetable oil. Place over medium-high heat. Add meat to hot skillet and cook for 3 minutes. Turn and cook 3 to 5 minutes more, or until meat reaches desired doneness. Remove meat from skillet and keep warm.

Add reserved marinade to skillet. Cook and stir over medium-high heat until marinade just begins to boil, about 3 minutes. To serve, pour hot marinade over meat.

NUTRIENT ANALYSIS
(PER SERVING)

Calories 224 kcal
Protein 21 g
Carbohydrate 19 g
Cholesterol 55 mg
Sodium 60 mg
Total fat 7 g
  Saturated 3 g
  Polyunsaturated 0 g
  Monounsaturated 3 g

Meats

Beef Tenderloin on Herbed White Beans

Use any combination of fresh herbs you like for the beans. Some possibilities are basil, oregano, marjoram, thyme, chives, and dill.

Vegetable oil spray
½ cup chopped red onion
½ teaspoon bottled minced garlic
15-ounce can navy or Great Northern beans
1 tablespoon chopped fresh herbs or 1 teaspoon dried herbs, crushed
1-pound beef tenderloin, all visible fat removed
Ground white, red, or black pepper to taste
Fresh herbs (optional)

Serves 4; ¼ pound tenderloin and ½ cup beans per serving

Preparation time: 10 minutes

Cooking time: 15 minutes

Spray a small saucepan with vegetable oil. Place over medium heat. Add onion and garlic and cook until onion is tender, about 3 minutes, stirring occasionally. Drain some of the liquid from the beans (about 1 inch off the top of the can) and discard it. Add the partially drained beans and the herbs to saucepan with onion mixture. Reduce heat to low and stir to mix well. Cook until heated through, about 5 minutes.

Meanwhile, cut meat into 4 slices crosswise. Lightly rub pepper all over meat.

Spray a large skillet with vegetable oil. Place over medium-high heat. Add meat to hot skillet and cook on one side for 3 minutes. Turn and cook 3 to 5 minutes more or until meat reaches desired doneness.

To serve, spoon one-fourth of the bean mixture onto each individual plate. Top with meat. Garnish with fresh herbs if desired.

NUTRIENT ANALYSIS
(PER SERVING)
Calories 261 kcal
Protein 27 g
Carbohydrate 21 g
Cholesterol 55 mg
Sodium 221 mg
Total fat 7 g
  Saturated 3 g
  Polyunsaturated 0 g
  Monounsaturated 3 g

Steak with Sun-Dried Tomatoes

The assertive flavor of the sun-dried tomato filling is delicious with beef. For convenience, this recipe uses tomatoes that are packed in oil, but you can substitute cellophane-wrapped dried tomatoes. Simply follow the rehydrating directions on the package.

Serves 4; ¼ pound steak per serving

Preparation time: 10 minutes

Cooking time: 12 to 14 minutes

4 sun-dried tomatoes, packed in oil
1 small carrot, shredded
1 green onion, sliced
2 teaspoons chopped fresh basil or ½ teaspoon dried basil, crushed
1-pound lean boneless top sirloin steak, cut 1 inch thick, all visible fat removed
1 teaspoon bottled minced garlic

Remove as much oil as possible from tomatoes by patting them with paper towels. Coarsely chop the tomatoes. In a small bowl, combine tomatoes, carrot, green onion, and basil. Set aside.

Cut the steak in half crosswise. Cut a large slit horizontally in each half to form a pocket. Spoon the tomato mixture into the pocket. Secure opening with toothpicks.

Preheat broiler.

Lightly spread each side of steak with garlic.

Place steaks on the unheated rack of a broiler pan. Broil 4 inches from the heat for 6 minutes. Turn and broil 6 to 8 minutes more or until steaks reach desired doneness. Remove toothpicks and cut each piece of steak in half.

NUTRIENT ANALYSIS (PER SERVING)

Calories 197 kcal
Protein 23 g
Carbohydrate 5 g
Cholesterol 59 mg
Sodium 97 mg
Total fat 9 g
  Saturated 3 g
  Polyunsaturated 1 g
  Monounsaturated 4 g

Meats

Beef Fajitas in Lettuce

These fresh-tasting fajitas are served in lettuce instead of tortillas.

Serves 4; 2 fajitas per serving

Preparation time: 10 minutes

Cooking time: 10 to 11 minutes

Vegetable oil spray
12-ounce lean boneless top round steak, all visible fat removed
1 teaspoon cooking oil
1 large onion, thinly sliced
1 medium red, yellow, or green bell pepper, cut into strips
1 teaspoon bottled minced garlic
2 tablespoons lime juice
½ teaspoon ground cumin
8 medium romaine or leaf lettuce leaves
½ cup nonfat or low-fat sour cream (optional)

Spray a large skillet with vegetable oil. Place over medium-high heat. Thinly slice steak across the grain into 2- or 3-inch strips. Add meat to hot skillet and cook 2 to 3 minutes or until it reaches desired doneness, stirring often. Remove meat from skillet and drain off any fat. Wipe skillet with a paper towel.

Add the 1 teaspoon cooking oil to skillet and return skillet to burner. Add onion, bell pepper, and garlic. Cook until onion is tender, about 5 minutes. Return meat to skillet. Add lime juice and cumin. Cook and stir until heated through, about 3 minutes.

To serve, spoon hot meat mixture onto center of lettuce leaves. Add sour cream if desired. Fold lettuce around meat mixture.

NUTRIENT ANALYSIS
(PER SERVING)

Calories 149 kcal
Protein 21 g
Carbohydrate 6 g
Cholesterol 52 mg
Sodium 44 mg
Total fat 4 g
  Saturated 1 g
  Polyunsaturated 1 g
  Monounsaturated 1 g

Cook's Tip

Slicing the raw meat into thin strips will be easy if you put it in the freezer for about 30 minutes before beginning the recipe.

Coriander-Glazed Steak

This four-ingredient glaze is an easy way to turn a plain broiled steak into a special dinner entrée for four.

Serves 4; ¼ pound per serving

Preparation time: 5 minutes

Cooking time: 16 to 18 minutes

1 tablespoon frozen unsweetened pineapple-orange juice concentrate
1 tablespoon water
¼ teaspoon ground coriander or ginger
⅛ teaspoon black pepper
1-pound lean boneless top sirloin steak, all visible fat removed

Preheat broiler.

In a small bowl, combine all ingredients except meat. Place meat on the unheated rack of a broiler pan. Brush with some of the pineapple-orange mixture. Broil about 4 inches from the heat for 8 minutes.

Turn steak over and brush with more juice mixture. Broil for 8 to 10 minutes more or until steak reaches desired doneness.

NUTRIENT ANALYSIS (PER SERVING)

Calories 129 kcal
Protein 21 g
Carbohydrate 2 g
Cholesterol 56 mg
Sodium 41 mg
Total fat 3 g
  Saturated 1 g
  Polyunsaturated 0 g
  Monounsaturated 1 g

Healthy Joes

These are still sloppy and delicious, but they're lower in fat than traditional sloppy joes. Be sure to choose ground beef that is extra-lean, or 90 percent lean. The kids will never know you hid a whole zucchini in here.

Serves 4; 1 sandwich per serving

Preparation time: 10 minutes

Cooking time: 12 minutes

Microwave cooking time: 10 to 14 minutes

¾ pound lean ground beef
1 cup chopped onion
1 medium red, yellow, or green bell pepper, chopped
1½ cups low-fat meatless spaghetti sauce
1 medium zucchini, shredded
1 tablespoon chili powder
1 teaspoon paprika
½ teaspoon bottled minced garlic
⅛ teaspoon salt
4 whole-wheat hamburger buns, split
Alfalfa sprouts (optional)

In a large skillet, cook beef, onion, and bell pepper over medium-high heat until meat is brown and onion is tender, about 7 minutes, stirring occasionally. Place meat mixture in a colander and rinse under hot water. Drain well. Wipe skillet with a paper towel. Return meat mixture to skillet.

Stir in spaghetti sauce, zucchini, chili powder, paprika, garlic, and salt. Bring to a boil over high heat. Reduce heat and simmer, uncovered, for 5 minutes.

Spoon meat mixture onto buns. Top with alfalfa sprouts if desired.

NUTRIENT ANALYSIS (PER SERVING)

Calories 285 kcal
Protein 26 g
Carbohydrate 36 g
Cholesterol 50 mg
Sodium 663 mg
Total fat 6 g
  Saturated 2 g
  Polyunsaturated 1 g
  Monounsaturated 2 g

Microwave Method

Place meat, onion, and bell pepper in a 2½- to 3-quart microwave-safe casserole. Cover and cook on 100% power (high) for 6 to 8 minutes or until meat is brown and onion is tender, stirring twice. Place meat mixture in a colander and rinse under hot water. Drain well. Wipe casserole with a paper towel. Return meat mixture to casserole.

Stir in spaghetti sauce, zucchini, chili powder, paprika, garlic, and salt. Cook, uncovered, on high for 4 to 6 minutes or until bubbly, stirring twice.

Proceed as directed above.

Beef and Bean Enchiladas

Classic enchiladas are typically wrapped in flour tortillas. These Mexican bundles are encased in corn tortillas, which are lower in fat and higher in fiber than flour tortillas.

Serves 4; 2 enchiladas per serving

Preparation time: 10 minutes

Cooking time: 12 minutes

Standing time: 5 minutes

½ cup no-salt-added tomato sauce
½ cup commercial salsa or Fresh and Chunky Salsa (page 48)
8 6-inch corn tortillas
½ pound lean ground beef
1 cup canned nonfat refried beans
1 teaspoon chili powder
1 teaspoon ground cumin
⅛ teaspoon black pepper
½ cup shredded low-fat cheddar cheese

In a small bowl, stir together tomato sauce and salsa. Using about half the tomato sauce mixture, brush both sides of each tortilla. Stack tortillas on a plate and set aside. (This allows tortillas to soften.)

In a large skillet, cook beef over medium-high heat until brown, about 5 minutes, stirring occasionally. Place in a colander and rinse under hot water. Drain well. Wipe skillet with a paper towel. Return beef to skillet.

Stir in refried beans, chili powder, cumin, and pepper. Cook and stir for 2 minutes or until heated through.

Preheat broiler.

Spoon about ¼ cup of the mixture in a line down the center of each tortilla. Roll up tortillas and place, seam side down, in a 10×6×2-inch or 9×9×2-inch glass baking dish. Top with remaining tomato sauce mixture.

NUTRIENT ANALYSIS
(PER SERVING)

Calories 324 kcal
Protein 25 g
Carbohydrate 41 g
Cholesterol 40 mg
Sodium 643 mg
Total fat 7 g
 Saturated 3 g
 Polyunsaturated 1 g
 Monounsaturated 2 g

Broil 4 inches from the heat for 5 minutes or until browned. Sprinkle with cheese. Let stand 5 minutes before serving.

Cook's Tip

Not all baking dishes can take the intense heat of the broiler. Make sure the one you choose has tempered glass to withstand high heat. Look on the bottom of the dish for an indication or read the manufacturer's directions.

Cajun Meatloaf

Try to buy the leanest ground beef available, such as ground round or the new 90 percent fat-free ground beef.

1 pound lean ground beef
½ cup chopped onion
½ cup chopped celery
½ cup chopped red, yellow, or green bell pepper
½ cup plain dry bread crumbs
2 egg whites or egg substitute equivalent to 1 egg
1 tablespoon Worcestershire sauce
½ teaspoon black pepper
½ teaspoon ground cumin
¼ teaspoon ground red pepper

Serves 6; 1 slice per serving

Preparation time: 10 minutes

Cooking time: 45 minutes

Microwave cooking time: 8 to 10 minutes

Standing time: 5 minutes

Preheat oven to 350° F.

In a large bowl, combine all ingredients. Use your hands to mix until ingredients are well combined.

Shape meat mixture into a loaf and place in a shallow baking pan. Bake, uncovered, for 45 minutes or until no longer pink. Let stand 5 minutes. Drain off fat and remove loaf from pan. Pat loaf dry with paper towels and cut into 6 slices.

NUTRIENT ANALYSIS (PER SERVING)

Calories 191 kcal
Protein 18 g
Carbohydrate 9 g
Cholesterol 46 mg
Sodium 149 mg
Total fat 9 g
 Saturated 3 g
 Polyunsaturated 0 g
 Monounsaturated 4 g

Microwave Method

Prepare recipe as directed above, but use a 9-inch glass pie plate for a baking dish. Shape meat mixture into a ring that is 2 inches wide and 6 inches across. Cover with wax paper. Cook on 100% power (high) for 8 to 10 minutes or until no longer pink, rotating dish a quarter turn every 3 minutes. Let stand 5 minutes, then proceed as directed above.

Pork Roast with Horseradish and Herbs

A boneless pork rib roast, also called chef's prime, is the pork industry's version of prime rib. It's much leaner than its beefy counterpart. It ranges in weight from 2 to 4 pounds and makes great leftovers to use in sandwiches or casseroles.

Serves 8; ¼ pound per serving

Preparation time: 5 minutes

Cooking time: 1 hour

Standing time: 5 minutes

2-pound lean boneless pork rib roast or loin roast, all visible fat removed
1 teaspoon prepared horseradish
½ teaspoon dried marjoram, crushed
½ teaspoon dried basil, crushed
½ teaspoon dried oregano, crushed

Preheat oven to 350° F.

Place pork roast in a shallow baking pan. Spread horseradish over the surface of meat. Set aside.

In a small bowl, combine remaining ingredients. Sprinkle over roast.

Place roast, uncovered, in oven. Cook about 1 hour or until a meat thermometer registers 160° F. Let stand 5 minutes. Slice to serve.

NUTRIENT ANALYSIS (PER SERVING)

Calories 191 kcal
Protein 21 g
Carbohydrate 0 g
Cholesterol 71 mg
Sodium 55 mg
Total fat 11 g
 Saturated 4 g
 Polyunsaturated 1 g
 Monounsaturated 5 g

Cook's Tip

Pork is done when the meat is slightly pink and has an internal temperature of 160° F. For large cuts of meat, such as roasts, use a dependable meat thermometer. For smaller cuts of meat, such as chops, cook them until the meat is slightly pink and the juices run clear when the meat is pierced. Ground pork should always be cooked until well done with no pink remaining.

Sesame Pork Tenderloin

If your tenderloin comes in two portions, simply piece them together on the baking pan and secure with toothpicks to form one portion.

1½ pounds pork tenderloin, all visible fat removed
1 tablespoon molasses
1 tablespoon light soy sauce
¼ teaspoon sesame oil
1 tablespoon sesame seeds

Preheat oven to 425° F.

Place pork in a shallow baking pan. Set aside.

In a small bowl, stir together molasses, soy sauce, and sesame oil. Brush molasses mixture over meat and sprinkle with sesame seeds.

Place meat, uncovered, in oven and roast 45 minutes or until a meat thermometer registers 160° F. Let stand 5 minutes. Slice thinly to serve.

Serves 6; ¼ pound per serving

Preparation time:
5 minutes

Cooking time:
45 minutes

Standing time:
5 minutes

NUTRIENT ANALYSIS
(PER SERVING)

Calories 152 kcal
Protein 23 g
Carbohydrate 3 g
Cholesterol 74 mg
Sodium 155 mg
Total fat 5 g
 Saturated 1 g
 Polyunsaturated 1 g
 Monounsaturated 2 g

Pesto Pork Pinwheels

Pork tenderloin comes packaged two ways—either as a whole piece of pork or split into two pieces. For this recipe, we use one piece of pork tenderloin that weighs 1 pound. If your 1-pound package comes split into two pieces, make two smaller pork rolls and reduce the cooking time to about 25 minutes.

Serves 4; ¼ pound per serving

Preparation time: 10 minutes

Cooking time: 35 to 40 minutes

Standing time: 5 minutes

1-pound pork tenderloin, all visible fat removed
1 tablespoon commercial pesto or Homemade
    Pesto (see page 229)

Preheat oven to 425° F.

Butterfly tenderloin by cutting it lengthwise *almost* in half. Lay out flat. Cover meat with plastic wrap. Use a meat mallet to pound meat to a ¼-inch thickness.

Spread pesto over cut surface of tenderloin. Roll up tenderloin from one of the short ends and tie with string in several places to secure.

Place tenderloin on a rack in a shallow roasting pan. Roast, uncovered, 35 to 40 minutes or until a meat thermometer registers 160° F. Let stand 5 minutes. Cut into slices.

NUTRIENT ANALYSIS
(PER SERVING)

Calories 145 kcal
Protein 23 g
Carbohydrate 0 g
Cholesterol 74 mg
Sodium 78 mg
Total fat 5 g
    Saturated 2 g
    Polyunsaturated 1 g
    Monounsaturated 2 g

Meats

Pork Medallions with Sautéed Mushrooms

The mushrooms in this recipe need to be cooked quickly, so be sure to slice them thin.

Serves 4; 3 medallions and 2 tablespoons mushroom mixture per serving

Preparation time: 15 minutes

Cooking time: 15 minutes

Vegetable oil spray
1-pound pork tenderloin, all visible fat removed
1 tablespoon acceptable margarine
8 ounces fresh mushrooms, cleaned, trimmed, and thinly sliced
2 green onions, sliced
1 teaspoon chopped fresh rosemary or ¼ teaspoon dried rosemary
1 tablespoon dry sherry (optional)

Spray a 12-inch skillet with vegetable oil. Place over medium-high heat.

Cut pork into 12 slices and flatten each with the palm of your hand to about ¾-inch thickness. Add 6 pork slices to hot skillet and cook for 3 minutes on each side or until slightly pink. Remove from skillet and keep warm. Repeat with remaining pork slices.

Reduce heat to medium. Add remaining ingredients except sherry to skillet. Cook until mushrooms are tender. If desired, stir in sherry. Pour sautéed mushrooms over pork.

NUTRIENT ANALYSIS (PER SERVING)

Calories 170 kcal
Protein 24 g
Carbohydrate 3 g
Cholesterol 74 mg
Sodium 88 mg
Total fat 7 g
  Saturated 2 g
  Polyunsaturated 1 g
  Monounsaturated 3 g

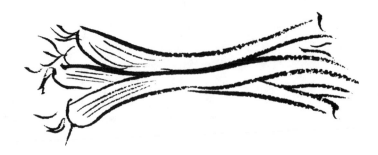

Three-Pepper Pork

This recipe may sound spicy, but it's not. The triple-pepper flavor comes from red bell pepper, yellow bell pepper, and mild poblano chili pepper. Look for poblano peppers in your grocer's produce section or in a specialty-food store.

Serves 4; ¼ pound per serving

Preparation time: 10 minutes

Cooking time: 10 minutes

1 pound lean boneless pork loin roast or chops, all
   visible fat removed
Vegetable oil spray
1 medium red bell pepper, cut into strips
1 medium yellow bell pepper, cut into strips
1 medium poblano chili pepper, chopped
1 tablespoon sugar
1 tablespoon light soy sauce
1 teaspoon finely shredded gingerroot
1 teaspoon sesame oil
1 teaspoon rice wine vinegar

Cut meat into strips and set aside.

Spray a large skillet with vegetable oil. Place over medium-high heat. Add pork strips to hot skillet and cook, stirring occasionally, for 5 minutes or until done. Remove from skillet.

Add bell pepper strips and chili pepper to hot skillet. Cook about 3 minutes or until bell peppers are slightly tender but still crisp.

In a small bowl, stir together remaining ingredients. Add to skillet with peppers and meat. Cook and stir until heated through, about 2 minutes.

NUTRIENT ANALYSIS (PER SERVING)

Calories 230 kcal
Protein 22 g
Carbohydrate 7 g
Cholesterol 71 mg
Sodium 206 mg
Total fat 12 g
  Saturated 4 g
  Polyunsaturated 2 g
  Monounsaturated 5 g

Cook's Tip

If you like fiery food, then you may want to spice up this recipe with some hot chili peppers. Just omit the poblano chili pepper and use fresh jalapeño or serrano peppers instead. For more intense heat, use the seeds and membranes of the peppers, which are the hottest parts.

Chili peppers contain volatile oils that can burn your skin and eyes, so it's very important to avoid

direct contact with the peppers as much as possible. One way is to clean and chop the peppers while holding them under cold running water. Another is to cover your hands with plastic gloves, rubber gloves, or plastic bags when you handle them. Be sure to wash your hands and under your fingernails well with soap and water when you are through. If you want to avoid handling peppers completely, look for jars of minced fresh jalapeño peppers in your grocer's produce section, near the jars of chopped fresh garlic.

Maple-Bourbon Pork Medallions

Serve this dish with your favorite cooked pasta so you can drizzle any extra maple-bourbon sauce over it.

Serves 4; 3 medallions and 2 tablespoons sauce per serving

1-pound pork tenderloin, all visible fat removed
⅓ cup maple syrup
⅓ cup bourbon or unsweetened apple juice
2 tablespoons whole-grain mustard or Dijon mustard
2 tablespoons ketchup
Vegetable oil spray

Preparation time:
10 minutes

Cooking time:
20 minutes

Cut pork into 12 slices and flatten each with the palm of your hand to about ¾-inch thickness. Set aside.

In a small bowl, stir together remaining ingredients except vegetable oil spray. Set aside.

Spray a large skillet with vegetable oil. Place over medium-high heat. Add 6 pork slices to hot skillet and cook for 3 minutes on each side or until slightly pink. Remove from skillet and keep warm. Repeat with remaining pork slices.

Add syrup mixture to skillet. Return to medium-high heat. Cook and stir until bubbly, about 5 minutes. Cook 2 minutes more, stirring constantly. Serve with tenderloin.

NUTRIENT ANALYSIS
(PER SERVING)

Calories 262 kcal
Protein 23 g
Carbohydrate 23 g
Cholesterol 74 mg
Sodium 268 mg
Total fat 4 g
  Saturated 1 g
  Polyunsaturated 1 g
  Monounsaturated 2 g

Cornbread-Coated Pork Chops

Instead of stuffing pork chops, use this streamlined recipe to coat the chops in store-bought cornbread stuffing mix. You get lots of flavor with little effort.

Serves 4; 1 chop per serving

Preparation time: 10 minutes

Cooking time: 45 minutes

¼ cup nonfat or low-fat sour cream
4 pork loin chops (5 ounces each), cut ¾ to 1 inch thick, all visible fat removed
1½ cups cornbread stuffing mix
Freshly ground black pepper

Preheat oven to 375° F.

Spread sour cream over pork chops, coating all sides. Coat with cornbread stuffing mix. Place coated pork chops on a rack in a shallow baking pan. Season with pepper.

Bake chops, uncovered, 45 minutes or until done. Serve immediately.

NUTRIENT ANALYSIS
(PER SERVING)

Calories 307 kcal
Protein 21 g
Carbohydrate 19 g
Cholesterol 73 mg
Sodium 738 mg
Total fat 16 g
  Saturated 6 g
  Polyunsaturated 2 g
  Monounsaturated 7 g

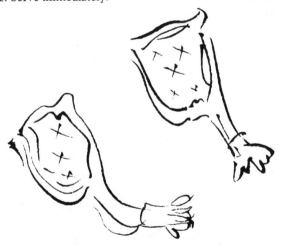

Pork Chops with Honey and Garlic

The tasty honey-and-garlic mixture used in this recipe would be good with chicken or turkey, too.

Serves 4; 1 chop and 2 tablespoons sauce per serving

Preparation time: 5 minutes

Cooking time: 18 minutes

Vegetable oil spray
4 center loin pork chops (5 ounces each), cut 1¼ to 1½ inches thick, all visible fat removed
¼ cup honey
¼ cup lemon juice
2 tablespoons light soy sauce
½ teaspoon bottled minced garlic

Spray a large skillet with vegetable oil. Place over medium-high heat. Add pork chops to hot skillet and brown for 1 minute on each side. Reduce heat to medium and cook about 8 minutes; turn and cook 5 minutes more or until done.

Meanwhile, in a small bowl, stir together remaining ingredients. Set aside.

Remove chops from skillet when they are done. Keep warm.

Add honey mixture to skillet. Cook 3 minutes, stirring occasionally. Pour over pork chops.

NUTRIENT ANALYSIS (PER SERVING)

Calories 227 kcal
Protein 18 g
Carbohydrate 19 g
Cholesterol 58 mg
Sodium 348 mg
Total fat 9 g
 Saturated 3 g
 Polyunsaturated 1 g
 Monounsaturated 4 g

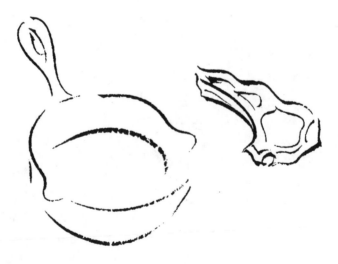

Tropical Broiled Chops

You can also grill these marinated chops by placing them over direct heat. Cover grill and cook 8 to 11 minutes or until chops are done, turning once.

Serves 4; 1 chop per serving
Preparation time: 10 minutes
Marinating time: 24 hours or overnight
Cooking time: 7 to 9 minutes

½ cup low-sodium chicken broth
½ cup unsweetened pineapple juice
2 tablespoons firmly packed brown sugar
2 tablespoons lime juice
½ teaspoon ground ginger
¼ teaspoon ground cloves
¼ teaspoon bottled minced garlic
⅛ teaspoon ground nutmeg
⅛ teaspoon crushed red pepper flakes
4 lean boneless pork loin chops (5 ounces each),
   cut about ¾ inch thick, all visible fat removed

In a large bag with a tight-fitting seal, combine all ingredients in the order listed. Seal bag and place it in the refrigerator for 24 hours or overnight, turning bag occasionally to distribute marinade.

Preheat broiler.

Remove chops from marinade and discard marinade. Place chops on the unheated rack of a broiler pan. Broil about 4 inches from the heat for 4 minutes. Turn chops and broil 3 to 5 minutes more or until done.

NUTRIENT ANALYSIS (PER SERVING)

Calories 154 kcal
Protein 17 g
Carbohydrate 0 g
Cholesterol 58 mg
Sodium 44 mg
Total fat 9 g
  Saturated 3 g
  Polyunsaturated 1 g
  Monounsaturated 4 g

Double Apricot-Ham Kabobs

This pretty dinner-on-a-stick features ham, fruit, and bell pepper glazed with an apricot mixture. Be sure to look for ham that is lower in fat and sodium than traditional ham. You can find spreadable fruit with the jams and jellies at your supermarket.

Serves 4; 2 kabobs per serving

Preparation time: 15 minutes

Cooking time: 15 minutes

Microwave cooking time: 5 to 6 minutes

¼ cup apricot spreadable fruit

1 tablespoon white wine vinegar or cider vinegar

¼ teaspoon dry mustard

8 ounces low-fat, low-sodium ham, cut into 16 bite-size pieces

20-ounce can pineapple chunks, canned in fruit juice, drained

16 dried apricots

1 medium red bell pepper, cut into 16 squares

In a small saucepan, stir together apricot spreadable fruit, vinegar, and mustard. Cook over low heat, stirring occasionally, while preparing kabobs. Preheat oven to 400° F.

Using 8 10-inch skewers, thread 2 ham chunks, 2 pineapple chunks, 2 apricots, and 2 bell pepper pieces alternately on each. Place skewers in a single layer in a shallow glass baking dish. Brush kabobs with apricot mixture. Bake 15 minutes or until kabobs are hot, brushing occasionally with any remaining apricot mixture. Serve warm.

NUTRIENT ANALYSIS (PER SERVING)

Calories 204 kcal
Protein 11 g
Carbohydrate 38 g
Cholesterol 27 mg
Sodium 473 mg
Total fat 2 g
  Saturated 1 g
  Polyunsaturated 0 g
  Monounsaturated 1 g

Microwave Method

Prepare recipe as directed above, but use 8 10-inch bamboo skewers or other microwave-safe skewers. Place apricot mixture in a 1-cup glass measure and cook, uncovered, on 100% power (high) for 30 to 60 seconds or until hot. Arrange kabobs on a 9-inch glass pie plate or other microwave-safe plate. Brush kabobs with apricot mixture. Cook, uncovered, on high for 2 minutes. Rotate plate a half turn and brush with any remaining apricot mixture. Cook on high 2 to 3 minutes more or until heated through.

Rosemary Lamb Chops with Lemon Sauce

Be sure to trim as much of the fat from the chops as possible before rubbing them with rosemary.

Serves 4; 1 chop and 1½ tablespoons sauce per serving

Preparation time: 10 minutes

Cooking time: 8 to 11 minutes

1 tablespoon snipped fresh rosemary or 1 teaspoon dried rosemary, crushed
4 lamb leg sirloin chops (approximately 1 pound), cut ¾ inch thick, all visible fat removed
⅓ cup low-sodium chicken broth
1 teaspoon cornstarch
¼ teaspoon finely shredded lemon peel
1 tablespoon lemon juice
1 teaspoon Dijon mustard

Preheat broiler.

Rub rosemary over chops. Place chops on the unheated rack of a broiler pan. Broil 3 to 4 inches from the heat for 5 to 6 minutes. Turn chops and broil 3 to 5 minutes more or until center of chop is slightly pink.

Meanwhile, in a small saucepan, stir together broth and cornstarch. Stir in remaining ingredients. Cook over medium heat, stirring constantly, until thickened and bubbly, about 3 minutes. Cook 2 minutes more, stirring constantly. Serve sauce with chops.

NUTRIENT ANALYSIS (PER SERVING)

Calories 113 kcal
Protein 15 g
Carbohydrate 1 g
Cholesterol 48 mg
Sodium 58 mg
Total fat 5 g
  Saturated 2 g
  Polyunsaturated 0 g
  Monounsaturated 2 g

Curried Lamb Stroganoff

This well-seasoned stroganoff is served with a raisin-studded brown rice mixture that cooks while you prepare the rest of the meal.

Serves 4; ¾ cup lamb mixture and ⅓ cup rice per serving

Preparation time: 15 minutes

Cooking time: 25 minutes

1¼ cups water
1 cup quick-cooking brown rice
¼ cup raisins or currants
12 ounces lean ground lamb
1 medium Granny Smith or other variety cooking apple, peeled and chopped
1 small onion, chopped
¾ cup low-sodium chicken broth
4 to 5 teaspoons curry powder
1 teaspoon bottled minced garlic
¼ teaspoon salt
¼ teaspoon ground cinnamon
⅛ teaspoon black pepper
¼ cup nonfat or low-fat sour cream or plain nonfat yogurt
1 tablespoon all-purpose flour

In a medium saucepan, bring water to a boil over high heat. Add rice and raisins. Reduce heat, cover, and simmer 10 minutes or until water is absorbed.

Meanwhile, in a large skillet over medium-high heat, cook lamb until brown, about 7 minutes. Place lamb in a colander. Rinse under hot water. Drain well. Wipe skillet with a paper towel. Return lamb to skillet. Add apple, onion, broth, curry powder, garlic, salt, cinnamon, and pepper. Bring to a boil over high heat. Reduce heat, cover, and simmer for 5 minutes.

In a small bowl, stir together sour cream and flour. Stir into meat mixture. Cook and stir over low heat until thickened and bubbly, about 2 minutes. Cook 1 minute more, stirring constantly. Serve with rice mixture.

NUTRIENT ANALYSIS
(PER SERVING)

Calories 372 kcal
Protein 23 g
Carbohydrate 53 g
Cholesterol 54 mg
Sodium 210 mg
Total fat 7 g
Saturated 2 g
Polyunsaturated 1 g
Monounsaturated 3 g

Kiwi Veal

Fresh kiwifruit is combined with tomato preserves to make a fabulous yet simple sauce for veal.

½ cup tomato preserves (see Cook's Tip)
1 kiwifruit, peeled and chopped
Vegetable oil spray
12 ounces veal scaloppine, cut ¼ inch thick

Serves 4; 3 veal scaloppine and 2 tablespoons preserve mixture per serving

Preparation time:
5 minutes

Cooking time:
7 minutes

In a small saucepan, combine tomato preserves and kiwifruit. Cook over low heat until heated through, about 3 minutes.

Meanwhile, spray a large skillet with vegetable oil. Place over medium-high heat. Add veal to hot skillet and cook 2 minutes. Turn and cook for 2 minutes more or until tender. Serve with sauce.

Cook's Tip

Tomato preserves are made with tomatoes, corn syrup, and lemon juice. They are not as sweet as other preserves and are the perfect balance to the kiwifruit in this recipe. Look for tomato preserves with other preserves at the supermarket. If they're not available, choose another lower-sugar preserve, such as apricot or jalapeño pepper.

NUTRIENT ANALYSIS
(PER SERVING)

Calories 155 kcal
Protein 14 g
Carbohydrate 18 g
Cholesterol 56 mg
Sodium 48 mg
Total fat 3 g
  Saturated 1 g
  Polyunsaturated 0 g
  Monounsaturated 1 g

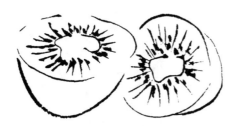

Veal Scaloppine in Shiitake Cream Sauce

Serve this elegant but easy entrée for a special-occasion dinner or celebration. The sauce can be made ahead and refrigerated. To serve, reheat the sauce in a skillet over low heat after the veal has been cooked.

Serves 4; 3 ounces veal and ⅓ cup sauce per serving

Preparation time:
10 minutes

Cooking time:
15 minutes

Vegetable oil spray
12 ounces veal scaloppine, cut ¼ inch thick
8 ounces fresh shiitake mushrooms or button mushrooms, cleaned, stemmed, and sliced
4 green onions, sliced
1 teaspoon bottled minced garlic
2 teaspoons all-purpose flour
½ teaspoon chopped fresh thyme or ¼ teaspoon dried thyme, crushed
¼ teaspoon salt
⅛ teaspoon black pepper
12-ounce can evaporated skim milk
1 tablespoon dry sherry (optional)

Spray a large skillet with vegetable oil. Place over medium-high heat. Add veal to hot skillet and cook 2 minutes. Turn and cook for 2 minutes more or until tender. Remove from skillet and keep warm.

Remove skillet from heat and wipe with a paper towel. Spray skillet with more vegetable oil. Place over medium heat. Add mushrooms, green onions, and garlic. Cook until tender, about 5 minutes. Stir in flour, thyme, salt, and pepper, then add evaporated skim milk all at once. Cook and stir until thickened and bubbly, about 3 minutes. Cook 1 minute more, stirring constantly. If desired, stir in dry sherry. Return veal to skillet; heat through, about 3 minutes.

NUTRIENT ANALYSIS
(PER SERVING)

Calories 180 kcal
Protein 22 g
Carbohydrate 15 g
Cholesterol 59 mg
Sodium 293 mg
Total fat 3 g
Saturated 1 g
Polyunsaturated 0 g
Monounsaturated 1 g

Veal Parmigiana with Fresh Tomatoes

Save time by buying tenderized veal cutlets that are ¼ inch thick. If you can't find them thin enough, simply cover them with plastic wrap and pound them with a meat mallet. Better yet, ask your butcher to pound them for you.

Serves 4; 1 cutlet per serving

Preparation time: 10 minutes

Cooking time: 5 minutes

Egg substitute equivalent to 1 egg
1 tablespoon skim milk
⅓ cup plain dry bread crumbs
⅓ cup grated Parmesan cheese
4 tenderized veal cutlets (about 12 ounces total),
    cut ¼ inch thick
Vegetable oil spray
4 large or 8 small tomato slices
1 tablespoon fresh snipped oregano or 1 teaspoon
    dried oregano, crushed
¼ teaspoon black pepper
2 slices part-skim mozzarella cheese, halved
    (3 ounces total)

In a shallow bowl, combine egg substitute and skim milk. In another shallow bowl, combine bread crumbs and Parmesan cheese. Dip each piece of veal in egg mixture, then coat with bread crumb mixture and shake off excess. Set aside.

Spray a large skillet with vegetable oil. Place over medium-high heat. Place veal in hot skillet and cook 2 minutes. Turn and cook 2 minutes more or until veal is tender. Transfer veal to a broiler-proof serving platter or casserole.

Preheat broiler. Arrange tomato slices over veal. Sprinkle with oregano and pepper. Top each cutlet with a piece of mozzarella cheese. Broil 3 to 4 inches from heat about 1 minute or until cheese melts.

NUTRIENT ANALYSIS
(PER SERVING)

Calories 222 kcal
Protein 25 g
Carbohydrate 9 g
Cholesterol 73 mg
Sodium 378 mg
Total fat 9 g
    Saturated 5 g
    Polyunsaturated 1 g
    Monounsaturated 3 g

One-Dish Meals

One-dish meals are a hurried cook's best friend. What could be easier than cooking your entire meal all at once? With these recipes, you rarely need to include a salad, vegetable, or starch to round out the meal.

In most recipes, the cooking times are longer than those for recipes in other sections of the book, but the preparation times remain short. Look for recipes with other time-saving cooking techniques, such as microwave and crockery cooker timings.

If you're looking for variety, you'll find it here. Seafood, poultry, beef, pork, and meatless recipes are all included in this chapter. Some stellar examples of each of these include Speedy Shrimp and Pasta, Poultry Pot Pies, Moroccan Beef and Barley, Ham and Rye Casserole, and Vegetarian Couscous Paella.

Orange Roughy Casserole

This pasta-generous casserole is layered with tomatoes, spinach fettuccine, summer squash, fish, and seasonings. If orange roughy is not available, any other white fish fillets can be substituted.

Serves 4; 1 cup per serving

Preparation time: 10 minutes

Cooking time: 35 to 40 minutes

Standing time: 5 minutes

1 pound orange roughy fillets
9-ounce package refrigerated spinach fettuccine
14½-ounce can Italian-style stewed tomatoes
2 small yellow summer squash, sliced
2 tablespoons chopped shallots
2 tablespoons snipped fresh basil or 1 teaspoon dried basil, crushed
2 tablespoons grated or shredded Parmesan or Romano cheese

Preheat oven to 425° F.

Rinse fish and pat dry. Cut into 4 serving-size pieces. Set aside.

Coarsely chop uncooked fettuccine. Set aside.

Place undrained tomatoes in the bottom of a 9-inch-square glass baking dish, cutting up any large tomatoes. Top with remaining ingredients except Parmesan or Romano cheese. Cover tightly with foil and bake 35 to 40 minutes or until fish flakes easily when tested with a fork.

Sprinkle with cheese. Cover and let stand 5 minutes before serving.

NUTRIENT ANALYSIS (PER SERVING)

Calories 336 kcal
Protein 29 g
Carbohydrate 36 g
Cholesterol 79 mg
Sodium 274 mg
Total fat 9 g
  Saturated 2 g
  Polyunsaturated 2 g
  Monounsaturated 3 g

One-Dish Meals

Speedy Shrimp and Pasta

If you want to make this recipe even speedier, simply use frozen shelled and deveined shrimp and increase the cooking time by 1 minute.

Serves 4; 1 cup per serving

Preparation time: 10 minutes

Cooking time: 6 to 7 minutes

16-ounce package frozen seasoned vegetables and pasta
12 ounces uncooked shelled and deveined medium shrimp
¼ cup water
¼ cup grated or shredded Parmesan or Romano cheese
¼ cup snipped fresh basil or parsley

In a large skillet, stir together vegetables and pasta, shrimp, and water. Bring to a boil over high heat. Reduce heat, cover, and simmer 3 minutes. Stir and cook 1 to 2 minutes more or until shrimp turn pink, vegetables are tender yet still crisp, and pasta is done. Sprinkle with cheese and basil.

NUTRIENT ANALYSIS (PER SERVING)

Calories 212 kcal
Protein 20 g
Carbohydrate 18 g
Cholesterol 130 mg
Sodium 562 mg
Total fat 7 g
  Saturated 3 g
  Polyunsaturated 2 g
  Monounsaturated 2 g

Salmon and Brown Rice Bake

This recipe is reminiscent of an old family favorite—tuna-noodle casserole. For a change of pace, it uses boneless, skinless canned salmon instead of tuna and brown rice instead of noodles.

Serves 3; 1¼ cups per serving

Preparation time: 5 minutes

Cooking time: 35 minutes

9- or 10-ounce package frozen no-salt-added corn
6½-ounce can boneless, skinless salmon, drained
¾ cup quick-cooking brown rice
⅔ cup water
2 tablespoons sliced green onions
½ teaspoon low-sodium chicken bouillon granules
¼ teaspoon dried dill weed
¼ cup shredded low-fat cheddar cheese
¼ teaspoon salt (optional)

Preheat oven to 375° F.

In a 1½-quart casserole, combine corn, salmon, uncooked rice, water, green onions, bouillon granules, and dill weed. Cover and bake 30 minutes or until rice is tender. Sprinkle with cheese. Bake, uncovered, 5 minutes more or until cheese melts. Season with salt if desired.

Tuna-Noodle Casserole

If you have trouble separating the frozen vegetables before adding them to the casserole, simply place them in a colander and run them under hot water for a few seconds or until they separate.

Serves 5; 1 cup per serving

Preparation time: 10 minutes

Cooking time: 40 minutes

2 6½-ounce cans water-packed low-salt tuna, drained

10½-ounce can reduced-fat and reduced-sodium condensed cream of chicken soup

1 cup skim milk

2 cups (3 ounces) medium no-cholesterol noodles, uncooked

½ cup chopped onion

½ cup chopped celery

10-ounce package frozen no-salt-added peas and carrots

¼ cup snipped fresh parsley (optional)

Preheat oven to 375° F.

In a 2-quart casserole or 9-inch-square glass baking dish, combine tuna, soup, and milk. Stir in remaining ingredients. Cover and bake about 25 minutes. Stir, replace cover, and cook 15 minutes more or until noodles are tender.

One-Dish Meals

Baked Chicken with Winter Vegetables

Serve this when you want to spend a little time preparing a dish and then sit back and relax while it bakes. It's great for a late supper after work or for a weekend dinner.

Serves 4; 1 to 2 pieces of chicken and ½ cup vegetables per serving

Preparation time: 20 minutes

Cooking time: 1¼ to 1½ hours

2½- to 3-pound cut-up chicken, skinned, all visible fat removed
4 to 6 small red potatoes, scrubbed and halved
4 large carrots, peeled and cut into 1-inch pieces
1 small acorn squash, quartered and seeded
1 medium onion or fresh fennel bulb, cut into 8 wedges
¼ cup water
¼ teaspoon salt
¼ teaspoon black pepper
Bottled low-fat chicken or turkey gravy (optional)

Preheat oven to 375° F.

Rinse chicken and pat dry. Place in a 13×9×2-inch glass baking dish or 3-quart casserole. Arrange potatoes, carrots, squash, and onion around chicken. Pour water over chicken and vegetables. Sprinkle with salt and pepper. Cover dish or casserole tightly with foil and bake 1¼ to 1½ hours or until chicken and vegetables are tender.

If desired, heat gravy according to package directions and serve with chicken and vegetables.

NUTRIENT ANALYSIS (PER SERVING)

Calories 433 kcal
Protein 40 g
Carbohydrate 49 g
Cholesterol 102 mg
Sodium 307 mg
Total fat 9 g
 Saturated 3 g
 Polyunsaturated 2 g
 Monounsaturated 2 g

Cook's Tip

Fennel is a creamy white or pale green vegetable of the carrot family. Cooking fennel makes its licorice-like flavor more delicate and its celery-like texture softer.

Baked Chicken and Rice with Herbs

You can save a few more minutes by purchasing boneless, skinless chicken breast halves and reducing cooking time to 35 to 45 minutes.

Serves 4; ½ chicken breast per serving

Preparation time: 5 minutes

Cooking time: 1 hour

2 whole medium chicken breasts, halved lengthwise (1½ pounds total), skinned, all visible fat removed
5-ounce package brown and wild rice or long-grain and wild rice
1½ cups water
9- or 10-ounce package frozen no-salt-added peas
¼ cup dry white wine or water
¾ teaspoon dried Italian seasoning

Preheat oven to 350° F.

Rinse chicken breasts, pat dry, and set aside.

In a 2-quart glass baking dish or casserole, combine rice and water. Discard seasoning packet that came with rice. Stir in remaining ingredients and arrange chicken on top. Cover dish and bake about 1 hour or until chicken and rice are tender.

NUTRIENT ANALYSIS (PER SERVING)

Calories 292 kcal
Protein 32 g
Carbohydrate 30 g
Cholesterol 66 mg
Sodium 115 mg
Total fat 4 g
  Saturated 1 g
  Polyunsaturated 1 g
  Monounsaturated 1 g

Plum Good Chicken

This Asian-inspired dish boasts a medley of noodles, vegetables, and chicken topped with a tasty plum sauce. There's no need to cook the noodles separately—everything bakes at once.

Serves 5; 1 chicken breast and 1 cup vegetable mixture per serving

Preparation time: 15 minutes

Cooking time: 50 minutes

5 boneless, skinless chicken breast halves (about 1 pound total), all visible fat removed
2 3-ounce packages ramen noodles
16-ounce bag frozen Asian-style mixed vegetables
10½-ounce can low-sodium chicken broth
½ cup bottled plum sauce or plum jam
1 tablespoon grated gingerroot
1 teaspoon finely shredded lemon peel
1 tablespoon lemon juice
1 teaspoon light soy sauce

Preheat oven to 350° F.

Rinse chicken and pat dry. Set aside.

Break up noodles and sprinkle them in the bottom of a 13×9×2-inch glass baking dish or shallow 3-quart baking dish. Discard seasoning packets. Spread vegetables over noodles. Pour broth over vegetables and noodles. Arrange chicken breasts on top of vegetable mixture. Set aside.

In a small bowl, stir together remaining ingredients. Spoon sauce over chicken breasts. Cover and bake about 50 minutes or until chicken, vegetables, and noodles are tender.

NUTRIENT ANALYSIS
(PER SERVING)
Calories 396 kcal
Protein 32 g
Carbohydrate 47 g
Cholesterol 66 mg
Sodium 171 mg
Total fat 9 g
Saturated 3 g
Polyunsaturated 2 g
Monounsaturated 2 g

Chicken with Broccoli and Bulgur

Try this recipe the next time you have very little time to spend fixing dinner.

12 ounces boneless, skinless chicken breasts, all visible fat removed
Vegetable oil spray
1 teaspoon bottled minced garlic
1½ cups water
¾ cup bulgur or couscous
1 teaspoon low-sodium chicken bouillon granules
1 teaspoon finely shredded lemon peel
¼ teaspoon dried sage, crushed
3 cups broccoli florets
Black pepper (optional)

Serves 4; 1½ cups per serving

Preparation time: 10 minutes

Cooking time: 9 to 13 minutes

Rinse chicken, pat dry, and cut into bite-size pieces. Set aside.

Spray a large skillet with vegetable oil. Place over medium-high heat. Add chicken and garlic to skillet and cook 2 to 3 minutes, turning once. Stir in water, bulgur, bouillon granules, lemon peel, and sage. Arrange broccoli on top. Bring to a boil over high heat. Reduce heat, cover, and simmer 7 to 10 minutes or until chicken, broccoli, and bulgur are tender. Season with pepper if desired.

NUTRIENT ANALYSIS (PER SERVING)

Calories 266 kcal
Protein 26 g
Carbohydrate 36 g
Cholesterol 47 mg
Sodium 67 mg
Total fat 3 g
 Saturated 1 g
 Polyunsaturated 1 g
 Monounsaturated 1 g

One-Dish Meals

Quick Cassoulet

A typical French cassoulet, a hearty mixture of meat, beans, and vegetables, can take up to 3 days to prepare. This easy version skimps on time but not on flavor.

Serves 5; 1 cup per serving

Preparation time: 15 minutes

Cooking time: 15 minutes

Vegetable oil spray
1 small onion, chopped
1 cup chopped carrots
1 cup chopped celery
1 teaspoon bottled minced garlic
8 ounces boneless, skinless chicken breasts, all visible fat removed
2 15-ounce cans Great Northern beans, rinsed and drained
8-ounce can no-salt-added tomato sauce
1 cup chopped low-fat, low-sodium ham
2 tablespoons firmly packed brown sugar
2 tablespoons molasses
¼ teaspoon ground allspice
¼ teaspoon dry mustard
¼ teaspoon black pepper

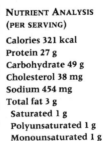

Spray a large skillet with vegetable oil. Place over medium-high heat. Add onion, carrots, celery, and garlic and cook and stir until tender, about 7 minutes.

Rinse chicken, pat dry, and cut into bite-size pieces. Add chicken to skillet with vegetables and cook and stir 2 to 3 minutes or until just tender.

Stir in remaining ingredients. Reduce heat to medium-low and cook 5 minutes, stirring occasionally.

NUTRIENT ANALYSIS
(PER SERVING)

Calories 321 kcal
Protein 27 g
Carbohydrate 49 g
Cholesterol 38 mg
Sodium 454 mg
Total fat 3 g
  Saturated 1 g
  Polyunsaturated 1 g
  Monounsaturated 1 g

Chicken Jambalaya

The Cajuns perfected this spicy chicken-and-rice dish. Now you can enjoy a quick and healthful version.

Serves 4; 2 cups per serving

Preparation time: 20 minutes

Cooking time: 22 minutes

12 ounces boneless, skinless chicken breasts or turkey breast tenderloins, all visible fat removed
Vegetable oil spray
1 medium onion, chopped
1 medium green bell pepper, chopped
1 medium red bell pepper, chopped
½ cup chopped celery
3 cloves garlic, minced
2 14½-ounce cans no-salt-added tomatoes, chopped (reserve liquid)
1 cup quick-cooking brown rice
1 teaspoon dried thyme, crushed
1 teaspoon black pepper
¼ teaspoon salt
¼ teaspoon ground red pepper
4 ounces Canadian bacon, chopped

Rinse chicken and pat dry. Cut into bite-size pieces. Set aside.

Spray a Dutch oven with vegetable oil. Place over medium-high heat. Add onion, bell peppers, celery, and garlic. Cook until tender, about 7 minutes.

Stir in chopped tomatoes and tomato liquid, rice, thyme, black pepper, salt, and ground red pepper. Stir in chicken and Canadian bacon. Bring to a boil over high heat. Reduce heat, cover, and simmer 15 minutes or until chicken and rice are tender and liquid is absorbed.

NUTRIENT ANALYSIS
(PER SERVING)

Calories 385 kcal
Protein 31 g
Carbohydrate 51 g
Cholesterol 60 mg
Sodium 584 mg
Total fat 6 g
  Saturated 2 g
  Polyunsaturated 2 g
  Monounsaturated 2 g

One-Dish Meals

Poultry Pot Pies

The little ones at your house will dig right in with the hungry adults when you serve this updated, home-style casserole.

Vegetable oil spray
1 small onion, chopped
½ teaspoon bottled minced garlic
1 pound boneless, skinless chicken breasts or
    turkey breast tenderloins, all visible fat removed
12-ounce bottle low-fat chicken or turkey gravy
10-ounce package frozen no-salt-added peas and
    carrots
2 cups reduced-fat buttermilk baking and pancake
    mix
⅔ cup skim milk
Black pepper (optional)

Serves 6; 1 cup per serving
Preparation time:
10 minutes
Cooking time:
28 minutes
Standing time:
5 minutes

Preheat oven to 450° F.

Spray a large saucepan with vegetable oil. Place over medium heat. Cook onion and garlic in hot saucepan for about 5 minutes or until tender.

Meanwhile, rinse chicken, pat dry, and cut into bite-size pieces. Add to skillet with onion mixture. Cook and stir 2 to 3 minutes or until chicken is just tender. Stir in gravy and vegetables. Heat through, about 5 minutes.

Meanwhile, in a medium bowl, stir together baking and pancake mix and milk until a soft dough forms. Set aside.

Transfer hot chicken or turkey filling to three 15-ounce casseroles or one 2-quart casserole. Drop dough by spoonfuls onto hot filling. Bake 15-ounce casseroles, uncovered, 10 to 15 minutes. Bake 2-quart casserole, uncovered, 15 to 20 minutes. Topping should be golden brown and filling should be hot. Let stand 5 minutes and season with pepper if desired.

NUTRIENT ANALYSIS
(PER SERVING)
Calories 305 kcal
Protein 24 g
Carbohydrate 36 g
Cholesterol 44 mg
Sodium 839 mg
Total fat 6 g
  Saturated 2 g
  Polyunsaturated 1 g
  Monounsaturated 2 g

Chicken Sausage Pizza

Enjoy the full flavor of sausage without the fat by combining lean ground poultry with sausage seasonings, such as fennel seed and flakes of crushed red pepper. It's spicy enough for adults but not too spicy for kids. If you like your meat spicier, increase the crushed red pepper to a half teaspoon.

Serves 4; 2 pieces per serving

Preparation time: 15 minutes

Cooking time: 27 minutes

12 ounces ground chicken or turkey, ground without skin
1 small onion, chopped
1 small green or red bell pepper, chopped
8 ounces sliced fresh mushrooms
1 teaspoon bottled minced garlic
8-ounce can no-salt-added tomato sauce
½ teaspoon fennel seeds, crushed
¼ teaspoon salt
¼ teaspoon crushed red pepper
Vegetable oil spray
10-ounce package refrigerated pizza dough
1 cup shredded part-skim mozzarella cheese

Preheat oven to 425° F.

Place chicken, onion, bell pepper, mushrooms, and garlic in a large skillet over medium-high heat. Cook chicken about 7 minutes or until no longer pink. Place chicken mixture in a colander and rinse under hot water. Drain well. Wipe skillet with a paper towel. Return chicken or turkey mixture to skillet. Stir in tomato sauce, fennel seeds, salt, and crushed red pepper.

Meanwhile, spray a 12-inch pizza pan with vegetable oil. Press dough evenly into prepared pan. Spoon chicken mixture over dough. Sprinkle with cheese. Bake about 20 minutes or according to package directions. Cut into 8 wedges.

NUTRIENT ANALYSIS (PER SERVING)

Calories 398 kcal
Protein 34 g
Carbohydrate 43 g
Cholesterol 63 mg
Sodium 684 mg
Total fat 10 g
  Saturated 4 g
  Polyunsaturated 2 g
  Monounsaturated 3 g

Cook's Tip

To end up with a crispier pizza, precook the pizza dough for 5 to 7 minutes before adding the toppings.

One-Dish Meals

Moroccan Beef and Barley

You can fix and forget this well-seasoned, one-dish meal whether you simmer it on the stove or cook it all day in an electric crockery cooker.

Serves 4; 2 cups per serving

Preparation time: 15 minutes

Cooking time: 1 hour 40 minutes

Crockery cooker time: 4½ to 5½ hours on high-heat setting

8½ to 10½ hours on low-heat setting

Vegetable oil spray
12 ounces lean boneless beef round steak, all visible fat removed
2 14½-ounce cans diced tomatoes
1½ cups water
1 small onion, sliced and separated into rings
½ cup pearl barley
1 teaspoon sugar
1 teaspoon ground cumin
1 teaspoon ground ginger
1 teaspoon bottled minced garlic
½ teaspoon ground turmeric
½ teaspoon paprika
½ teaspoon ground cinnamon
¼ teaspoon salt
10-ounce package frozen no-salt-added mixed vegetables

Spray a Dutch oven with vegetable oil. Set aside.

Cut meat into bite-size pieces. Place Dutch oven over medium-high heat. Add meat to hot Dutch oven and brown about 5 minutes, stirring frequently. Drain fat.

Stir in remaining ingredients except frozen vegetables. Bring to a boil over high heat. Reduce heat, cover, and simmer 1 hour.

Stir in frozen vegetables. Cover and simmer 30 minutes more or until meat, barley, and vegetables are tender and liquid is absorbed. Stir before serving.

NUTRIENT ANALYSIS (PER SERVING)

Calories 289 kcal
Protein 25 g
Carbohydrate 41 g
Cholesterol 47 mg
Sodium 223 mg
Total fat 4 g
 Saturated 1 g
 Polyunsaturated 1 g
 Monounsaturated 1 g

Crockery Cooker Method

Cut meat into bite-size pieces. (Do not brown.) Place meat and all remaining ingredients except frozen vegetables in a 3½- or 4-quart electric crockery cooker. Cover and cook on high-heat setting for 4 to 5 hours or on low-heat setting for 8 to 10 hours or until meat is fully cooked and tender. Stir in frozen vegetables and cook 30 minutes more or until vegetables are tender.

Skip-a-Step Pasta Pie

Don't worry about cooking the pasta for this casserole—a favorite with kids. Uncooked, refrigerated angel-hair (capellini) pasta forms a crust while the pie bakes. Be sure to use low-fat fresh pasta with 2 grams of fat or less per serving.

Serves 4; 1 wedge per serving

Preparation time:
10 minutes

Cooking time:
33 minutes

Standing time:
5 minutes

Vegetable oil spray
¼ cup water
1 egg white
4 ounces refrigerated angel-hair (capellini) pasta
⅓ cup grated Parmesan cheese
8 ounces lean ground beef
½ cup chopped onion
¾ cup low-fat meatless spaghetti sauce
½ cup shredded part-skim mozzarella cheese

Preheat oven to 350° F. Lightly spray a 9-inch pie plate with vegetable oil.

In a medium bowl, combine water and egg white. Stir until well combined. Stir in uncooked pasta and Parmesan cheese. Place pasta mixture in pie plate. Press mixture against the bottom and slightly up the sides of the pie plate to form an even crust. Set aside.

In a large skillet, cook ground beef and onion over medium-high heat until meat is brown and onion is tender, about 5 minutes. Place cooked meat mixture in a colander and rinse under hot water. Drain well. Wipe skillet with a paper towel. Return meat mixture to skillet. Stir in spaghetti sauce; heat through, about 3 minutes.

Spoon meat mixture over pasta crust. Bake, uncovered, 20 minutes. Sprinkle with mozzarella cheese and bake about 5 minutes more or until cheese melts. Let stand 5 minutes, then cut into 4 wedges and serve.

NUTRIENT ANALYSIS
(PER SERVING)

Calories 249 kcal
Protein 23 g
Carbohydrate 19 g
Cholesterol 46 mg
Sodium 251 mg
Total fat 9 g
    Saturated 4 g
    Polyunsaturated 1 g
    Monounsaturated 3 g

Cook's Tip

Ground meats, no matter how lean, always contain some fat, which cooks out of them and into the pan. Draining the fat is a good idea, but it doesn't get rid of all the fat. The best way to get rid of as much fat as possible is to drain the meat in a colander and rinse under hot water. Don't forget to wipe the skillet or saucepan with paper towels to get rid of any fat that clings to the skillet or saucepan. Another handy way to cook ground meat is in your microwave oven. Put the meat in a microwave-safe colander or steamer set in a microwave-safe bowl. As the meat cooks, the fat drains right into the bowl. Place 1 pound of ground meat in the colander and cook on 100% power (high) for 10 minutes, stirring occasionally.

Southwest Shepherd's Pie

This classic "comfort food" recipe has gone south with its seasonings.

Serves 6; 1½ cups per serving

Preparation time: 15 minutes

Cooking time: 40 minutes

8 ounces lean ground beef
½ cup chopped onion
2 cups packaged instant mashed potatoes (enough for 6 servings)
2 cups water
¾ cup skim milk
16-ounce can kidney beans, rinsed and drained
10¾-ounce can low-fat condensed cream of tomato soup
12-ounce can no-salt-added whole-kernel corn, drained
4-ounce can chopped green chili peppers, drained
¼ cup water
1 teaspoon ground cumin
¼ teaspoon salt
⅛ teaspoon black pepper
¼ cup shredded low-fat cheddar cheese

Preheat oven to 375° F.

In a large skillet over medium-high heat, cook ground beef and onion until meat is brown and onion is tender, about 5 minutes.

Meanwhile, prepare potatoes according to package directions, but use 2 cups water and ¾ cup skim milk and omit butter or margarine and salt.

Place cooked meat mixture in a colander and rinse under hot water. Drain well. Wipe skillet with a paper towel. Return meat mixture to skillet over medium heat. Stir in remaining ingredients, except cheese, and heat through, about 7 minutes.

Transfer meat mixture to a 2-quart casserole. Drop potato mixture in mounds on meat mixture or spread it over meat mixture. Bake, uncovered, 25 to 30 minutes or until hot. Sprinkle with cheese.

NUTRIENT ANALYSIS (PER SERVING)

Calories 269 kcal
Protein 18 g
Carbohydrate 42 g
Cholesterol 25 mg
Sodium 564 mg
Total fat 4 g
  Saturated 1 g
  Polyunsaturated 1 g
  Monounsaturated 1 g

Pork and Rhubarb Bake

If you're lucky enough to have fresh rhubarb, use 3 cups of bite-size pieces in place of the frozen. Serve this unique dish with two cups of hot cooked brown rice.

Serves 4; ⅔ cup per serving

Preparation time: 10 minutes

Cooking time: 25 to 30 minutes

12 ounces lean boneless pork loin roast or chops, all visible fat removed
Vegetable oil spray
16-ounce package frozen no-sugar-added cut rhubarb, thawed and drained
¼ cup sugar
2 tablespoons all-purpose flour
½ teaspoon ground cinnamon
Cinnamon stick (optional)

Preheat oven to 350° F.

Cut pork into bite-size cubes. Set aside.

Spray a large skillet with vegetable oil. Place over medium-high heat. Add pork and brown in hot skillet about 5 minutes, stirring frequently. Drain fat.

In a large bowl, stir together rhubarb, sugar, flour, and ground cinnamon. Place half the rhubarb mixture in the bottom of a 1½-quart casserole. Arrange pork over rhubarb mixture. Top with remaining rhubarb mixture. Cover and bake 20 to 25 minutes or until pork and rhubarb are tender. Garnish with cinnamon stick if desired.

NUTRIENT ANALYSIS
(PER SERVING)

Calories 216 kcal
Protein 17 g
Carbohydrate 19 g
Cholesterol 55 mg
Sodium 45 mg
Total fat 9 g
  Saturated 3 g
  Polyunsaturated 1 g
  Monounsaturated 4 g

Pork Chop-Sweet Potato Skillet

Warm a loaf of hearty whole-grain bread or rolls to serve with this recipe. Then you'll have a great cool-weather dinner in minutes.

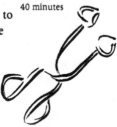

Serves 4; 1 chop per serving

Preparation time: 10 minutes

Cooking time: 40 minutes

Vegetable oil spray
4 lean boneless pork loin or sirloin chops, cut ½ to ¾ inch thick (about 12 ounces total), all visible fat removed
1 large sweet potato, peeled and chopped
1 medium onion, chopped
16-ounce can Italian-style stewed tomatoes
½ cup water

Spray a large skillet with vegetable oil. Place over medium-high heat. Brown chops in hot skillet for 5 minutes; turn and brown for 5 minutes more. Remove chops; drain fat, if necessary.

Place sweet potato and onion in skillet. Arrange pork chops over potato mixture. Pour tomatoes and water over pork chops and bring to a boil over high heat. Reduce heat, cover, and simmer about 25 minutes or until pork and potatoes are tender.

NUTRIENT ANALYSIS
(PER SERVING)

Calories 226 kcal
Protein 19 g
Carbohydrate 18 g
Cholesterol 55 mg
Sodium 232 mg
Total fat 9 g
  Saturated 3 g
  Polyunsaturated 1 g
  Monounsaturated 4 g

One-Dish Meals

Ham and Rye Casserole

Take your choice: Bake this savory egg dish and serve it right away for dinner, or cover, refrigerate, and bake it in the morning for breakfast or brunch.

Serves 6; ¾ cup per serving

Preparation time: 10 minutes

Cooking time: 45 to 50 minutes

Standing time: 10 minutes

Vegetable oil spray
4 slices seeded rye bread, cut into bite-size cubes
2 cups diced low-fat, low-sodium ham
1 cup shredded low-fat Swiss cheese
1 cup skim milk
Egg substitute equivalent to 4 eggs
¼ teaspoon black pepper

Preheat oven to 325° F. Lightly spray an 8-inch-square glass baking dish with vegetable oil.

Layer half the bread, half the ham, and half the cheese in baking dish. Repeat with remaining bread, ham, and cheese. Set aside.

In a medium bowl, stir together milk, egg substitute, and pepper. Gently pour egg mixture over ham mixture.

Bake, uncovered, 45 to 50 minutes or until set and lightly browned. Let stand 10 minutes before serving.

NUTRIENT ANALYSIS
(PER SERVING)

Calories 174 kcal
Protein 20 g
Carbohydrate 13 g
Cholesterol 29 mg
Sodium 634 mg
Total fat 5 g
  Saturated 2 g
  Polyunsaturated 1 g
  Monounsaturated 2 g

Healthful Macaroni and Cheese

Choose the frozen vegetable or vegetables that your family likes best. Mixed vegetables, peas, broccoli, and green beans all taste great in this simple one-dish meal.

Serves 4; 1 cup per serving

Preparation time: 5 minutes

Cooking time: 10 to 15 minutes

6 cups water
9- or 10-ounce package frozen no-salt-added vegetables
7¼-ounce package macaroni-and-cheese dinner mix
¼ cup skim milk
¼ cup nonfat or low-fat sour cream
¼ teaspoon dried Italian seasoning (optional)
¼ teaspoon black pepper (optional)
½ cup shredded low-fat cheddar cheese

In a large saucepan, bring water to a boil over high heat. Add vegetables and macaroni, reserving the cheese-sauce mix. Return to a boil. Reduce heat, cover, and simmer 7 to 10 minutes or until vegetables are tender yet crisp and macaroni is tender. Drain.

Return macaroni mixture to saucepan. Place over medium heat and stir in milk, sour cream, and reserved cheese-sauce mix from package. Heat through, about 3 to 5 minutes. If desired, stir in Italian seasoning and pepper. Sprinkle each serving with 2 tablespoons shredded cheese.

NUTRIENT ANALYSIS (PER SERVING)

Calories 281 kcal
Protein 15 g
Carbohydrate 43 g
Cholesterol 12 mg
Sodium 337 mg
Total fat 5 g
  Saturated 3 g
  Polyunsaturated 0 g
  Monounsaturated 1 g

Black Bean Lasagna

When you can't decide between Mexican and Italian food, choose this tasty combination. A spicy black bean mixture replaces the meat in this healthful lasagna, which features "no-cook" noodles. Made especially for use in casseroles, these time-saving noodles bake with the other ingredients. If you can't find "no-cook" noodles, buy regular noodles and soak them in hot water while you prepare the sauce. Remove the noodles from the water just before assembling the lasagna.

Serves 9; 1 cup per serving

Preparation time: 20 minutes

Cooking time: 40 minutes

Microwave cooking time: 17 to 19 minutes

Standing time: 5 minutes

2 16-ounce cans black beans, rinsed, drained, and slightly mashed
1 cup commercial salsa or Fresh and Chunky Salsa (page 48)
2 cups low-fat meatless spaghetti sauce
1 teaspoon bottled minced garlic
1 teaspoon ground cumin
15-ounce container low-fat, low-salt ricotta cheese
⅓ cup grated or shredded Parmesan or Romano cheese
1 egg white
¼ cup skim milk
Vegetable oil spray
6 no-cook lasagna noodles (3½×6½ inches)
1 cup shredded low-fat Monterey Jack cheese
1 cup shredded part-skim mozzarella cheese

Preheat oven to 350° F.

In a large bowl, stir together beans, salsa, spaghetti sauce, garlic, and cumin. Set aside.

In a medium bowl, stir together ricotta, Parmesan, egg white, and milk.

To assemble lasagna, spray a 13×9×2-inch baking pan or glass baking dish with vegetable oil. Spread about 1 cup bean mixture in the bottom of dish. Cover with 3 uncooked lasagna noodles, making sure noodles do not touch edges of dish. Cover noodles with half of the remaining bean

NUTRIENT ANALYSIS
(PER SERVING)

Calories 333 kcal
Protein 23 g
Carbohydrate 39 g
Cholesterol 31 mg
Sodium 800 mg
Total fat 10 g
  Saturated 6 g
  Polyunsaturated 1 g
  Monounsaturated 3 g

mixture, making sure bean mixture covers noodles completely. Spread with half of the ricotta cheese mixture and sprinkle with half of the Monterey Jack and half of the mozzarella. Repeat layers of noodles, bean mixture, ricotta mixture, Monterey Jack, and mozzarella.

Cover dish tightly with foil and bake 30 minutes. Uncover and bake 10 minutes more or until noodles are done and lasagna is heated through. Let stand 5 minutes before serving.

Microwave Method

Assemble recipe as directed above, but cover glass baking dish with plastic wrap. Cook on 100% power (high) 17 to 19 minutes or until noodles are done and lasagna is heated through; give dish a quarter turn twice. Let stand 5 minutes before serving.

Meatless Tamale Pie

Using packaged corn-muffin mix for the casserole topping saves precious minutes in the kitchen.

Serves 6; 1 cup per serving

Preparation time: 10 minutes

Cooking time: 30 minutes

Vegetable oil spray
1 cup chopped onion
½ cup chopped carrot
2 15-ounce cans kidney beans, rinsed and drained
12-ounce can no-salt-added corn, drained
8-ounce can no-salt-added tomato sauce
1 to 2 teaspoons chili powder
1 teaspoon ground cumin
8¼-ounce package corn-muffin mix
2 egg whites
⅓ cup skim milk

Preheat oven to 400° F.

Spray a 9-inch-square glass baking dish with vegetable oil. Set aside.

Spray a large skillet with vegetable oil. Place over medium-high heat. Add onion and carrot and cook in hot skillet until almost tender, about 5 minutes. Stir in beans, corn, tomato sauce, chili powder, and cumin. Heat through, about 5 minutes.

Meanwhile, combine corn-muffin mix with egg whites and skim milk. Mix as directed on the package. Set aside.

Spoon the hot bean mixture into prepared baking dish. Spread cornmeal mixture evenly over the top of the bean mixture.

Bake, uncovered, about 20 minutes or until golden brown.

NUTRIENT ANALYSIS
(PER SERVING)

Calories 323 kcal
Protein 14 g
Carbohydrate 63 g
Cholesterol 0 mg
Sodium 421 mg
Total fat 3 g
  Saturated 0 g
  Polyunsaturated 1 g
  Monounsaturated 1 g

Fresh Tomato Pizza

For best results, use fresh Italian plum tomatoes, which are available all year.

Vegetable oil spray
10-ounce package refrigerated pizza dough
3 or 4 medium Italian plum tomatoes, thinly
  sliced
¼ cup snipped fresh basil or parsley
Freshly ground black pepper
1 cup shredded part-skim mozzarella cheese

Preheat oven to 425° F.

Spray a 12-inch pizza pan with vegetable oil. Press dough evenly into prepared pan. Arrange tomato slices on top. Sprinkle with basil and season with pepper. Sprinkle with cheese. Bake 15 to 20 minutes or according to package directions. Cut into 8 wedges.

Serves 4; 2 pieces per serving

Preparation time: 10 minutes

Cooking time: 15 to 20 minutes

NUTRIENT ANALYSIS (PER SERVING)

Calories 284 kcal
Protein 15 g
Carbohydrate 40 g
Cholesterol 16 mg
Sodium 500 mg
Total fat 7 g
  Saturated 3 g
  Polyunsaturated 1 g
  Monounsaturated 2 g

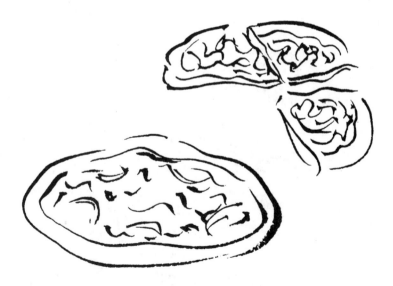

Green Chili and Tortilla Casserole

This pretty layered casserole has a slight tang from the buttermilk. Although it sounds rich and full of fat, buttermilk weighs in at only 100 calories and 2 grams of fat per cup.

Serves 4; 1 cup per serving

Preparation time: 10 minutes

Cooking time: 30 to 35 minutes

Vegetable oil spray
8 6-inch corn tortillas
4-ounce can chopped green chili peppers, drained
1 cup shredded low-fat cheddar cheese
1 medium red bell pepper, chopped
4 green onions, sliced
1 whole egg and 2 egg whites, or egg substitute
   equivalent to 2 eggs
1 cup low-fat buttermilk

Preheat oven to 325° F.

Spray a 9-inch-square glass baking dish with vegetable oil. Tear tortillas into bite-size pieces. Arrange half of the tortillas in baking dish. Top with half the green chilies, half the cheese, half the bell pepper, and half the green onions. Repeat layering. Set aside.

Stir together egg, egg whites, and buttermilk. Gently pour over tortilla mixture. Bake, uncovered, for 30 to 35 minutes or until a knife inserted near the center comes out clean. Serve warm.

NUTRIENT ANALYSIS (PER SERVING)

Calories 258 kcal
Protein 17 g
Carbohydrate 29 g
Cholesterol 71 mg
Sodium 575 mg
Total fat 9 g
  Saturated 4 g
  Polyunsaturated 1 g
  Monounsaturated 2 g

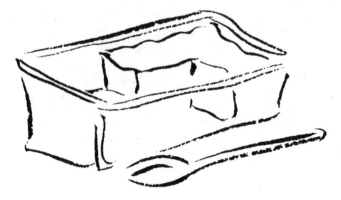

Curried Lentils and Vegetables

Lentils are a powerhouse of important nutrients, such as iron and vitamin B. Unlike dried beans, they don't require soaking and long cooking times. Try them in this easy stovetop meal.

Serves 4; 1¼ cups per serving

Preparation time: 10 minutes

Cooking time: 35 to 40 minutes

1 cup dry green lentils, rinsed and drained
2 cups water
1 medium onion, chopped
¼ cup currants or raisins
1 teaspoon bottled minced garlic
½ teaspoon curry powder
¼ teaspoon salt
¼ teaspoon black pepper
8-ounce package frozen no-salt-added cut green
    beans
4 carrots, peeled and sliced ½ inch thick

In a large saucepan or Dutch oven, combine lentils, water, onion, currants, garlic, curry powder, salt, and pepper. Bring to a boil over high heat. Reduce heat, cover, and simmer 20 minutes. Add green beans and carrots. Cover and simmer 15 to 20 minutes more or until lentils and vegetables are tender, stirring occasionally.

NUTRIENT ANALYSIS
(PER SERVING)

Calories 243 kcal
Protein 15 g
Carbohydrate 48 g
Cholesterol 0 mg
Sodium 190 mg
Total fat 1 g
  Saturated 0 g
  Polyunsaturated 0 g
  Monounsaturated 0 g

Vegetarian Couscous Paella

Couscous replaces the rice in this traditional saffron-spiced Spanish dish. Made of ground semolina, couscous is usually located in the rice or pasta section of your supermarket.

Serves 4; 1¼ cups per serving

Preparation time:
10 minutes

Cooking time:
15 minutes

Standing time:
5 minutes

Vegetable oil spray
1 small red onion, chopped
2 teaspoons bottled minced garlic
1½ cups low-sodium chicken broth
9-ounce package frozen baby lima beans (with trace of salt necessary for processing)
1 cup frozen no-salt-added peas
¼ teaspoon salt
⅛ teaspoon powdered saffron or ½ teaspoon ground turmeric
⅛ teaspoon ground red pepper
1 cup couscous
1 medium tomato, chopped
¼ cup snipped fresh cilantro or parsley

Spray a large saucepan or Dutch oven with vegetable oil. Place over medium-high heat. Add onion and garlic and cook until onion is tender, about 5 minutes. Add broth, lima beans, peas, salt, saffron, and red pepper. Bring to a boil over high heat. Reduce heat, cover, and simmer 10 minutes or until lima beans are tender.

Remove from heat and stir in uncooked couscous, tomato, and cilantro. Cover and let stand 5 minutes before serving.

NUTRIENT ANALYSIS
(PER SERVING)

Calories 293 kcal
Protein 13 g
Carbohydrate 57 g
Cholesterol 0 mg
Sodium 228 mg
Total fat 1 g
  Saturated 0 g
  Polyunsaturated 0 g
  Monounsaturated 0 g

Vegetables

At last vegetables are getting the recognition they deserve. Not content to play second fiddle in any meal, vegetables are edging out meat for more space on our dinner plates. They add variety, nutrition, and texture to our meals without much fat or sodium.

Look to these recipes when you need a sensational side dish to go with your grilled lean meat or other low-fat main dish. Choose from steal-the-show recipes such as Roasted Asparagus and Mushrooms with Rosemary, Cauliflower with Peanut Dipping Sauce, Sugar-Kissed Peas and Carrots, and Greek Spinach.

Roasted Asparagus and Mushrooms with Rosemary

Roasting vegetables instead of steaming them brings out their natural sugars and gives them a deliciously sweet flavor.

Serves 4; ¾ cup per serving

Preparation time: 10 minutes

Cooking time: 10 minutes

1 pound trimmed fresh asparagus
8 ounces shiitake or button mushrooms, cleaned and trimmed
2 teaspoons olive oil or other acceptable vegetable oil
½ teaspoon chopped fresh rosemary or ¼ teaspoon dried rosemary, crushed
Freshly ground black pepper
Garlic powder (optional)

Preheat oven to 500° F.

Place asparagus spears and mushrooms in a large plastic bag with a tight-fitting seal. Drizzle oil over asparagus mixture in bag. Add rosemary. Seal bag tightly and shake gently until asparagus and mushrooms are coated lightly with oil.

Arrange asparagus and mushrooms in a single layer on a large baking sheet. Season with pepper and, if desired, garlic powder. Bake about 10 minutes or until asparagus is tender yet crisp.

NUTRIENT ANALYSIS (PER SERVING)

Calories 56 kcal
Protein 4 g
Carbohydrate 6 g
Cholesterol 0 mg
Sodium 4 mg
Total fat 3 g
  Saturated 0 g
  Polyunsaturated 0 g
  Monounsaturated 2 g

Broccoli with Easy Mustard Sauce

The vegetables and creamy sauce are cooked in the same saucepan, making cleanup a snap.

½ cup low-sodium chicken broth, plus more if needed for thinning sauce
½ teaspoon dried thyme, crushed
3 cups broccoli florets
2 tablespoons nonfat or low-fat sour cream
2 teaspoons all-purpose flour
2 teaspoons Dijon mustard

Serves 4; ⅔ cup per serving

Preparation time: 10 minutes

Cooking time: 8 minutes

In a medium saucepan, bring the ½ cup broth and the thyme to a boil over high heat. Add broccoli. Return to a boil. Reduce heat, cover, and simmer 5 minutes or until tender yet crisp. Do not drain. With a slotted spoon, remove broccoli from saucepan. Set aside and keep warm.

Meanwhile, in a small bowl, stir together remaining ingredients. Stir sour-cream mixture into cooking liquid remaining in saucepan. Cook and stir over medium heat until thickened, about 2 minutes. Do not let it boil. Cook 1 minute more, stirring constantly. (If sauce is too thick, add more broth, 1 tablespoon at a time, until desired consistency is reached.)

Return broccoli to saucepan with sauce. Stir gently until well coated.

NUTRIENT ANALYSIS (PER SERVING)

Calories 32 kcal
Protein 3 g
Carbohydrate 5 g
Cholesterol 0 mg
Sodium 59 mg
Total fat 0 g
  Saturated 0 g
  Polyunsaturated 0 g
  Monounsaturated 0 g

New Potatoes with Easy Mustard Sauce

Prepare recipe as directed above except omit broccoli and thyme. Use 1 pound tiny new potatoes, scrubbed and cut into bite-size pieces, and ¼ teaspoon dried dill weed. Cook potatoes for 10 to 15 minutes or until tender.

NUTRIENT ANALYSIS (PER SERVING)

Calories 100 kcal
Protein 3 g
Carbohydrate 22 g
Cholesterol 0 mg
Sodium 49 mg
Total fat 0 g
  Saturated 0 g
  Polyunsaturated 0 g
  Monounsaturated 0 g

Orange-Buttered Brussels Sprouts

The easy orange mixture in this recipe also makes a delicious accompaniment to other cooked vegetables, such as broccoli, carrots, or snow pea pods.

Serves 4; ⅔ cup per serving

Preparation time: 5 minutes

Cooking time: 7 minutes

10-ounce package frozen no-salt-added brussels sprouts
2 teaspoons water
2 teaspoons frozen orange juice concentrate
1 teaspoon acceptable margarine
¼ teaspoon sesame seeds

Cook brussels sprouts according to package directions; drain.

Meanwhile, in a small saucepan, combine remaining ingredients. Cook and stir over low heat until margarine melts.

To serve, toss orange juice mixture with brussels sprouts.

Microwave Method for Sauce

Place orange juice mixture in a 1-cup glass measure. Microwave on 100% power (high) about 30 seconds or until margarine melts. Proceed as directed above.

NUTRIENT ANALYSIS
(PER SERVING)

Calories 43 kcal
Protein 3 g
Carbohydrate 7 g
Cholesterol 0 mg
Sodium 27 mg
Total fat 1 g
Saturated 0 g
Polyunsaturated 0 g
Monounsaturated 0 g

Cauliflower with Peanut Dipping Sauce

This peanut sauce with lime and curry steals its flavors from Indonesian satés (sah-TAYS). It turns cooked cauliflower into a unique side dish.

Serves 4; ⅔ cup cauliflower and 1 tablespoon sauce per serving

Preparation time: 10 minutes

Cooking time: 8 minutes

3 cups cauliflower florets
Water
⅓ cup unsweetened apple juice
1 tablespoon peanut butter
½ teaspoon finely shredded lime peel
1 teaspoon lime juice
½ teaspoon bottled minced garlic
¼ teaspoon curry powder
Dash ground red pepper

In a medium saucepan over medium-high heat, cook cauliflower in a small amount of boiling water for 8 minutes, or until tender yet crisp. Drain and set aside.

Meanwhile, in a small saucepan, combine remaining ingredients. Cook over low heat until it reaches desired thickness, stirring occasionally.

Place sauce in four small dishes and serve alongside cauliflower for dipping.

NUTRIENT ANALYSIS
(PER SERVING)

Calories 52 kcal
Protein 3 g
Carbohydrate 7 g
Cholesterol 0 mg
Sodium 37 mg
Total fat 2 g
  Saturated 0 g
  Polyunsaturated 1 g
  Monounsaturated 1 g

Baked Endive with Oregano

Belgian endive, also called French endive, has a slightly bitter flavor even when it's cooked. Serve this unusual recipe with a light and creamy pasta main dish, such as Speedy Shrimp and Pasta (page 176).

2 medium heads Belgian endive (about 3 ounces each)
Vegetable oil spray
¼ teaspoon dried oregano, crushed
Freshly ground black pepper
¼ cup shredded or grated Parmesan cheese

Serves 4; ½ head per serving

Preparation time:
5 minutes

Cooking time:
30 minutes

Standing time:
2 to 3 minutes

Preheat oven to 375° F.

Cut each head of endive lengthwise in half and remove outer leaves. Place, cut side up, on a piece of foil large enough to fold over all four halves. Lightly spray the cut surfaces with vegetable oil. Sprinkle with oregano and pepper. Wrap endive tightly in foil.

Bake for 30 minutes or until tender. Unwrap foil and sprinkle endive with Parmesan cheese. Rewrap and let stand before serving for 2 to 3 minutes or until Parmesan cheese melts.

NUTRIENT ANALYSIS
(PER SERVING)

Calories 35 kcal
Protein 3 g
Carbohydrate 1 g
Cholesterol 5 mg
Sodium 120 mg
Total fat 2 g
  Saturated 1 g
  Polyunsaturated 0 g
  Monounsaturated 1 g

Crispy Skin-On Oven Fries

When the urge for French fries hits, turn to this recipe for a crispy, low-fat version. To make these less spicy, omit some of the paprika, garlic powder, or pepper.

Serves 4; 6 potato wedges per serving

Preparation time: 10 minutes

Cooking time: 20 minutes

Microwave cooking time: 8 to 10 minutes plus 3 to 4 minutes for broiling

3 medium baking potatoes
¼ teaspoon salt
¼ teaspoon paprika
¼ teaspoon garlic powder
⅛ teaspoon black pepper
Vegetable oil spray

Preheat oven to 450° F.

Scrub potatoes; pat dry. Cut each potato into 8 wedges. Arrange, skin side down, in a single layer on a baking sheet.

In a small bowl, stir together remaining ingredients except vegetable oil spray. Spray potatoes lightly with vegetable oil. Sprinkle salt mixture over potatoes.

Bake, uncovered, for 20 minutes or until potatoes are tender and skin is crisp.

Microwave Method

Prepare recipe as directed above, but arrange potatoes in a 2-quart microwave-safe casserole. Spray potatoes with vegetable oil and sprinkle with salt mixture. Cover and cook on 100% power (high) for 8 to 10 minutes or until tender; give dish a half turn once.

Meanwhile, preheat broiler. Using a spatula, carefully transfer cooked potatoes to the unheated rack of a broiler pan. Broil 4 to 6 inches from the heat for 3 to 4 minutes or until brown and crisp.

NUTRIENT ANALYSIS (PER SERVING)

Calories 101 kcal
Protein 2 g
Carbohydrate 23 g
Cholesterol 0 mg
Sodium 141 mg
Total fat 0 g
  Saturated 0 g
  Polyunsaturated 0 g
  Monounsaturated 0 g

Quick Green Bean Casserole

This healthful version of the classic potluck vegetable dish uses low-fat soup and fat-free popcorn cakes or rice cakes. Since this recipe is for four servings, you don't have to wait for a potluck dinner to try it.

Serves 4; ½ cup per serving

Preparation time: 5 minutes

Cooking time: 35 minutes

Microwave cooking time: 9 to 11 minutes

9- or 10-ounce package frozen no-salt-added cut green beans

½ of a 10¾-ounce can (about ½ cup) reduced-fat and reduced-sodium condensed cream of mushroom soup

¼ teaspoon dried tarragon, crushed

1 cup crumbled fat-free popcorn cakes or rice cakes

Preheat oven to 350° F.

In a 1-quart casserole, combine green beans, soup, and tarragon. Cover and bake for 30 minutes or until beans are tender and mixture is bubbly. Sprinkle with crumbled popcorn cakes. Continue baking, uncovered, 5 more minutes.

Microwave Method

Prepare recipe as directed above, but place beans, soup, and tarragon in a 1-quart microwave-safe casserole. Cover and cook on 100% power (high) for 5 minutes. Stir, re-cover, and cook 3 to 5 minutes more or until bubbly. Top as directed above. Microwave, uncovered, 1 more minute.

NUTRIENT ANALYSIS (PER SERVING)

Calories 55 kcal
Protein 2 g
Carbohydrate 11 g
Cholesterol 2 mg
Sodium 179 mg
Total fat 1 g
  Saturated 0 g
  Polyunsaturated 0 g
  Monounsaturated 0 g

Vegetables

Sugar-Kissed Peas and Carrots

Peeling and slicing full-size carrots can be laborious and time-consuming. This recipe uses small carrots. Try to choose small carrots that are similar in size. Or use near-bite-sized miniatures that come already scrubbed and peeled.

Serves 4; ½ cup per serving

Preparation time: 10 minutes

Cooking time: 10 minutes

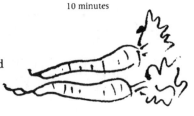

1 cup water
8 ounces peeled small carrots
4 ounces fresh snow pea pods, trimmed
1 tablespoon acceptable margarine
1 teaspoon sugar

In a large saucepan, bring water to a boil over high heat. Add carrots and return to a boil. Reduce heat, cover, and simmer for 5 minutes. Add pea pods to saucepan and bring to a boil over high heat. Reduce heat, cover, and simmer for 3 minutes more or until tender yet crisp. Drain in a colander.

Place margarine and sugar in the saucepan in which vegetables were cooked. Place over medium heat. When margarine is melted, add cooked vegetables. Cook and stir about 2 minutes or until vegetables are glazed.

NUTRIENT ANALYSIS (PER SERVING)

Calories 64 kcal
Protein 1 g
Carbohydrate 8 g
Cholesterol 0 mg
Sodium 69 mg
Total fat 3 g
  Saturated 1 g
  Polyunsaturated 1 g
  Monounsaturated 1 g

Greek Spinach

Serve this light and lemony side dish with lean roasted lamb or pork.

10-ounce package frozen no-salt-added chopped spinach
½ cup frozen no-salt-added pearl onions
½ teaspoon dried oregano, crushed
½ teaspoon finely shredded lemon peel
1 tablespoon lemon juice
½ teaspoon bottled minced garlic
¼ cup crumbled feta cheese (1 ounce)

Cook spinach according to package directions, but add onions to saucepan. Drain well, squeezing as much moisture as possible from the mixture. Add remaining ingredients except feta cheese and stir until well combined. Sprinkle with feta cheese and toss to combine.

Serves 4; ½ cup per serving

Preparation time: 5 minutes

Cooking time: 5 to 10 minutes

NUTRIENT ANALYSIS (PER SERVING)

Calories 45 kcal
Protein 3 g
Carbohydrate 5 g
Cholesterol 8 mg
Sodium 141 mg
Total fat 2 g
Saturated 1 g
Polyunsaturated 0 g
Monounsaturated 0 g

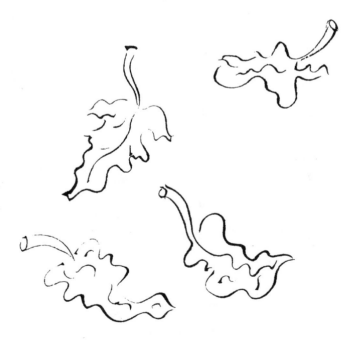

Italian-Style Spaghetti Squash

Busy cooks should prepare spaghetti squash in a microwave oven—it's twice as fast as conventional cooking, and the squash comes out moist and delicious.

Serves 6; ½ cup per serving

Preparation time: 5 minutes

Cooking time: 30 to 40 minutes

Microwave cooking time: 10 to 14 minutes

½ medium spaghetti squash (about 1½ pounds) (see Note)
2 tablespoons water
14½-ounce can Italian-style stewed tomatoes, drained
¼ cup grated or shredded Parmesan cheese (optional)

Remove seeds from squash. Place squash, cut side down, in a microwave-safe baking dish. Add water. Cover and microwave on 100% power (high) for 10 to 14 minutes or until pulp can just be pierced with a fork; give dish a half turn twice during cooking. Drain.

Using a pot holder, hold squash in one hand and with a fork shred squash pulp into strands, letting them fall into the baking dish. Add drained tomatoes, tossing to coat. Sprinkle with Parmesan cheese if desired.

NUTRIENT ANALYSIS
(PER SERVING)

Calories 42 kcal
Protein 1 g
Carbohydrate 9 g
Cholesterol 0 mg
Sodium 112 mg
Total fat 1 g
  Saturated 0 g
  Polyunsaturated 0 g
  Monounsaturated 0 g

Conventional Oven Cooking Method

Prepare recipe as above except prick the squash skin all over with a fork. Bake, uncovered, in a glass baking dish in a preheated 350° F oven for 30 to 40 minutes or until tender. Complete recipe as above.

Note: Buy a 3-pound squash and cut it in half lengthwise. Use one piece for this recipe, and cover and refrigerate the other piece to try another time. The uncooked squash will stay fresh for up to 1 week.

Pasta, Rice, and Grains

Turn to this chapter when you want high-energy, low-fat foods to help round out any meal. Italian Pasta with Greens, Southwestern Rice, Gingered Bulgur with Apricots, and Garlic Quinoa are just a few satisfying examples, each taking 10 minutes or less to prepare.

Their quick-to-the-table status is no trick. Pasta, noodles, couscous, and bulgur are naturally quick-cooking. Brown rice typically takes 45 minutes to cook, but quick-cooking brown rice takes only 5 to 10 minutes. Stay on the lookout for other fast-to-fix rice or grain mixes at your supermarket. Discard the high-sodium flavor packets that come with some of them and add your own no-salt flavorings, such as garlic, herbs, and spices.

German-Style Noodles

Try these delicious noodles with lean broiled pork chops.

6 cups water
3 cups medium no-cholesterol noodles
½ cup sliced carrots
1 cup chopped cabbage
½ cup nonfat or low-fat sour cream or plain nonfat
  yogurt
2 green onions, sliced
½ teaspoon caraway seeds
½ teaspoon salt
⅛ teaspoon black pepper

Serves 4; ¾ cup per serving

Preparation time: 5 minutes

Cooking time: 10 to 15 minutes

In a large saucepan, bring water to a boil over high heat. Add noodles and carrots. Reduce heat slightly and boil gently, uncovered, 5 minutes. Add cabbage and cook 3 to 5 minutes more or until noodles are tender. Drain. Return to saucepan. Stir in remaining ingredients and heat 1 to 2 minutes over low heat or until heated through (do not boil).

NUTRIENT ANALYSIS
(PER SERVING)

Calories 139 kcal
Protein 6 g
Carbohydrate 27 g
Cholesterol 1 mg
Sodium 303 mg
Total fat 1 g
 Saturated 0 g
 Polyunsaturated 0 g
 Monounsaturated 0 g

Italian Pasta with Greens

Keep this colorful recipe in mind for a company-special dinner side dish or a satisfying lunch entrée.

Serves 5; 1 cup per serving

Preparation time: 10 minutes

Cooking time: 9 minutes

6 cups water
2 cups bow-tie or medium shell pasta
½ teaspoon bottled minced garlic
1 teaspoon olive oil
1 to 2 tablespoons balsamic vinegar
2 cups torn fresh spinach
1 cup torn radicchio
¼ cup shredded or grated Parmesan cheese

In a large saucepan, bring water to a boil over high heat. Add pasta. Reduce heat slightly and boil gently, uncovered, about 8 minutes or until pasta is al dente. Drain.

Meanwhile, in a small skillet, cook garlic in oil over medium heat until tender, about 1 minute. Stir in vinegar.

Place spinach and radicchio in a large bowl. Add hot pasta. Pour hot garlic mixture over pasta and spinach mixture; toss to mix well. Sprinkle with Parmesan cheese.

NUTRIENT ANALYSIS
(PER SERVING)

Calories 238 kcal
Protein 10 g
Carbohydrate 42 g
Cholesterol 4 mg
Sodium 114 mg
Total fat 3 g
  Saturated 1 g
  Polyunsaturated 1 g
  Monounsaturated 1 g

Cook's Tip

When cooking pasta, take a tip from the Italians: cook it until it is "al dente," which means "to the tooth." In other words, pasta is done when it offers some resistance when it is bitten.

Sesame Pasta and Vegetables

A little bit of sesame oil goes a long way in this peppery pasta side dish. Choose the blend of frozen vegetables that your family likes best.

Serves 4; 1 cup per serving

Preparation time: 5 minutes

Cooking time: 8 minutes

8 cups water
16-ounce package frozen no-salt-added vegetables
4 ounces dried fettuccine or linguine, broken up
1 tablespoon acceptable margarine
1 teaspoon sesame seeds
½ teaspoon sesame oil
⅛ to ¼ teaspoon crushed red pepper flakes

In a large saucepan, bring water to a boil over high heat. Add vegetables and pasta. Return to a boil. Reduce heat slightly and boil gently, uncovered, 8 minutes, or until pasta is al dente and vegetables are tender yet crisp. Drain.

Return mixture to saucepan. Add remaining ingredients. Toss gently to coat.

NUTRIENT ANALYSIS (PER SERVING)

Calories 209 kcal
Protein 7 g
Carbohydrate 37 g
Cholesterol 0 mg
Sodium 73 mg
Total fat 4 g
  Saturated 1 g
  Polyunsaturated 1 g
  Monounsaturated 2 g

Peppery Spaetzle

Spaetzle (SHPET-sluh) is a classic German dumpling or noodle that is made by pressing batter through a colander into boiling water. Use these plump morsels the same way you use noodles.

Serves 4; ½ cup per serving

Preparation time: 10 minutes

Cooking time: 5 minutes

2 quarts water
1 cup all-purpose flour
¼ teaspoon black pepper
⅛ teaspoon salt
Egg substitute equivalent to 1 egg
⅓ cup skim milk
2 tablespoons grated or shredded Parmesan cheese

In a Dutch oven, bring water to a boil over high heat.

Meanwhile, in a medium bowl, combine flour, pepper, and salt. Make a well in the center. Set aside.

In a small bowl, stir together egg substitute and milk. Pour into flour well. Mix well.

Hold colander with large holes over boiling water. Pour batter into colander. Using a large spoon, press batter through holes in colander so batter falls into the water. Be careful not to splatter boiling water. Cook 5 minutes, occasionally stirring gently. Drain well.

Sprinkle with Parmesan cheese and serve hot.

NUTRIENT ANALYSIS
(PER SERVING)

Calories 139 kcal
Protein 6 g
Carbohydrate 25 g
Cholesterol 2 mg
Sodium 154 mg
Total fat 1 g
  Saturated 1 g
  Polyunsaturated 0 g
  Monounsaturated 0 g

Brown Rice Pilaf with Mushrooms

Quick-cooking brown rice makes this a fast side dish to serve with lean roasted beef or pork.

Vegetable oil spray
8 ounces sliced fresh mushrooms
1 bunch (6 to 8) green onions, sliced
1 teaspoon bottled minced garlic
1¼ cups water
1 teaspoon low-sodium beef bouillon granules
¼ teaspoon salt
¼ teaspoon dried thyme, crushed
1½ cups quick-cooking brown rice
¼ cup chopped fresh parsley (optional)

Serves 4; ¾ cup per serving

Preparation time: 10 minutes

Cooking time: 12 minutes

Microwave cooking time: 8 minutes

Standing time: 5 minutes

Spray a medium saucepan with vegetable oil. Place over medium-high heat. Add mushrooms, green onions, and garlic. Cook until mushrooms are tender, about 5 minutes. Add water, bouillon granules, salt, and thyme. Bring to a boil over high heat. Add rice and return to a boil. Reduce heat, cover, and simmer 5 minutes. Remove from heat and let stand, covered, 5 minutes. Stir in parsley if desired.

Microwave Method

Omit vegetable oil spray. Place all other ingredients except parsley in a 1½-quart microwave-safe casserole. Cover and cook on 100% power (high) for 4 minutes. Rotate dish a half turn and cook 4 minutes more. Let stand 5 minutes. Stir in parsley if desired.

NUTRIENT ANALYSIS (PER SERVING)

Calories 283 kcal
Protein 8 g
Carbohydrate 58 g
Cholesterol 0 mg
Sodium 150 mg
Total fat 3 g
  Saturated 1 g
  Polyunsaturated 1 g
  Monounsaturated 1 g

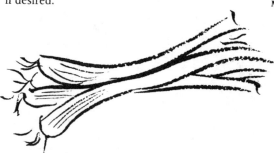

Southwestern Rice

Aromatic rice smells like popcorn or nuts when it's cooked. Regular long-grain rice can be substituted for the aromatic rice.

Serves 4; ¾ cup per serving

Preparation time:
5 minutes

Cooking time:
25 minutes

2 cups low-sodium chicken broth
⅛ teaspoon salt
1 cup white or brown aromatic rice, such as basmati or Texmati
½ teaspoon ground cumin
1 tomatillo or tomato, chopped
1 to 2 tablespoons snipped fresh cilantro
½ teaspoon finely shredded lime peel
1 teaspoon lime juice
½ teaspoon bottled minced jalapeño pepper (optional)

NUTRIENT ANALYSIS
(PER SERVING)

Calories 205 kcal
Protein 6 g
Carbohydrate 42 g
Cholesterol 0 mg
Sodium 102 mg
Total fat 1 g
  Saturated 0 g
  Polyunsaturated 0 g
  Monounsaturated 0 g

In a medium saucepan, bring broth and salt to a boil over high heat. Add rice and cumin and return to a boil. Reduce heat, cover, and simmer 20 minutes or until rice is tender and liquid is absorbed. Stir in remaining ingredients.

Cook's Tip

Tomatillos (toe muh TEE yos), also called Mexican green tomatoes, are small olive-green fruits encased in thin, papery husks. Their texture is like a firm tomato, and they have a slightly acidic flavor with hints of lemon and apple. Look for them in your grocer's produce section. Remove the husks before using.

Toasted Barley Pilaf

Browning the barley before cooking it gives this dish a nutty flavor similar to brown rice pilaf. Try this delightfully chewy dish instead of rice tonight.

Serves 4; ½ cup per serving

Preparation time: 10 minutes

Cooking time: 30 minutes

1 cup pearl barley
2 cups low-sodium chicken broth
½ cup sliced celery
¼ teaspoon snipped fresh rosemary or ⅛ teaspoon dried rosemary, crushed
⅛ teaspoon salt
⅛ teaspoon black pepper

NUTRIENT ANALYSIS
(PER SERVING)

Calories 191 kcal
Protein 6 g
Carbohydrate 40 g
Cholesterol 0 mg
Sodium 112 mg
Total fat 1 g
  Saturated 0 g
  Polyunsaturated 0 g
  Monounsaturated 0 g

Place barley in a large, heavy skillet. Cook over medium heat about 10 minutes or until lightly toasted, stirring occasionally. Slowly stir in the broth and then add remaining ingredients. Bring to a boil over high heat. Reduce heat, cover, and simmer 20 minutes or until liquid is absorbed and barley is pleasantly chewy.

Gingered Bulgur with Apricots

Fresh gingerroot and dried apricots provide the flavor boost to fiber-rich bulgur (also known as precooked cracked wheat). Substitute dried fruit bits for the apricots, if you prefer.

Serves 4; ¾ cup per serving

Preparation time: 5 to 7 minutes

Cooking time: 5 minutes

2 cups water
1 cup bulgur
¼ cup chopped dried apricots
1 tablespoon chopped fresh gingerroot
¼ teaspoon salt
¼ teaspoon ground cinnamon

NUTRIENT ANALYSIS
(PER SERVING)

Calories 203 kcal
Protein 7 g
Carbohydrate 46 g
Cholesterol 0 mg
Sodium 144 mg
Total fat 1 g
  Saturated 0 g
  Polyunsaturated 0 g
  Monounsaturated 0 g

In a medium saucepan, combine all ingredients. Bring to a boil over high heat. Reduce heat, cover, and simmer 5 minutes or until liquid is absorbed.

Pasta, Rice, and Grains

Fresh Herb Polenta

Serve this creamy cornmeal concoction just as you would serve mashed potatoes.

2 cups water
⅔ cup finely ground yellow cornmeal
⅔ cup cold water
¼ teaspoon salt
¼ cup grated or shredded Parmesan cheese
2 tablespoons snipped fresh or 1 teaspoon dried basil, crushed
1 teaspoon snipped fresh or ¼ teaspoon dried thyme, crushed

Serves 6; ½ cup per serving

Preparation time: 10 minutes

Cooking time: 5 to 7 minutes

Baking time: 30 minutes

In a medium saucepan, bring 2 cups water to a boil over high heat.

Meanwhile, in a large liquid measuring cup, combine the cornmeal, ⅔ cup cold water, and the salt. Slowly pour cornmeal mixture into boiling water, stirring constantly. Return just to boiling. Reduce heat to low and cook, uncovered, about 5 minutes or until thick, stirring frequently. Stir in remaining ingredients.

NUTRIENT ANALYSIS (PER SERVING)

Calories 72 kcal
Protein 3 g
Carbohydrate 12 g
Cholesterol 3 mg
Sodium 152 mg
Total fat 1 g
  Saturated 1 g
  Polyunsaturated 0 g
  Monounsaturated 0 g

Baked Polenta

Follow the recipe above, then transfer hot mixture to a 9-inch pie plate that has been sprayed with vegetable oil. Cover and chill until firm at least 1 hour, or overnight. Bake, uncovered, in a preheated 350° F oven about 30 minutes or until heated through.

Cook's Tip

An easy way to speed up the boiling of water is to put a lid on the saucepan as you heat the water. We tested this theory on 2 cups of water in a small, heavy saucepan. The water in the pot with the lid took 4 minutes to come to a boil. The water in the pot without a lid took 5 minutes. So cover the pan and you'll save time.

Colorful Lemon Couscous

Serve this pretty side dish along with grilled fish or chicken.

Vegetable oil spray
1 small green bell pepper, chopped
1 small red or yellow bell pepper, chopped
1 teaspoon bottled minced garlic
1 cup low-sodium chicken broth
⅛ teaspoon salt
1 cup couscous
1 teaspoon finely shredded lemon peel
1 tablespoon lemon juice

Spray a medium saucepan with vegetable oil. Place over medium-high heat. Add bell peppers and garlic. Cook until tender, about 5 minutes. Stir in broth and salt and bring to a boil over high heat. Add remaining ingredients, stir, and remove from heat. Cover and let stand 5 minutes or until liquid is absorbed.

Serves 4; ¾ cup per serving

Preparation time: 10 minutes

Cooking time: 8 minutes

Standing time: 5 minutes

NUTRIENT ANALYSIS
(PER SERVING)

Calories 188 kcal
Protein 7 g
Carbohydrate 37 g
Cholesterol 0 mg
Sodium 87 mg
Total fat 1 g
  Saturated 0 g
  Polyunsaturated 0 g
  Monounsaturated 0 g

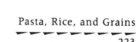

Garlic Quinoa

Quinoa (KEEN-wah) is a high-protein, calcium-rich grain from South America with a wonderful crunchy texture and subtle nutty taste. Before cooking quinoa, rinse it in a colander under running water to remove its bitter-tasting coating. Look for quinoa in a health-food store or gourmet shop.

Serves 4; ⅔ cup per serving

Preparation time: 10 minutes

Cooking time: 18 minutes

Vegetable oil spray
½ cup chopped onion
2 teaspoons bottled minced garlic
1 cup quinoa, rinsed and drained
2 cups water
¼ teaspoon salt

Spray a medium saucepan with vegetable oil. Place over medium heat. Add onion and garlic. Cook until onion is just tender, about 3 minutes. Add quinoa, water, and salt. Bring to a boil over high heat. Reduce heat, cover, and simmer 15 minutes or until water is absorbed. Serve with a saucy main dish, such as Chinese-Style Chicken Thighs (page 118).

NUTRIENT ANALYSIS
(PER SERVING)

Calories 170 kcal
Protein 5 g
Carbohydrate 35 g
Cholesterol 0 mg
Sodium 139 mg
Total fat 1 g
　Saturated 0 g
　Polyunsaturated 0 g
　Monounsaturated 0 g

Sauces

Sauces have a way of adding a special touch to ordinary foods. The savory and sweet sauces in this chapter are a great way to dress up any main dish or dessert without spending too much time in the kitchen. Here's positive proof that sauces don't need to be laden with butter or fat to make them taste good. Red Pepper and Tomato Sauce relies on the natural flavor of a fresh red bell pepper. Fresh Strawberry Sauce uses only three simple ingredients to make a refreshing sauce to spoon over fresh fruit or frozen yogurt.

All these sauces can be made ahead and chilled until serving time. To serve warm, simply reheat the chilled sauce in a saucepan over low heat.

Lemony Horseradish Sauce

Dollop this spicy sauce on top of lean grilled burgers or steamed new potatoes.

⅓ cup nonfat or low-fat sour cream
⅓ cup fat-free, cholesterol-free mayonnaise
2 tablespoons prepared horseradish
½ teaspoon finely shredded lemon peel
1 teaspoon lemon juice

In a small bowl, stir together all ingredients. Serve immediately or cover and refrigerate until serving time.

Makes ⅔ cup

Serves 10; 1 tablespoon per serving

Preparation time: 5 minutes

NUTRIENT ANALYSIS (PER SERVING)

Calories 12 kcal
Protein 1 g
Carbohydrate 3 g
Cholesterol 0 mg
Sodium 111 mg
Total fat 0 g
 Saturated 0 g
 Polyunsaturated 0 g
 Monounsaturated 0 g

Mango-Lime Cream Sauce

Serve this sauce as a unique accompaniment to quesadillas or roasted or grilled chicken. Look for bottled fresh mango slices in your grocer's produce section.

½ cup coarsely chopped mango
¼ cup nonfat or low-fat sour cream
1 tablespoon mango juice
½ teaspoon finely shredded lime peel
1 teaspoon lime juice

In a blender or the work bowl of a food processor fitted with a metal blade, combine all ingredients. Cover and process until well combined. Serve immediately or cover and refrigerate until serving time.

Makes ½ cup

Serves 8; 1 tablespoon per serving

Preparation time: 5 minutes

NUTRIENT ANALYSIS (PER SERVING)

Calories 12 kcal
Protein 1 g
Carbohydrate 3 g
Cholesterol 0 mg
Sodium 6 mg
Total fat 0 g
 Saturated 0 g
 Polyunsaturated 0 g
 Monounsaturated 0 g

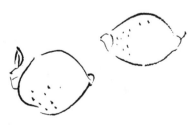

Red Pepper and Tomato Sauce

Serve this eye-catching sauce over grilled fish or poultry or toss with hot pasta.

Makes ⅔ cup

Serves 5; 2 tablespoons per serving

Preparation time: 5 minutes

Cooking time: 5 minutes

1 medium red bell pepper, chopped
½ cup low-sodium chicken broth
¼ teaspoon salt
⅛ teaspoon black pepper
Dash ground red pepper
1 tablespoon no-salt-added tomato paste

In a medium saucepan, combine all ingredients except tomato paste. Bring to a boil over high heat. Reduce heat, cover, and simmer for 5 minutes or until bell pepper is tender.

Transfer mixture to a blender or the work bowl of a food processor fitted with a metal blade. Add tomato paste. Cover and process until smooth. Serve immediately (sauce will still be warm) or cover and refrigerate for later use. Reheat in a small saucepan over low heat before serving.

NUTRIENT ANALYSIS
(PER SERVING)

Calories 9 kcal
Protein 1 g
Carbohydrate 2 g
Cholesterol 0 mg
Sodium 115 mg
Total fat 0 g
  Saturated 0 g
  Polyunsaturated 0 g
  Monounsaturated 0 g

Homemade Pesto

We slashed half the oil and replaced it with low-sodium chicken broth in this classic Italian sauce. Use it in the recipes throughout this cookbook that call for pesto, or toss some with hot cooked pasta or spaghetti squash.

Makes ¾ cup

Serves 12: 1 tablespoon per serving

Preparation time: 10 minutes

1 cup firmly packed fresh basil leaves
½ cup firmly packed fresh parsley sprigs, preferably Italian flat-leaf, stems removed
½ cup grated Parmesan cheese
¼ cup walnut pieces
1 teaspoon bottled minced garlic
2 tablespoons olive oil
2 tablespoons low-sodium chicken broth or water

In the work bowl of a food processor fitted with a metal blade, combine basil, parsley, Parmesan, walnuts, and garlic. Cover and process until a paste forms, scraping sides as necessary. With machine running, gradually add oil and broth. Process until smooth.

Serve immediately or cover and refrigerate until serving time.

NUTRIENT ANALYSIS
(PER SERVING)

Calories 54 kcal
Protein 2 g
Carbohydrate 1 g
Cholesterol 3 mg
Sodium 65 mg
Total fat 5 g
  Saturated 1 g
  Polyunsaturated 1 g
  Monounsaturated 2 g

Fresh Strawberry Sauce

This fresh sauce is great served chilled with fresh fruit. You can also warm it in a saucepan and spoon it over nonfat frozen yogurt or ice milk.

2 cups fresh strawberries, hulled
2 tablespoons sugar
2 tablespoons orange-flavored liqueur or orange
   juice

Place all ingredients in a blender or the work bowl of a food processor fitted with a metal blade. Cover and process until smooth. Serve immediately or cover and refrigerate until serving time.

Makes 1¼ cups

Serves 10; 2 tablespoons per serving

Preparation time: 5 minutes

NUTRIENT ANALYSIS
(PER SERVING)

Calories 27 kcal
Protein 0 g
Carbohydrate 6 g
Cholesterol 0 mg
Sodium 0 mg
Total fat 0 g
  Saturated 0 g
  Polyunsaturated 0 g
  Monounsaturated 0 g

Dessert Sauce

What could be easier? Stir together a few ingredients, and you have a rich-tasting sauce to serve with your favorite dessert.

½ cup ready-to-eat nonfat vanilla or chocolate
   pudding
2 tablespoons skim milk or desired liqueur
Dash ground nutmeg

In a small bowl, stir together all ingredients. Serve immediately or cover and refrigerate until serving time. Serve over fresh fruit or angel food cake.

Makes ½ cup

Serves 4; 2 tablespoons per serving

Preparation time: less than 5 minutes

NUTRIENT ANALYSIS
(PER SERVING)

Calories 32 kcal
Protein 1 g
Carbohydrate 7 g
Cholesterol 1 mg
Sodium 54 mg
Total fat 0 g
  Saturated 0 g
  Polyunsaturated 0 g
  Monounsaturated 0 g

Breads

Fresh home-baked bread is a treat at any meal, even if you take some shortcuts to make it. You may not think of bread as an important part of your daily diet, but think again. Bread helps fuel your body with carbohydrates and has little or no fat. It's the high-fat butter and spreads that tarnish bread's reputation.

Most of these recipes rely on a few time-saving ingredients, such as quick bread mix, refrigerated French loaf dough, hot-roll mix, reduced-fat baking and pancake mix, and muffin mix. You'll find these products in the baking aisle of most supermarkets.

So go ahead. Make some homemade bread for dinner. You and your family will be glad you did.

Oat Bran Soda Bread

This coarsely textured bread tastes just right with a bowl of hearty soup or stew.

Serves 10; 1 wedge per serving

Preparation time: 10 minutes

Baking time: 35 minutes

Vegetable oil spray
1½ cups all-purpose flour
½ cup oat bran, plus 1 tablespoon for sprinkling on top of loaf
1 teaspoon baking powder
½ teaspoon baking soda
¼ teaspoon salt
3 tablespoons acceptable margarine
Egg substitute equivalent to 1 egg
¾ cup low-fat buttermilk
1 egg white

Preheat oven to 375° F. Lightly spray a baking sheet with vegetable oil. Set aside.

In a large bowl, stir together flour, ½ cup of the oat bran, baking powder, baking soda, and salt. Cut in margarine until mixture resembles coarse crumbs. Set aside.

In a small bowl, stir together egg substitute and buttermilk. Stir into flour mixture just until moistened. On a lightly floured surface, knead dough gently for 12 strokes.

Place dough on prepared baking sheet and shape into a 6-inch round loaf. With a sharp knife cut an X about ¼ inch deep on the top of the dough. Brush loaf with egg white. Sprinkle with the remaining 1 tablespoon oat bran. Bake 35 minutes or until toothpick inserted near the center comes out clean. Remove bread from baking sheet and cool slightly on a wire rack. Cut into 10 wedges. Serve warm.

NUTRIENT ANALYSIS (PER SERVING)

Calories 124 kcal
Protein 4 g
Carbohydrate 19 g
Cholesterol 1 mg
Sodium 209 mg
Total fat 4 g
  Saturated 1 g
  Polyunsaturated 1 g
  Monounsaturated 2 g

Easy Mexican Cornbread

You don't need to use a fat-laden cornbread mix for quick and easy cornbread. You can make a more healthful version from scratch in less than ten minutes of preparation time.

Serves 12; 1 piece per serving

Preparation time: 5 to 10 minutes

Baking time: 25 to 30 minutes

Vegetable oil spray
1 cup cornmeal
1 cup whole-wheat flour
¼ cup sugar
½ teaspoon baking soda
½ teaspoon chili powder
½ teaspoon ground cumin
Egg substitute equivalent to 1 egg or 2 egg whites
1½ cups low-fat buttermilk
11-ounce can whole-kernel corn with red and
    green bell peppers, drained
⅓ cup acceptable vegetable oil
4-ounce can chopped green chili peppers, drained

Preheat oven to 425° F. Lightly spray a 9-inch-square glass baking dish with vegetable oil. Set aside.

In a large bowl, stir together cornmeal, flour, sugar, baking soda, chili powder, and cumin. Set aside.

In a medium bowl, combine remaining ingredients. Add to cornmeal mixture, stirring until well combined.

Pour batter into prepared baking dish. Bake 25 to 30 minutes or until a toothpick inserted near the center comes out clean. Cut into 12 squares. Serve warm.

NUTRIENT ANALYSIS
(PER SERVING)

Calories 177 kcal
Protein 4 g
Carbohydrate 26 g
Cholesterol 1 mg
Sodium 155 mg
Total fat 7 g
  Saturated 1 g
  Polyunsaturated 4 g
  Monounsaturated 2 g

Pecan-Topped Pumpkin Bread

No one will suspect that this home-baked bread came from a box or that it's low in fat and cholesterol. Plan to make this bread in the fall when the pumpkin quick-bread mix is most readily available.

Makes 1 loaf

Serves 12; 1 slice per serving

Preparation time: 10 minutes

Baking time: 45 to 60 minutes

¼ teaspoon acceptable margarine
1 teaspoon all-purpose flour
14-ounce package pumpkin quick-bread mix
½ cup shredded carrot
1 to 2 teaspoons finely shredded orange peel
3 tablespoons unsweetened applesauce
Egg substitute equivalent to 2 eggs
2 tablespoons chopped pecans

Preheat oven to 350° F. Spread margarine on bottom and sides of a 9×5×3-inch loaf pan. Sprinkle flour over margarine. Set aside.

Prepare quick-bread mix according to package directions (using amount of water specified on package), but add the shredded carrot and orange peel, substitute the 3 tablespoons applesauce for the oil, and use the egg substitute for the eggs.

Pour batter into prepared loaf pan. Sprinkle top with pecans. Bake for 45 to 60 minutes or according to package directions.

NUTRIENT ANALYSIS (PER SERVING)

Calories 158 kcal
Protein 3 g
Carbohydrate 32 g
Cholesterol 0 mg
Sodium 183 mg
Total fat 2 g
  Saturated 0 g
  Polyunsaturated 1 g
  Monounsaturated 1 g

Crusty Herb French Loaf

A mere five minutes of your time will yield a hot loaf of fresh-baked bread when you start with refrigerated French-loaf dough.

Serves 13; 1 slice per serving

Preparation time: 5 minutes

Baking time: 28 to 33 minutes

11-ounce package refrigerated French-loaf dough
⅛ teaspoon dried basil, oregano, or thyme, crushed
Dash garlic powder

Breads

Preheat oven to 350° F.

Prepare French loaf according to package directions, but sprinkle with desired dried herb and garlic powder after making slashes on top of dough. Bake for 28 to 33 minutes or according to package directions.

NUTRIENT ANALYSIS
(PER SERVING)

Calories 66 kcal
Protein 2 g
Carbohydrate 14 g
Cholesterol 0 mg
Sodium 140 mg
Total fat 0 g
  Saturated 0 g
  Polyunsaturated 0 g
  Monounsaturated 0 g

Peppery Parmesan Pan Rolls

If you have a few extra minutes, make these easy rolls into cloverleaf or crescent shapes according to the package directions.

Serves 16; 1 roll per serving

Preparation time: 15 minutes

Rising time: 20 to 30 minutes

Baking time: 15 to 20 minutes

16-ounce package hot-roll mix
¼ cup grated Parmesan cheese
½ teaspoon coarsely cracked black pepper
2 tablespoons acceptable margarine, softened
Egg substitute equivalent to 1 egg

Preheat oven to 375° F.

Prepare hot-roll mix according to package directions, but stir Parmesan cheese and pepper into bowl with hot-roll mix, substitute acceptable margarine for the margarine or butter, and use egg substitute for the egg.

Shape dough according to package directions for pan rolls. Bake for 15 to 20 minutes or according to package directions.

NUTRIENT ANALYSIS
(PER SERVING)

Calories 119 kcal
Protein 4 g
Carbohydrate 21 g
Cholesterol 1 mg
Sodium 243 mg
Total fat 2 g
  Saturated 1 g
  Polyunsaturated 0 g
  Monounsaturated 1 g

Garden Herb Biscuits

You'll find tasty flecks of green onion, carrot, and dill weed in each tender biscuit.

Serves 12; 1 biscuit per serving

Preparation time: 5 to 10 minutes

Baking time: 8 to 10 minutes

Vegetable oil spray
1 cup reduced-fat baking and pancake mix
¾ cup all-purpose flour
2 green onions, finely chopped
1 small carrot, finely shredded
¼ teaspoon dried dill weed
¾ cup skim milk

Preheat oven to 450° F. Lightly spray a baking sheet with vegetable oil. Set aside.

In a medium bowl, stir together all ingredients except milk. Add milk. Stir just until a soft dough forms. If dough is sticky, gradually stir in more baking mix (up to 2 tablespoons) to make dough easier to handle.

Drop dough by tablespoonfuls onto prepared baking sheet. Bake for 8 to 10 minutes or until biscuits are lightly browned on top. Remove biscuits from baking sheet and cool slightly on a wire rack.

Cook's Tip

You can freeze any leftover biscuits. Simply defrost them and place them, uncovered, in a preheated 350° F oven for 3 to 5 minutes before serving.

NUTRIENT ANALYSIS
(PER SERVING)

Calories 74 kcal
Protein 2 g
Carbohydrate 14 g
Cholesterol 0 mg
Sodium 121 mg
Total fat 1 g
  Saturated 0 g
  Polyunsaturated 0 g
  Monounsaturated 0 g

Breads

237

Refrigerator Bran Muffins

Keep this handy muffin batter in the refrigerator all week and dip into it to bake as many muffins as you need.

Serves 15; 1 muffin per serving

Preparation time:
15 minutes

Baking time:
15 to 18 minutes

Microwave cooking time: 30 to 60 seconds

Standing time:
5 minutes

1 cup all-purpose flour
¾ cup unprocessed wheat bran (see Note)
½ cup whole-wheat flour
2½ teaspoons baking powder
1 teaspoon ground cinnamon
¼ teaspoon salt
1 cup skim milk
Egg substitute equivalent to 2 eggs
⅓ cup firmly packed light brown sugar
¼ cup unsweetened applesauce
2 tablespoons acceptable vegetable oil
⅓ cup raisins, chopped dates, or mixed dried fruit bits
Vegetable oil spray or paper bake cups

In a large bowl, stir together all-purpose flour, wheat bran, whole-wheat flour, baking powder, cinnamon, and salt. Make a well in the center. Set aside.

In a medium bowl, stir together milk, egg substitute, brown sugar, applesauce, and oil. Add to flour mixture, stirring just until moistened. Batter should be thick and lumpy. Fold in raisins. Use batter immediately or store in an airtight container in the refrigerator for up to 1 week.

To bake, preheat oven to 400° F. Do NOT stir batter. Lightly spray desired number of muffin cups with vegetable oil or line with paper bake cups. Fill muffin cups two-thirds full. Bake 15 to 18 minutes or until brown. If making only a few muffins, fill empty muffin cups with water for even baking.

Nutrient Analysis
(PER SERVING)

Calories 107 kcal
Protein 3 g
Carbohydrate 20 g
Cholesterol 0 mg
Sodium 126 mg
Total fat 2 g
  Saturated 0 g
  Polyunsaturated 1 g
  Monounsaturated 0 g

Microwave Method

Mix together ingredients as directed above. Line one or two 6-ounce custard cups with paper bake cups. Spoon 3 tablespoons batter into each cup. For one muffin, cook on 100% power (high) for 30 to 50 seconds or until done. For two muffins, cook for 50 to 60 seconds or until done. Let stand 5 minutes.

Note: The wheat bran used in this recipe is not a ready-to-eat dry cereal. It is unprocessed wheat bran, which can be found in most supermarkets.

Wild Blueberry Cornmeal Muffins

By cutting the fat and adding cornmeal, we've come up with a simple-to-make, healthful muffin you can really sink your teeth into.

Serves 12; 1 muffin per serving

Preparation time: 15 minutes

Baking time: 15 to 20 minutes

Vegetable oil spray (optional)
16½-ounce package light wild blueberry muffin
   mix
⅓ cup cornmeal
Egg substitute equivalent to 1 egg or 2 egg whites
2 tablespoons water

Preheat oven to 425° F. Spray bottoms of muffin cups with vegetable oil or use paper bake cups.

   Prepare muffin mix. Follow the package directions but make these changes: stir cornmeal into bowl with dry muffin mix; use egg substitute or egg whites in place of the egg; and add 2 tablespoons water (in addition to the liquid called for on the package). Bake for 15 to 20 minutes or according to package directions.

NUTRIENT ANALYSIS (PER SERVING)

Calories 108 kcal
Protein 3 g
Carbohydrate 24 g
Cholesterol 0 mg
Sodium 197 mg
Total fat 0 g
  Saturated 0 g
  Polyunsaturated 0 g
  Monounsaturated 0 g

Heart-Healthful Croutons

Don't limit these crispy morsels to a salad. Toss them into a bowl of soup or grab a handful for a quick snack.

Makes about 3 cups

Serves 12; ¼ cup per serving

3 slices whole-wheat bread
Vegetable oil spray
Garlic powder (optional)

Preparation time: Less than 5 minutes

Cooking time: 20 to 25 minutes

Cooling time: 10 minutes

Preheat oven to 300° F.

Cut bread into ½-inch cubes. Arrange in a single layer on a baking sheet. Spray bread lightly with vegetable oil. If desired, sprinkle lightly with garlic powder.

Bake for 10 minutes. Remove from oven and stir bread cubes. Return to oven and bake for 10 to 15 minutes more or until bread cubes are dry and crisp.

Cool completely before using. The croutons can be stored in an airtight container at room temperature for up to 3 weeks or in the freezer for up to 2 months.

NUTRIENT ANALYSIS
(PER SERVING)

Calories 17 kcal
Protein 1 g
Carbohydrate 3 g
Cholesterol 0 mg
Sodium 38 mg
Total fat 0 g
  Saturated 0 g
  Polyunsaturated 0 g
  Monounsaturated 0 g

Desserts

Wouldn't it be great to indulge in delicious desserts without feeling guilty? Wouldn't it be even better if you didn't have to spend a lot of time in the kitchen? In this chapter, your wishes can come true. You'll find delicious yet healthful desserts that are quick and easy to prepare.

How? We did it by relying on fresh or canned fruits and avoiding time-consuming techniques. We also capitalized on convenience products, such as graham cracker crusts, light cake mixes, ready-to-eat breakfast cereals, and gingerbread cake and cookie mixes. It's as easy as substituting egg whites or egg substitutes for whole eggs in Confetti Cupcakes with Chocolate Glaze or the Upside-Down Gingerbread with Pears and Raisins. It's as clever as cutting the margarine in half and replacing it with maple syrup in the Crispy Cereal Treats. Use our recipes as inspiration and then go ahead and "lighten up" some of your own family favorites. Smart eating has never been sweeter.

Fitness Flan

For a pretty presentation, serve the whole flan on a platter surrounded by fresh fruit.

½ cup granulated sugar
1½ cups skim milk
Egg substitute equivalent to 3 eggs
⅓ cup firmly packed brown sugar
1 teaspoon vanilla

Serves 8; 1 wedge per serving

Preparation time: 5 minutes

Cooking time: 46 to 50 minutes

Cooling time: 15 minutes

Chilling time: At least 1 hour

Preheat oven to 325° F.

To caramelize granulated sugar, place it in a heavy medium skillet. Cook over medium-high heat 3 to 5 minutes, or until sugar starts to melt, shaking the skillet occasionally but not stirring. Reduce heat to medium-low. Cook and stir with a wooden spoon until sugar is golden brown and completely melted, about 3 to 5 minutes. Remove from heat and quickly pour into an 8-inch round baking pan, tilting pan to evenly distribute sugar. (The sugar will harden quickly.)

In a medium bowl, stir together remaining ingredients. Pour over caramelized sugar. Place the 8-inch baking pan in a 13×9×2-inch baking pan. Add hot water to the larger pan until water reaches halfway up the side of the smaller pan. Bake, uncovered, about 40 minutes or until a knife inserted near the center comes out clean. Remove pan from water and cool. Cover surface with plastic wrap and chill at least 1 hour or until serving time. To serve, invert pan onto a serving plate and cut into 8 wedges.

NUTRIENT ANALYSIS (PER SERVING)

Calories 110 kcal
Protein 4 g
Carbohydrate 24 g
Cholesterol 1 mg
Sodium 72 mg
Total fat 0 g
   Saturated 0 g
   Polyunsaturated 0 g
   Monounsaturated 0 g

Desserts

Balsamic Berries Brûlée

Have you ever used balsamic vinegar? Here's your chance to try it. You'll love what it can do for fresh strawberries.

Serves 4; ½ cup per serving

Preparation time: 10 minutes

Cooking time: 1 to 2 minutes

2 cups fresh strawberries, hulled and thinly sliced
1 teaspoon sugar
2 tablespoons balsamic vinegar
1 teaspoon chopped fresh mint
Freshly ground black pepper
⅓ cup nonfat or low-fat sour cream
⅓ cup plain nonfat yogurt
2 tablespoons firmly packed brown sugar

In a 9-inch pie plate, combine berries and sugar. Let stand 5 minutes. Stir in balsamic vinegar and mint. Season with pepper.

Meanwhile, preheat broiler.

In a small bowl, stir together sour cream and yogurt. Spoon evenly over berries. Sprinkle with brown sugar.

Broil berries 4 to 6 inches from the heat for 1 to 2 minutes or until sugar melts. Serve immediately.

NUTRIENT ANALYSIS
(PER SERVING)

Calories 79 kcal
Protein 3 g
Carbohydrate 17 g
Cholesterol 1 mg
Sodium 35 mg
Total fat 0 g
  Saturated 0 g
  Polyunsaturated 0 g
  Monounsaturated 0 g

Frosty Fruit

For best results, choose firm, ripe (but not overripe) fruit with no signs of bruises or blemishes.

2 cups fresh fruit, such as grapes, whole small strawberries, blueberries, raspberries, melon chunks, sliced peaches, or peeled kiwifruit chunks

Serves 4; ½ cup per serving

Preparation time: Less than 5 minutes

Freezing time: At least 1 hour

Standing time: 2 minutes

If necessary, rinse fruit and pat dry. Arrange fruit in a single layer on a baking sheet. Freeze, uncovered, about 1 hour or until firm.

To serve, remove fruit from freezer and let stand for 2 minutes. (Fruit should be served frozen but not rock hard.)

Transfer any leftovers to freezer containers or bags. Seal, label, and freeze for a few hours or several days. You can thaw the fruit (it will be soft) for recipes such as cooked sauces.

NUTRIENT ANALYSIS (PER SERVING)

WITH GRAPES:
Calories 57 kcal
Protein 1 g
Carbohydrate 14 g
Cholesterol 0 mg
Sodium 2 mg
Total fat 0 g
  Saturated 0 g
  Polyunsaturated 0 g
  Monounsaturated 0 g

WITH STRAWBERRIES:
Calories 22 kcal
Protein 0 g
Carbohydrate 5 g
Cholesterol 0 mg
Sodium 1 mg
Total fat 0 g
  Saturated 0 g
  Polyunsaturated 0 g
  Monounsaturated 0 g

WITH MIXED FRUITS:
Calories 33 kcal
Protein 1 g
Carbohydrate 8 g
Cholesterol 0 mg
Sodium 3 mg
Total fat 0 g
  Saturated 0 g
  Polyunsaturated 0 g
  Monounsaturated 0 g

Fresh Fruit Tarts

Choose a variety of festive fruits, such as assorted berries, melon cubes, pineapple chunks, star fruit, and peach chunks.

½ cup nonfat or low-fat sour cream
2 tablespoons confectioners' sugar
1 teaspoon chopped fresh mint or ¼ teaspoon dried mint, crushed
4-ounce package single-serve graham cracker crusts (6 small crusts)
1 cup assorted cut-up fresh fruit
⅓ cup nonfat or low-fat lemon yogurt

In a small bowl, stir together sour cream, confectioners' sugar, and mint. Spoon into graham cracker crusts. Arrange fruit over sour cream mixture. Serve immediately or cover and refrigerate until serving time.

Just before serving, stir yogurt and drizzle over fruit.

Serves 6; 1 tart per serving

Preparation time: 10 minutes

NUTRIENT ANALYSIS (PER SERVING)

WITH MIXED FRUIT:
Calories 139 kcal
Protein 3 g
Carbohydrate 19 g
Cholesterol 4 mg
Sodium 82 mg
Total fat 6 g
Saturated 3 g
Polyunsaturated 1 g
Monounsaturated 3 g

WITH MIXED BERRIES:
Calories 129 kcal
Protein 3 g
Carbohydrate 16 g
Cholesterol 4 mg
Sodium 82 mg
Total fat 6 g
Saturated 2 g
Polyunsaturated 1 g
Monounsaturated 3 g

Frozen Yogurt Pie

Be sure to read the labels on the various graham cracker crusts available at your grocery store. Choose the crust with the lowest number of grams of fat per serving. You can find the spreadable fruit in the store's jelly section.

1 quart (4 cups) peach nonfat or low-fat frozen yogurt or ice milk, or a flavor of your choice
1 purchased 8- or 9-inch graham cracker pie crust
⅔ cup raspberry spreadable fruit or a flavor of your choice

Serves 10; 1 wedge per serving

Preparation time: 5 minutes

Cooking time: 2 to 3 minutes

Freezing time: At least 2 hours

Place yogurt or ice milk in a large mixing bowl and stir or beat with an electric mixer until softened. Spoon into graham cracker pie crust. Cover and freeze at least 2 hours or until serving time.

To serve, let pie stand at room temperature for 5 minutes. Meanwhile, place spreadable fruit in a small saucepan and cook over low heat 2 to 3 minutes or until heated. Cut pie into 10 wedges and drizzle about 1 tablespoon spreadable fruit over each piece.

NUTRIENT ANALYSIS
(PER SERVING)

Calories 206 kcal
Protein 4 g
Carbohydrate 35 g
Cholesterol 4 mg
Sodium 91 mg
Total fat 7 g
 Saturated 2 g
 Polyunsaturated 1 g
 Monounsaturated 3 g

Dried Fruit Truffles

The combination of orange-flavored fruit coated with cocoa powder gives this bite-size dessert a surprising richness. Children might prefer a coating of graham cracker crumbs instead of cocoa powder.

Serves 12; 2 truffles per serving

Preparation time: 10 minutes

1 cup dried orange-essence pitted prunes or regular dried pitted prunes
½ cup dried pitted whole dates
2 tablespoons unsweetened cocoa powder

NUTRIENT ANALYSIS
(PER SERVING)

In the work bowl of a food processor fitted with a metal blade, combine prunes and dates. Cover and process until finely chopped, scraping sides as necessary.

Shape mixture into 24 nuggets 1 inch in diameter. Roll in cocoa powder to coat. Place on wax paper. The truffles can be stored in an airtight container in the refrigerator for up to 2 weeks.

Calories 55 kcal
Protein 1 g
Carbohydrate 14 g
Cholesterol 0 mg
Sodium 1 mg
Total fat 0 g
 Saturated 0 g
 Polyunsaturated 0 g
 Monounsaturated 0 g

Easy Apple-Cinnamon Crisp

Serve this warm, home-style dessert with a scoop of vanilla ice milk or nonfat frozen yogurt.

⅔ cup multigrain rolled oats or regular rolled oats
⅓ cup all-purpose flour
2 tablespoons firmly packed brown sugar
1 teaspoon ground cinnamon
¼ cup acceptable margarine
16-ounce can water-packed sliced apples, drained

Serves 9; ½ cup per serving

Preparation time: 5 minutes

Cooking time: 30 minutes

Preheat oven to 375° F.

In a medium bowl, stir together oats, flour, brown sugar, and cinnamon. Cut in margarine until mixture is crumbly.

Place drained apples in an 8-inch-square baking pan or glass baking dish. Sprinkle with oat mixture. Bake, uncovered, 30 minutes or until topping is light brown. Serve warm.

NUTRIENT ANALYSIS
(PER SERVING)

Calories 124 kcal
Protein 2 g
Carbohydrate 18 g
Cholesterol 0 mg
Sodium 62 mg
Total fat 6 g
  Saturated 1 g
  Polyunsaturated 1 g
  Monounsaturated 2 g

Easy Cherry-Cinnamon Crisp

Prepare recipe as directed above except use canned tart red cherries, drained, in place of the apples.

NUTRIENT ANALYSIS
(PER SERVING)

Calories 113 kcal
Protein 2 g
Carbohydrate 14 g
Cholesterol 0 mg
Sodium 61 mg
Total fat 6 g
  Saturated 1 g
  Polyunsaturated 1 g
  Monounsaturated 2 g

Crispy Cereal Treats

Here's a recipe for a family favorite with a new twist— less fat. We took out half the margarine and used syrup in its place. Maple syrup gives the bars a sweet, fresh flavor. If you like yours less sweet, use corn syrup instead.

Serves 32; 1 bar per serving

Preparation time: 5 minutes

Cooking time: 8 minutes

Cooling time: 30 minutes

Vegetable oil spray
¼ cup light maple syrup or corn syrup
2 tablespoons acceptable margarine
40 regular marshmallows or 4 cups miniature marshmallows
3 cups toasted rice cereal
3 cups toasted chocolate rice cereal
Vegetable oil spray

Spray a 13×9×2-inch baking pan with vegetable oil. Set aside.

In a large saucepan or Dutch oven, cook maple syrup and margarine over medium-low heat until margarine melts, about 3 minutes. Add marshmallows and stir until completely melted, about 5 minutes. Remove from heat.

Add cereals and stir until well coated. Transfer to baking pan. Spray the back of a metal spoon with vegetable oil. Use it to press mixture evenly into prepared pan. Cover and refrigerate at least 30 minutes. Cut into 32 bars. The bars can be stored, covered tightly, in the refrigerator for up to 1 week.

NUTRIENT ANALYSIS (PER SERVING)

Calories 63 kcal
Protein 0 g
Carbohydrate 14 g
Cholesterol 0 mg
Sodium 69 mg
Total fat 1 g
  Saturated 0 g
  Polyunsaturated 0 g
  Monounsaturated 0 g

Confetti Cupcakes with Chocolate Glaze

These festive cupcakes make great party food. Try drizzling the glaze in a pattern to match the theme of the party.

Serves 24; 1 cupcake per serving

Preparation time:
10 minutes

Cooking time:
15 to 20 minutes

Cooling time:
30 minutes

Vegetable oil spray (optional)
18¼-ounce package light white cake mix (see Note)
1½ cups water
3 egg whites
2 tablespoons multicolored candy sprinkles
¼ cup milk chocolate or semisweet chocolate
  chips

Preheat oven to 350° F.

Line 24 muffin cups with paper bake cups or spray with vegetable oil. Set aside.

In a large mixing bowl, combine cake mix, water, and egg whites. Beat with an electric mixer on low speed until combined. Beat on medium speed for 2 minutes. Fold in candy sprinkles. (Do not overmix or candy will bleed into batter.) Divide batter evenly among 24 muffin cups or make 12 cupcakes and refrigerate the remaining batter, covered, for up to 5 days.

Bake cupcakes 15 to 20 minutes or until a toothpick inserted near the center comes out clean. Cool at least 30 minutes on a wire rack.

Meanwhile, place chocolate chips in a small plastic bag with a tight-fitting seal. Seal bag. Place bag in a bowl of hot water; let stand about 5 minutes or until chips soften and melt. Wipe bag dry. Cut a small tip off one corner of the bag. Drizzle melted chocolate over cooled cupcakes. Allow glaze to set. The cupcakes can be stored, loosely covered, for 3 to 4 days.

Note: If you are using a light cake mix that specifies different amounts, ingredients, and/or directions, follow the package directions.

NUTRIENT ANALYSIS
(PER SERVING)

Calories 105 kcal
Protein 1 g
Carbohydrate 20 g
Cholesterol 2 mg
Sodium 170 mg
Total fat 2 g
  Saturated 1 g
  Polyunsaturated 0 g
  Monounsaturated 1 g

Cook's Tip

What's the best way to fill muffin cups? Transfer some or all of the batter to a large measuring cup, then pour the batter into the prepared muffin cups.

Upside-Down Gingerbread with Pears and Raisins

Gingerbread gets even better when you treat it like an upside-down cake and add pears and raisins.

Serves 12

Preparation time: 10 minutes

Cooking time: 30 to 40 minutes

Cooling time: 5 minutes

16-ounce can pear halves, canned in fruit juice
2 tablespoons firmly packed brown sugar
1 tablespoon lemon juice
2 tablespoons raisins
14½-ounce package gingerbread cake and cookie mix
1¼ cups water
Egg substitute equivalent to 1 egg or 2 egg whites

Preheat oven to 350° F.

Drain pears, reserving 1 tablespoon of the liquid. Slice pears horizontally in half. In an 8- or 9-inch baking pan, stir together brown sugar, lemon juice, and reserved pear liquid. Arrange pears in pan, flat side down. Sprinkle with raisins and set aside.

In a medium bowl, combine gingerbread mix, water, and egg substitute. Stir with a fork until combined. Stir 2 more minutes. Spoon batter into pan over pears and raisins. Bake 30 to 40 minutes or until a toothpick inserted near the center comes out clean. Cool on a wire rack for 5 minutes. Loosen sides with a knife; invert onto a plate. If any fruit sticks to the bottom of the pan, use a spoon to transfer it to the top of the cake. Cut into 12 slices. Serve warm.

NUTRIENT ANALYSIS (PER SERVING)

Calories 173 kcal
Protein 2 g
Carbohydrate 32 g
Cholesterol 0 mg
Sodium 252 mg
Total fat 5 g
  Saturated 1 g
  Polyunsaturated 1 g
  Monounsaturated 2 g

Golden Pumpkin Bundt Cake

There's no need to frost this moist cake since it's topped with crunchy sugared pecans.

Serves 14

Preparation time:
10 minutes

Cooking time: 1 hour

Cooling time:
45 minutes

Vegetable oil spray
18½-ounce package light yellow cake mix (see Note)
1⅓ cups water
¾ cup canned pumpkin (*not* pumpkin-pie filling)
Egg substitute equivalent to 2 eggs
1 teaspoon ground cinnamon
½ teaspoon ground ginger
½ teaspoon ground nutmeg
¼ cup acceptable margarine
¼ cup firmly packed brown sugar
¼ cup finely chopped pecans

Preheat oven to 350° F. Spray a Bundt pan with vegetable oil.

In a large mixing bowl, combine cake mix, water, pumpkin, egg substitute, cinnamon, ginger, and nutmeg. Beat with an electric mixer on low speed until well combined. Beat on high speed for 2 minutes.

Pour batter into pan. Bake for 1 hour or until a toothpick inserted near the center comes out clean. Cool cake in pan on a wire rack for 25 minutes. Remove from pan. Let stand 20 minutes or until completely cooled.

In a small skillet or saucepan, melt margarine. Stir in brown sugar and pecans. Cook and stir over medium heat until sugar dissolves, about 3 minutes. Spoon nut mixture over the top of the cooled cake. Cut into 14 slices before serving.

Note: If you are using a light cake mix with different amounts, ingredients, and/or directions, follow the package directions.

NUTRIENT ANALYSIS
(PER SERVING)
Calories 219 kcal
Protein 2 g
Carbohydrate 37 g
Cholesterol 3 mg
Sodium 323 mg
Total fat 7 g
 Saturated 2 g
 Polyunsaturated 1 g
 Monounsaturated 3 g

Oatmeal-Carrot Cake

This unconventional, reduced-fat carrot cake contains a cup of rolled oats for extra fiber and texture. For best results, use freshly grated carrots. They are moister than packaged shredded carrots. The cake is moist enough to eat unfrosted as a snack cake, but if you would like to frost it, use the Low-Fat Cream Cheese Frosting. (Nutritional analysis is given separately for the cake and the frosting.)

Serves 15; 1 2 × 3-inch piece per serving

Preparation time: 5 to 10 minutes

Cooking time: 35 to 40 minutes

Cooling time: 45 minutes

Vegetable oil spray
18½-ounce package light yellow cake mix (see Note)
1⅓ cups water
Egg substitute equivalent to 2 eggs
2 teaspoons ground cinnamon
½ teaspoon ground nutmeg
2 cups finely shredded carrots
1 cup quick-cooking rolled oats
Low-Fat Cream Cheese Frosting (page 254) (optional)

Preheat oven to 350° F. Spray a 13×9×2-inch baking pan or glass baking dish with vegetable oil.

In a large mixing bowl, combine cake mix, water, egg substitute, cinnamon, and nutmeg. Beat with an electric mixer on low speed until well combined. Beat on high speed for 2 minutes. Add carrots and rolled oats; beat on low speed until well combined.

Pour batter into prepared pan. Bake 35 to 40 minutes or until a toothpick inserted near the center comes out clean. Let cake cool slightly in pan on a wire rack. Eat warm or let cool completely and frost with Low-Fat Cream Cheese Frosting.

Note: If you are using a light cake mix with different amounts, ingredients, and/or directions, follow the package directions.

NUTRIENT ANALYSIS (PER SERVING)

Calories 177 kcal
Protein 3 g
Carbohydrate 36 g
Cholesterol 3 mg
Sodium 279 mg
Total fat 3 g
  Saturated 1 g
  Polyunsaturated 0 g
  Monounsaturated 1 g

Low-Fat Cream Cheese Frosting

This version of the classic high-fat frosting uses two secrets to reduce the fat. First, use low-fat cream cheese. Second, use less frosting, spread thinly over the cake.

Makes quantity sufficient to frost a 13×9×2-inch cake

Serves 15

Preparation time: 10 minutes

½ of an 8-ounce container light cream cheese
2 tablespoons acceptable margarine
1 teaspoon vanilla
2½ cups sifted confectioners' sugar

In a medium mixing bowl, beat cream cheese, margarine, and vanilla with an electric mixer at high speed until light and fluffy, about 2 minutes. Gradually add 1 cup of the confectioners' sugar, beating well, at medium speed about 2 minutes. Gradually beat in remaining confectioners' sugar to make frosting of spreading consistency, about 2 minutes.

Cook's Tip

Fat-free cream cheese contains more moisture than regular and light cream cheese. It isn't a good substitute in some frosting recipes, such as this one, because it produces a thin, runny frosting.

NUTRIENT ANALYSIS
(PER SERVING)

Calories 111 kcal
Protein 1 g
Carbohydrate 20 g
Cholesterol 6 mg
Sodium 48 mg
Total fat 3 g
 Saturated 1 g
 Polyunsaturated 0 g
 Monounsaturated 1 g

Fudge Brownie Sundaes

The raspberry sauce from Sherbet Parfaits (see page 256) goes well with this recipe, too. Simply use the sauce instead of the chocolate syrup.

Serves 15; 1 sundae per serving

Preparation time:
8 minutes

Cooking time:
25 minutes

Cooling time:
30 minutes

Vegetable oil spray
20½-ounce package light fudge brownie mix (see Note)
⅔ cup water
2 pints nonfat or low-fat vanilla frozen yogurt or a flavor of your choice
1 cup chocolate-flavored syrup
Maraschino cherries, drained (optional)

Preheat oven to 350° F. Spray a 13×9×2-inch glass baking dish with vegetable oil.

In a medium bowl, combine brownie mix and water. Stir with a spoon just until moistened, or mix according to package directions. Pour batter into prepared pan.

Bake 25 minutes. Cool in pan on a wire rack, about 30 minutes, or use warm.

To make sundaes, cut brownies into 15 pieces and set aside. Place about ¼ cup frozen yogurt in each bowl and drizzle with about 1 tablespoon chocolate syrup. Place brownie in bowl, next to frozen yogurt. Garnish with a cherry if desired.

Note: If you are using a light brownie mix with different amounts, ingredients, and/or directions, follow the package directions.

NUTRIENT ANALYSIS (PER SERVING)

Calories 240 kcal
Protein 4 g
Carbohydrate 55 g
Cholesterol 1 mg
Sodium 183 mg
Total fat 2 g
  Saturated 1 g
  Polyunsaturated 1 g
  Monounsaturated 1 g

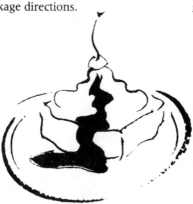

Sherbet Parfaits

Any sherbet will go nicely with the sweetened fruit, but rainbow sherbet looks especially pretty.

2 cups fresh raspberries or blueberries
2 tablespoons sugar
1 pint frozen rainbow sherbet or a flavor of your choice

In a medium bowl, combine berries and sugar. Using a potato masher or fork, mash berries slightly. Layer the berries with the sherbet in 4 6-ounce parfait or decorative glasses. Serve immediately or freeze until serving time. If frozen, let stand at room temperature for 10 minutes before serving.

Serves 4; 1 6-ounce parfait per serving

Preparation time:
5 minutes

NUTRIENT ANALYSIS
(PER SERVING)

Calories 187 kcal
Protein 2 g
Carbohydrate 43 g
Cholesterol 5 mg
Sodium 44 mg
Total fat 2 g
  Saturated 1 g
  Polyunsaturated 0 g
  Monounsaturated 1 g

Cookies-and-Cream Milk Shakes

Nonfat frozen yogurt takes on a whole new richness in these thick, delicious shakes. If you like thin shakes, add more milk, a few tablespoons at a time, and blend until desired consistency is reached.

1 pint vanilla, chocolate, or coffee nonfat or low-fat frozen yogurt or ice milk
¼ cup skim milk
2 chocolate sandwich cookies

In a blender container, combine frozen yogurt and skim milk. Cover and blend until smooth. Add cookies. Cover and blend just until cookies are coarsely chopped. Serve immediately.

Serves 4; ½ cup per serving

Preparation time:
5 minutes

NUTRIENT ANALYSIS
(PER SERVING)

Calories 112 kcal
Protein 5 g
Carbohydrate 22 g
Cholesterol 3 mg
Sodium 82 mg
Total fat 1 g
  Saturated 1 g
  Polyunsaturated 0 g
  Monounsaturated 0 g

Appendix A
Dining Out

More people are eating outside the home, thanks to Americans' on-the-go lifestyle. Sometimes there are simply not enough hours in the day to prepare a home-cooked meal. So, naturally, eating out is a quick and easy option. Here are a few ways to make sure these excursions don't undermine your heart-smart eating goals.

- Order foods that are steamed, broiled, grilled, stir-fried, or roasted. Or ask the chef to prepare the food with very little butter or oil or none at all.
- Drink two full glasses of water before your food arrives.
- Avoid foods described in the following way: buttery, buttered, fried, pan-fried, creamed, escalloped, au lait, or à la mode.
- Ask the chef to remove the skin from poultry or remove it yourself at the table.
- Request that sauces and salad dressings be served on the side. Then use them sparingly or not at all.
- Good bread-basket choices are melba toast and whole-grain rolls. Avoid muffins and croissants and skip the butter or margarine.
- Be selective at salad bars and choose fresh greens, raw vegetables, fresh fruits, garbanzo beans, and low-fat dressing. Avoid cheeses, marinated salads, pasta salads, and fruit salads with whipped cream.
- Skip dessert or order fresh seasonal fruit without whipped cream or a topping.

Appendix B
Menus

Here's just a small sampling of the ways to toss together the recipes in this book to create lively dinner menus. Choose from the seven below or invent your own. When devising your own menus, select recipes according to your likes and dislikes. Also, consider the various tastes and textures of the foods when you combine them.

Recipes with an asterisk (*) can be found in this cookbook.

Family Fajita Feast
Beef Fajitas in Lettuce*
Southwestern Rice*
Assorted greens tossed with Honey-Lime Vinaigrette*

Speedy and Spicy Supper
Spicy Sole and Tomatoes*
Colorful Lemon Couscous*
Tossed salad with Orange-Chèvre Salad Dressing*

Busy Night Meat Loaf
Fresh Herb Turkey Loaf*
Mashed potatoes (made with acceptable margarine and skim milk)
Mustard-Marinated Vegetable Salad*

Dash Home Dinner
Pork Chops with Honey and Garlic*
Gingered Bulgur with Apricots*
Steamed broccoli

Matchless Meatless Meal
Three-Bean Chili*
Easy Mexican Cornbread*
Light and Lemony Caesar Salad*

Special-Occasion Dinner	Lemon-Sauced Chicken with Asparagus* Steamed rice Assorted greens drizzled with Orange-Chèvre Salad Dressing*

Football Get-Together	Savory Snack Mix* Moroccan Beef and Barley* Assorted vegetable crudités

Appendix C
Equivalents

▬ ▬ ▬ ▬ ▬ ▬ ▬ ▬ ▬ ▬ ▬

Weights and Measures

Dash	= 2 to 4 drops		
3 teaspoons	= 1 tablespoon	= ½ fluid ounces	= 15 ml
4 tablespoons	= ¼ cup	= 2 fluid ounces	= 59 ml
16 tablespoons	= 1 cup (½ pint)	= 8 fluid ounces	= 237 ml
2 cups	= 1 pint	= 16 fluid ounces	= 473 ml
2 pints	= 1 quart	= 32 fluid ounces	= 946 ml
			= 0.95 l
4 quarts	= 1 gallon	= 128 fluid ounces	= 3785 ml
			= 3.8 l

Beans

	DRIED	COOKED
Kidney beans	1 pound (2¼ cups)	5½ cups
Lima beans	1 pound (2½ cups)	5½ cups
Navy beans	1 pound (2⅓ cups)	5½ cups
Soybeans	1 pound (2 cups)	4½ cups

Rice, Wheat, and Pasta

	DRY	COOKED
Rice	1 pound (2½ cups)	8 cups
Macaroni	1 pound (3¼ cups)	9 cups
Spaghetti	1 pound (4½ cups)	9 cups
Bulgur	1 pound (2¼ cups)	8 cups

Flour

	WEIGHT	VOLUME
Enriched white	1 pound	4 cups sifted
Enriched cake	1 pound	4½ cups sifted
Whole-wheat	1 pound	3⅓ cups stirred
Whole-wheat pastry	1 pound	4½ cups sifted

Miscellaneous

	WEIGHT	GRATED
Cheese	1 pound	4 cups

Appendix D
For Further
Information

For further information about American Heart Association programs and services, call 1-800-AHA-USA1 (1-800-242-8721) or contact us online at http://www.americanheart.org. For information about the American Stroke Association, a division of the American Heart Association, call 1-888-4STROKE (1-888-478-7653).

National Center
American Heart Association
7272 Greenville Avenue
Dallas, TX 75231-4596
214-373-6300

Operating Units of National Center
Office of Public Advocacy
Washington, DC

American Heart Association, Hawaii
Honolulu, HI

Affiliates
Desert/Mountain Affiliate
Arizona, Colorado, New Mexico, Wyoming
Denver, CO

Florida/Puerto Rico Affiliate
St. Petersburg, FL

Heartland Affiliate
Arkansas, Iowa, Kansas, Missouri, Nebraska, Oklahoma
Topeka, KS

Heritage Affiliate
Connecticut, New Jersey, New York City, Long Island
New York, NY

Mid-Atlantic Affiliate
Maryland, District of Columbia, North Carolina, South Carolina,
  Virginia
Glen Allen, VA

Midwest Affiliate
Illinois, Indiana, Michigan
Chicago, IL

New England Affiliate
Maine, Massachusetts, New Hampshire, Rhode Island, Vermont
Framingham, MA

New York State Affiliate
Syracuse, NY

Northland Affiliate
Minnesota, North Dakota, South Dakota, Wisconsin
Minneapolis, MN

Northwest Affiliate
Alaska, Idaho, Montana, Oregon, Washington
Seattle, WA

Ohio Valley Affiliate
Kentucky, Ohio, West Virginia
Columbus, OH

Pennsylvania Delaware Affiliate
Delaware, Pennsylvania
Wormleysburg, PA

Southeast Affiliate
Alabama, Georgia, Louisiana, Mississippi, Tennessee
Marietta, GA

Texas Affiliate
Austin, TX

Western States Affiliate
California, Nevada, Utah
Los Angeles, CA

Index

‑‑‑‑‑‑‑‑‑‑‑‑‑‑‑‑‑‑‑‑